A GIRL AND A GUN

"All you need to make a film is a girl and a gun."

—JEAN LUC GODARD

A Girl and a Gun

The Complete Guide to Film Noir on Video

Archive Photos

David N. Meyer

AVON BOOKS
A division of
The Hearst Corporation
1350 Avenue of the Americas
New York, New York 10019

Front cover photograph by Archive Photos
Published by arrangement with the author
Visit our website at **http://www.AvonBooks.com**
ISBN: 0-380-79067-X

Library of Congress Cataloging in Publication Data:

Meyer, David N.
A girl and a gun : the complete guide to film noir on video / David N. Meyer.
p. cm.
Includes bibliographical references.
1. Film noir—Catalogs. I. Title.
PN1995.9.F54M48 1998 97-34771
016.79143'655—dc21 CIP

First Avon Books Trade Printing: May 1998

Printed in the U.S.A.

QPM 10 9 8 7 6 5 4 3 2 1

Dedicated to:
Ida Lupino
&
Samuel Fuller

WARNER BROS./ARCHIVE PHOTOS

FOTOS INTERNATIONAL/ARCHIVE PHOTOS

"If there are two, one betrays."
—Jean-Pierre Melville

ARCHIVE PHOTOS

Lori Martin and Robert Mitchum in *Cape Fear.*

Contents

Acknowledgments

Many thanks to my parents, Anne and Sylvan Meyer of Miami Beach, Florida and Gainesville, Georgia, for their love and support.

Thanks again to Michael Shulman of Archive Photo in Manhattan, for his enthusiasm for this book, his quick response to my many requests and for these extraordinary photos.

There is no noir scholarship or research in America without *Film Noir: An Encyclopedic Reference to the American Style,* the seminal work by Alain Silver and Elizabeth Ward. It was their thinking on noir that inspired this book, and I referred to their volume a hundred times. Also indispensable is Alain Silver and James Ursini's *Film Noir Reader*. Mr. Silver was quite gracious and helpful in my quest for certain photographs. I am grateful for his work and for his assistance.

A writer survives on the few he can trust to read his work with care and to comment honestly. I'm lucky; but can the same be said for the Brain Trust upon whom I inflicted review after review via email and even read-aloud phone calls? I doubt it, but I could not have written this without the unflagging support and shocking patience of Tessa De Carlo in Napa; Tom Prassis, Dewey Thompson and Godfrey Cheshire in Manhattan; and Julie Ardery in Lexington.

Elsie Mac Adam of Manhattan read many of these reviews and her insights were very helpful, as were those of Alison

PARAMOUNT PICTURES/ARCHIVE PHOTOS

Payback is a bitch; Faye Dunaway in *Chinatown*

McClean of Manhattan and Deborah Hamilton of Stinson Beach, CA.

Tessa De Carlo in particular saw almost every review in draft form, and her guidance was essential. How she found time to do her own writing with me bothering her every day, I cannot imagine.

Both Tom Prassis and Godfrey Cheshire provided hours of thoughtful discussion and commentary on the issue of ''what is noir?'' Both offered suggestions of films I had overlooked and argued against films I intended to include. This book bears the marks of their generous enthusiasm and is more accurate and clear-headed because of their friendship. I owe them both a great debt of gratitude.

Likewise, my endless parsing of popular culture with Brother Cleve of Boston and Randall Rothenberg of Manhattan helped shape my ideas on noir more than either might realize. Both were steadfast in their encouragment and willingness to put aside their own projects for the inspirational email bullshitting that only the self-employed appreciate at its true priceless value.

Laura Blum of the Center for Communication in Manhattan had, as always, no shortage of opinions, most of them quite discerning. The Center for Communication staged a noir panel that enabled me to discuss noir with Paul Schrader and Donald Westlake. My heartfelt appreciation to Laura and to the Center.

My twin rocks of support, Rick Slone and Tim Bailey of Ketchum, Idaho, got me past my own demons once more, with their usual love and tact. Judy Fox, that shining example of artistic dedication, was always there. *Namasté,* and gratitude, again. Thanks to Kim Howard, Laird Erman and Michael & Ruthann Saphire in Ketchum for their encouragement.

Thanks to my community at Cinemax/HBO: Mark Davidson, Alberto Ferreras, Geoff Bird, Susan Walker and Heather Laird.

Introduction

At the end of a mainstream Hollywood film, the viewer knows everything of importance and is offered a vision of social harmony. Neither desire is satisfied here.

—R. BARTON PALMER

Hollywood's Dark Cinema: The American Film Noir

A dark, subversive whisper softly calling from beneath the glossy surface of American mainstream movie-dom, film noir revels in the glamour of hopelessness, the romance of clinging to a failed past, and the seductiveness of the futile. Exemplifying the great American tradition of using low culture to comment on profound themes and issues, noir began as B movies, pulp thrillers, and as a haven for the disaffected: writers, actors, and directors banned from more sanctified work by Joseph McCarthy's House Un-American Activities Committee, the resultant Communist witch-hunt, and the Hollywood blacklisting of the late 1940s and 1950s.

Using the narrative conventions of the crime thriller—the honorable hoodlum, the crooked cop, the femme fatale, the untrustworthy pal, illicit sex, and sexy violence—noir presents the dark side of the American soul. What studio pictures never dared address, noir took as its *raison d'être:* lust, murder, betrayal, weird kicks, compulsive obsessions, loss of faith, failed redemption, uncertain identity, the end of romance, the inevitable betrayal of love, and the transcendent allure of cheap sex.

Might as well blame Einstein. The struggles in noir take place between the poles of his discoveries. From them spring the key torments of our half of this century: the end of absolute morality (in the face of the theory of relativity) and the certainty of Armageddon (in the form of the A-bomb). Film noir seems a spontaneous reaction to the addled postwar morality, nuclear paranoia, and the weakening of traditionally held religious ideas that resulted. Noir's critical themes include postwar guilt, with its by-product of the rejection of the middle-class values that served as the rallying cry for the war, an apocalyptic sensibility, and a strong belief in the power of fate to shape events.

ARCHIVE PHOTOS

In a world without certainty, noir embraces the unpredictable. It provided an outlet for America's postwar confusions over an unknown future, the demise of any demarcation between right and wrong, the shifting roles of men and women, the frustrations of nonconformity, and the poetic alienation of the outsider. The first hipsters, and the delineation of what would become the hipster sensibility, appear in noir.

As purely an American art form as jazz or the Western, noir sprang from a specific set of social and creative circumstances: the end of World War II, the impact of European refugees on an American art form, the mainstream film studios' need for a steady supply of low budgets, lurid pictures, and the ascendance of a particular writing style.

That authorial voice—described by author Mike Davis in his study of Los Angeles, *City of Quartz,* as "existentialized Marxism"—derived from another fortuitous clash of cultures. The hard-bitten, American pulp energy of James M. Cain, Mickey Spillane, Jim Thompson, Dashiell Hammett, B. Traven, Raymond Chandler, and others was filtered through the refined, ironic sensibilities of cultured European directors. The writers created heroes who dealt with spiritual crisis (caused by the emptiness of American middle-class life) by alternating between emotional withdrawal and physical attack. The refugee directors preferred a more sardonic, alienated approach.

The combining of these sensibilities helped create one of the great creative outpourings in American history. As Alain Silver points out in his comprehensive overview, *Film Noir: An Encyclopedic Reference to the American Style,* noir is not based on any preexisting notions of American heroism or narrative. Unlike the Western, noir has no real-world precursors in mythology, history, or in social fact. Its stories, characters, and issues reflect the era of its creation.

Noir debuted new (and enduring) ideas of heroism and villainy, and offered new moral solutions, or proof that none existed. Noir stories offer powerful metaphors for the undercurrent of violence in American life and for a deep dissatisfaction with widely espoused (though entrapping) middle-class values.

Noir functioned not only as a haven for the blacklisted, but also as a pulpit from which they might speak. Never before had American pulp enjoyed such an infusion of creative genius and thoughtful artists. The result was an unusually high quality of writing, acting, camera work, and directorial execution in low-budget films. It also resulted in a certain amount of self-righteous schlock, but what's more American than that?

Life is in color, but black & white is more realistic.

—SAMUEL FULLER

The State of Things

Noir scholars generally agree that the classical period of film noir lasted from 1941 to 1958, from *The Maltese Falcon* to *Touch of Evil. The Maltese Falcon* is a private eye picture in the existing tradition. Within that familiar form, however, director John Huston and star Humphrey Bogart created something new. They suggested, for the first time, a genuine humanity behind the *pro forma* toughness of the hard-bitten private eye. This humanity permitted Bogart to be capable of experiencing loss, and to grieve for that loss. In grieving, Bogie recognized his own mortality, and mortality's inevitable companion, dread. Huston's and Bogart's twin discoveries fueled what would become classical noir. Those discoveries were (1) use of the thriller to address profound philosophical, moral, and social issues (while providing all the thrills expected of a thriller), and (2) the motivating power of dread.

By 1958, noir had provided a catalogue of cynical crime movie kicks and had explored every nook and cranny of humanity's dark side. *Touch of Evil* stands as the diametrical opposite of *The Maltese Falcon. Falcon* is shot simply, with basic setups that put the characters front and center in the frame. *Touch*'s style could not be more baroque. In accordance with its simple look, *Falcon* offers a hero and several villains. *Touch* presents a moral universe in which such childish terms hardly apply.

Touch is a fitting end to the classical cycle. What film could top its convoluted visual, spiritual, and moral riot? Though the essence of noir might be described as films with simple plots presenting complex issues, Orson Welles made a picture that reflected the complexity of its subject in its style. This, critic and director Paul Schrader writes, is the core of noir: a cinematic movement wherein style counts for more than story.

Film noir was an immensely creative period—probably the most creative in Hollywood's history . . . picked at random, a film noir is likely to be a better-made film than a randomly selected silent comedy, musical, Western and so on. Taken as a whole period, film noir achieved an unusually high level of artistry.

—PAUL SCHRADER

"Notes on Film Noir"

Since ironies abound in noir, it's suitably ironic that this quintessentially American art form was discovered by the French. No American director of the mid-forties thought he was making a "film noir." Of course, writers, directors, and cameramen were aware of other films with similar themes, and many were aware of the opportunities for expression that pulp and B movies provided, but the early films of noir did not emerge from a self-conscious, self-defined "movement."

The first recognition of noir as a body of work came from Europe after World War II. Unable to see American films during the war, postwar French film critics were struck by a wave of commercial thrillers and melodramas with dark themes, films in which the action took place mostly at night, films with profoundly unhappy endings whose visuals were marked by high-contrast B/W cinematography that featured strange compositions, deep shadows, and darkened looming cityscapes. The first published recognition of these themes appeared in *Panorama du Film Noir Américain*, a 1955 volume written by Raymond Borde and Étienne Chaumeton.

Contemporary American critics were much slower to recognize either a cogent body of work or its values. They tended to see noir as second-rate pulp, B thrillers intended for downmarket theaters and therefore not worthy of further scrutiny.

Both studios and movie theaters welcomed noir, however. The studios needed cheap product, and low budgets doomed early noir to be the province of outsiders, inspired hacks, and sophisticated unhireables. It is their combined vision that created film noir.

• What Is Noir? •

THE BOGART SUSPENSE PICTURE
WITH THE SURPRISE FINISH!
COLUMBIA PICTURES presents
HUMPHREY
BOGART
In A Lonely Place
with
Gloria GRAHAME
FRANK LOVEJOY · CARL BENTON REID · ART SMITH · JEFF DONNELL · MARTHA STEWART
Screen Play by Andrew Solt
A SANTANA PRODUCTION
ROBERT LORD · NICHOLAS RAY

ARCHIVE PHOTOS

What makes noir, noir? Noir scholarship is marked by its continual effort to define film noir. Is it a genre, a motif, a style? Like chic or cool, noir is difficult to define, but easy to recognize. . . .

While Westerns are simple—mix horses, open landscapes, and violent heroics, and a Western will emerge—noir proves considerably more slippery. Some private eye movies are noir, some aren't. Some women's melodramas (*Caught, Mildred Pierce*) are noir. Certain films from the classical period feature rainy streets, guys in dark suits, shadowy cinematography, carefully planned capers, and unthinkable betrayals, but they aren't noir. Noir is not made from a recipe; a film noir is always more than the sum of its parts. The surface material must be there, but noir uses crime capers only as vehicles to present other, deeper concerns.

Noir is nothing so recognizable or limited as a genre, motif, or style. Noir's mysterious nature identifies it as a subculture, a constantly mutating form (containing genre, motif, and style) that by mutating seeks to avoid co-option by the omnivorous mainstream. In the face of mass-produced Hollywood culture, noir remains steadfastly individual. Its themes have little to do with the sleek surfaces and happy faces of mainstream studio releases.

Watch five noir films in a row and you will see they will have little in common, save that are all fueled by heartfelt existential terror. The characters in noir struggle against their own mortality, against their fear of and need for intimacy, against the fleeting pleasures of the illicit, and against a larger society that seeks to define them against their will.

Gangster movies are not noir films; they are too melodramatic. The gangster film loads up a villainous character with a wide range of loathsome aspects and worships a hero who has no flaws. As a modern example, think of Brian DePalma's *The Untouchables.*

Our hero is cop Kevin Costner: lean, handsome, gallant, well-spoken, loving, brave, an admired leader of men. Opposing him is Robert De Niro: fat, psychotic, gruntingly inarticulate, homicidal, alienated, a feared despot. There is no connection, no similarity, no unifying human aspect that might lead to confusing one man with the other. An audience instantly recognizes which one they should identify with, and applaud. In noir, such identification can be problematic, if not impossible. Noir blurs the lines and defies melodramatic conventions.

Noir heroes and villains are vested with qualities both admirable and despicable, whereas gangster films tend toward moral simplifications. Noir presents compelling protagonists who have virtually no classically heroic aspects. The few noir heroes who possess heroic virtues squander them in service of the lowest aims. Sterling Hayden in *The Killing,* for example, displays courage, ingenuity, perseverance, and imagination, but in pursuit of robbery and murder. In *T-Men,* heroic cops demonstrate their abilities to lie, betray, and deceive, all in the name of the law. In *The Big Heat,* Glenn Ford plays a cop who abandons any civilizing notions that might stand between him and revenge.

Whereas gangster films—especially prenoir gangster movies—are action-based, noir's tensions and excitements spring from character and mood. The action in noir defines the characters and sets the mood but never dominates either. While noir features car chases, shoot-outs, bank robberies, jewel heists, kidnappings, murders, seductions, plane crashes, and punch-ups, these are almost always secondary to the heart of the story, wherein some poor fool tries to work out his various confusions and is condemned to failure.

Another key noir characteristic is the tragic, unhappy, or morally ambiguous ending. What makes several Hitchcock films not quite noir is his preference for neatly wrapped finales in which the guilty are punished and the innocent go free (*Spellbound*). When Hitchcock is less sentimental, his works number among the masterpieces of noir (*Vertigo*).

Noir is deliberately intelligent. No matter how down-market the intended audience or source material, a noir usually offers a subtextual message in addition to the overt story material. As the only movement in cinema history to make its main thematic points by style, rather than story, a noir may feature a happy ending that rings blatantly false, or a tragic ending that seems to restore the universe to its proper order. The supposedly happy ending of *Caught* is played in the darkest shadow and suggests strongly that the audience should disregard the pleasant conclusion and study the visual world—impenetrable, claustrophobic, hopeless—in which that "happy" ending occurs.

In noir, right and wrong are not clearly defined. Indeed, they exist as points on a wheel that spins so fast, there is no telling them apart. John Garfield's character in *Force of Evil* does harm when he tries to do good. Unlike the actions of a conventional hero, Garfield's acts generate consequences he never imagined.

Noir's plots are often morality tales of a bleak sensibility. They present a harsh and randomly condemning universe (*Scarlet Street, Raw Deal, Caught*). While wrongdoing may or may not be punished (*Double Indemnity, Kansas City Confidential*), those who try to rise above their station or who succumb to their greed (for money, sex, or power) will usually suffer the consequences (as does Edward G. Robinson in *The Woman in the Window* or Bruce Dern in *After Dark, My Sweet*). At the same time, the "little guy" who lacks the guts to stand up for himself (Robinson in *Scarlet Street*) is as likely to be crushed by an indifferent fate as the daring striver who risks all (Richard Widmark in *Night and the City*).

The rise of existentialism profoundly influenced noir. In the absence of a defined moral order and in the certainty of our own demise, humans must devise their own morality, must determine what each regards as good and evil. The forces of fate operate apart from our control, and so in the face of an absurd universe, we must find meaning in our own actions and in the codes that govern them. Noir heroes make their own moral choices, and for these choices, dues must be paid, large and small.

ARCHIVE PHOTOS

Noir provided a forum for presenting issues that seldom found a voice in major studio productions, including the difficulty of assimilating the veterans returning from the war (*The Blue Dahlia*); anti-Semitism (*Crossfire*); sexual hostility (*Gilda*); economic repression (*Force of Evil*); exploitation of one class by another (*Body and Soul*); the exhilaration of law-breaking (*Gun Crazy*); pointless violence (*The Big Combo*); betrayal (*The Big

Clock); and adult, loveless sex (*The Postman Always Rings Twice*). By its nature, noir is virulently anti-middle-class, non-conformist, and outlaw. Though noir honors men who live self-defined lives in defiance of the conformist culture, noir plots often turn on how diligently society (and fate) strives to crush such men. The more free the man, the more thorough will be his undoing.

Noirs usually take place in an urban environment, at night. The look of noir includes shadowy frames, dark images, somber moods, street locations (rather than sets), neorealist dialogue, gritty characters, and blatant sexuality.

Noir depends upon a carefully aligned relationship between bleak content and shadowy form. Noir cinematography is unusually expressive and direct. In *Invasion of the Body Snatchers,* as Kevin McCarthy flees the alien hordes, he moves through a series of shots that grow ever tighter around him, increasing his and our sense of claustrophobia. In *City That Never Sleeps,* the massive buildings and overwhelming shadows they cast serve to entrap the tiny souls who live among them.

The face of a noir character may appear half in close-up and half in light, to suggest the moral ambiguity within. Objects—furniture, mirrors, cars, guns—often loom as large in the frame as do faces or bodies, suggesting that the humans shown are at the mercy of their environment. The camera may suddenly become the subjective viewpoint of the protagonist (as often occurs in *Taxi Driver*), thus hurling the viewer more deeply in the story. As with good and evil, form and content in noir are closely related, and one constantly impacts the other.

Another key element is the flashback. Flashbacks are usually narrated by the hero as he contemplates the mess he has made of things. The ultimate flashback noir, *D.O.A.*, begins when a man reports his own murder to the police. He then decribes the twenty-four hours that precede his death. Flashbacks suggest a preference for a failed, romantic past over an uncertain future, a desire to reshape the past, the cleansing power of confession, a dislocated sense of time and place, a rejection of the prenoir private eye with his careful, linear pursuit of clues, and a chance to put a rueful, romantic—though often self-serving—spin on the hero's life.

There is a surprisingly wide range of crudity and sophistication in noir filmmaking. Great geniuses (Orson Welles, for one) and desperate hacks (please supply your own example) made noir. Masters of cinematographic storytelling and larger-than-life metaphor might prove incapable of, or uninterested in, directing actors (Anthony Mann leads this school). Other directors might be skilled at infusing every moment with sweaty tension, but prove unable to direct a cogent action sequence or follow a rational time line (Phil Karlson springs to mind).

ARCHIVE PHOTOS

Among the myriad writing on noir, few approach the brevity, clarity, and common sense of Paul Schrader's 1971 essay "Notes on Film Noir." Those familiar with Schrader's career as a screenwriter (*Taxi Driver, Raging Bull*) and director (*Light of Day, The Comfort of Strangers, American Gigolo*) may be unaware that for years he was a lucid and astute film critic. His analysis of the factors that helped create film noir is unmatched. I paraphrase Schrader with gratitude and urge everyone to seek out his two books, *Schrader on Schrader* and *Transcendental Style in Film*.

Schrader lists four factors as key to the creation of the noir style. The first is World War II and postwar disillusionment. In this view, the cheer-up movies of the Depression and the propaganda films produced during the war led to a backlash among filmmakers and audiences. Films that accurately reflected a sense of dislocation, the sense of exploitation for all that had been suffered during the war, the stress of returning to an unwelcoming society, and the shock of leaving the comforting, hierarchical camaraderie of the military for the anarchic, dog-eat-dog world of American success and striving, met with a welcoming reception.

Though Schrader does not address this issue, the struggles with feminine power and sexuality in film noir are an important aspect of the disillusionment they express. Women newly empowered by their productive war years in the workplace were forced to return to a more servile social position at war's end. Noir films suggest that men in the postwar era were inordinately afraid of strong women. Ambitious, sexually potent women are uniformly presented as evil and destructive. (No woman in noir takes power without stealing it from a man.)

The next factor Schrader cites is postwar realism. Neorealism swept cinema, forging a new style out of location shoots, natural lighting, nonactors in performing roles, and dialogue that mimicked natural speech. Schrader maintains that American audiences were tired of seeing the same old studio streets and welcomed movies that more accurately reflected the reality of the current place and time. The development of smaller cameras and cranes (which could be more easily maneuvered on location) and high-speed film stocks (which did not require huge studio lights) made it much simpler to shoot on location, to move the camera to express a character's emotions, and to merge characters with the urban environments in which they appeared. In *D.O.A.*, for example, Edmond O'Brien runs down the real streets of San Francisco. In *The Third Man*, the streets of Vienna become another character in the story. This mania for accuracy and naturalist location later led to counter-noir movements, such as the police procedural (*He Walked By Night*), with its mock-documentary fixation on re-creating every move a real-life policeman might make.

Schrader then cites the profound influence of German refugees on American cinema. Many writers, directors, and cinematographers were forced to flee Germany before and after the war. Their dramatic sensibility was steeped in the deep shadows, bizarre camera angles, and gloom-ridden alienation of Expressionism. The mix of this florid visual style with American tendencies for realistic naturalism in setting and dialogue created the baroque contradictions that are the essence of film noir.

These artists were also marked by a refugee's permanent-outsider stance and a misanthropic view of national, class, and/or ethnic loyalty with no faith whatsoever in society as an enforcer of the moral good. German émigrés critical to noir include directors Fritz Lang, Robert Siodmak, Billy Wilder, Max Ophuls, Edgar Ulmer, and Otto Preminger. Cinematographers include the masterful John Alton, Karl Freund, and Fritz Wagner.

And finally, Schrader cites the popular writers of the hard-boiled tradition. Post-Hemingway pulp authors such as Dashiell Hammett (*The Maltese Falcon*), Raymond Chandler (*The Big Sleep*), James M. Cain (*The Postman Always Rings Twice*), Jim Thompson (*The Killer Inside Me*), Mickey Spillane (*Kiss Me Deadly*), and Cornell Woolrich (*The Black Angel*) brought a tough, mean-spirited sensibility to the movies. Their terse dialogue, short sentences, and sparse descriptions were the written equivalent of the visuals of noir.

These writers created fatalistic, pre-existential heroes who walked their own roads. The hard-boiled school specialized in world-weary men whose disillusionment was their only armor, and man-eating women whose sexuality was their only weapon. By book's (or movie's) end, neither the armor nor the weapon would prove effective against the weight of fate or character. These were not literary writers condescending to write crime capers, suspense thrillers, murder mysteries, or psychotic fantasies. Like noir filmmakers, they saw a unique opportunity to address profound themes through the vehicle of pulp. Their rigorous love of pulp and their understanding of its demands make their work powerful and enduring.

ARCHIVE PHOTOS

• Noir Themes •

I like the futility of effort. The uphill road to failure is a very human thing.

—JEAN-PIERRE MELVILLE

The disparate films of noir share a common lexicon of themes. These themes are often self-contradictory and reflect noir's absence of faith in the ability of humankind to sort out any of its self-created problems. Noir themes include:

No good deed goes unpunished. The surest guarantee of disaster is a simple act of kindness. To his infinite regret, Tom Neal picks up a hitchhiker in *Detour*. Jack Nicholson abandons his cynicism and acts as protector for Faye Dunaway in *Chinatown*. Both are punished for their generosity. This suggests a nation in retreat from the all-together-now spirit of the war. It underlines the shocking atmosphere of ''every man for himself'' that became the rule in the postwar marketplace.

A detached ironic view is the only refuge. Noir protagonists pretend that the events of the world do not touch their emotions. They suppress their feelings, and whenever they allow themselves to genuinely interact, they risk either death or heartbreak. Mike Hammer in *Kiss Me Deadly* protects himself by his sarcasm and lack of compassion. Walter Neff in *Double Indemnity* pretends to be less passionate about his murderous lover than he really is. Raymond Chandler's Philip Marlowe became the archetype for all private detectives: distant, bemused, and uninvolved. It's axiomatic in noir that whenever the facade cracks, trouble follows.

Crime doesn't pay, but normal life is an experiential/existential straitjacket. Nothing is more likely to drive a man to crime than the soul-numbing ordinariness of existence. Men who race to the deadly flame of a femme fatale do so because she represents a change from the daily grind. And any change, no matter how destructive, is preferred to the sucker's life of nine to five. Thematically, this leaves no safe middle ground for a noir hero: Commit to the outlaw life and suffer dramatically; commit to the square life and suffer incrementally.

Character determines fate. In noir, no one escapes their true nature, even if they don't know what it is. The discovery of one's essence will assuredly come at the worst possible time. A character who sins in the past must pay for those sins in the future. Yet, at the same time, fate dispenses favor or misfortune according to its own whims. Efforts may be rewarded (*Kansas City Confidential*) or a man may be ruined through no fault of his own (*Detour*). The wheels of existence turn with no consideration man's plans or needs.

Though love might seem to be the only redeeming aspect of human existence, it's not. In the end, love will always be betrayed. In the few noir films in which love prevails (*On Dangerous Ground*), the sufferings that lead to love hardly justify its rewards.

Kicks count for something. The momentary exhilaration of violence or revenge or cheap sex is worth the inevitable price that must be paid. Those willing to pay that price remain free (of society's chains), even if they become slaves to the urges that drive them. Again, this illustrates the recurring antibourgeois underpinnings of noir. Anyone who accepts the morality of the conformist *über*-culture is presented as a serf; anyone who revels in the id is a martyr, no matter how despicable they may be otherwise.

Alienation rules. The noir protagonist is often alienated from self, from society, and even from those whose world he shares. In *Out of the Past*, Robert Mitchum finds himself cast out of the world of hoodlums in which he once thrived. Nor can he return to the "straight" world; he is marked by his criminal past. This alienation is a forceful presentation of the existential dilemma: If hell is other people (and in noir, it always is), where can the protagonist find the community he needs in order to survive? Since love is never faithful, families count for nothing, and money severs all loyalties, the answer is: He cannot.

This alienation leads to the more important noir theme of *fatalism*. In noir, few shape events to their preference. The assumption of failure is paramount. As a result, noir protagonists develop a hard shell of resigned fatalism in order to deal with cruel fate.

Among the attitudes held are: "I've done my best by my own (private, inexplicable) moral code, so screw the results." Or, "The world is bankrupt, so who cares if I'm an amoral pig?" Or, "The forces of fate/evil will undo all my efforts, so it doesn't matter what I do." Or, "I'm going to die, anyway, so I might as well get killed over this insignificant moral/style/revenge issue that nobody but me regards as worthwhile.''

In the face of this absence of control, the noir protagonist seldom blames the villain for his troubles. He recognizes that the villain is not evil unto himself (as are the villains in conventional Westerns, for instance), but instead the actualizer of evil forces extant in the universe. The result of this moral free-for-all (or morals-free universe) grants the protagonist the right to create his own moral code.

Other recurrent themes include: the transcendence of violence, sexual obsession, paranoia, greed, distrust among men, distrust between men and women, the essentially doomed nature of any of man's endeavors, the dominant role of luck, the pointlessness of heroism or of obeying social conventions, and the corruption of everybody and of every social institution.

• The Noir "Hero" •

Noir protagonists are mostly men. The exceptions—in *Mildred Pierce, Caught, Undercurrent, The Man I Love,* and *Raw Deal* (which is unusual for being narrated by a woman) prove the rule. Noir heroes are not all that heroic. They're cowards, drunkards, liars, outlaws, sexual dysfunctionals, sex maniacs, slobs, bullies, violence-prone, and lacking in ambition. In short, noir heroes are everything men of the repressive Fifties could never permit themselves to be. Noir heroes represent the id for their audience—just check out Mike Hammer in *Kiss Me Deadly*.

They also represent a different sort of male freedom from that of their duty-bound, romantic but asexual counterparts in Westerns. A noir protagonist may suffer a more suffocating sense of duty than any sheriff, but he can be romantically deluded or led astray by sexual desire as no cowboy ever was.

Noir codified the antihero. The protagonist follows his own moral code, as antiheroes must. The (anti)-hero's code is well-defined, often obsessively so, but remains opaque or inexplicable to others in the film (or even to viewers). The noir protagonist will die before he violates his code. At the film's climax, the antihero will encounter an ultimate barrier, a test to his code. Only two outcomes are possible: Either he, his world, and his self-construction will be crushed (*Homicide*), or he will smash through triumphantly, only to find that his life is in no way altered and that his victory is hollow and transitory (*The Big Heat*).

ARCHIVE PHOTOS

Lee Marvin in *Point Blank*

As antiheroes, noir protagonists live by certain rules. Their distaste for hypocrisy (and their innate honesty) force them to live outside of mainstream culture. By dint of their lifestyle (and their sense of humor) they are social critics. The pleasure principle drives them: dames, booze, money, kicks, and cars. . . . At the same time, the noir hero has swapped material success for a life of dubious personal freedom. Materialism is useful only when it aids hedonism or the hero's romantic quest. This freedom demands that he substitute style for substance, because the transitory nature of his human relationships means he never develops any connection of depth. Devotion to style is his only refuge. And the noir hero, however otherwise pathetic, regards selling out in any form as the absolute loss of identity and soul.

Where action is concerned, things get a bit trickier and self-contradictory. Most noir men justify their actions as means to an end. They do what they want. Many times, the criminals behave as heroes in a Horatio Alger story: They use their skills to get ahead no matter what the obstacles.

Finally, the noir hero may find himself paralyzed by passivity. This passivity stems from the understanding that *any* action will lead to uncontrollable consequences, and so avoiding action is the only safe course. This spiritual malaise should never be mistaken for a lack of physical courage.

When we look to the prototype of the cool modern guy, we find it hasn't changed much in the fifty-plus years since noir debuted. Cool guys now are as cool guys were then: detached, sardonic, ironic, and slightly embittered.

• Women in Noir •

Noir paints a curiously ambivalent portrait of women. Celebrated and desired for their blatant sexual hunger and passion, women are simultaneously vilified and feared for the same reasons. Adored for their loyalty and constancy, they are mocked for their mercurial nature and lack of courage. Women are shown as both more violent and more dependent than men; less capable of commitment and more so. Rita Hayworth as *Gilda* carries all these contradictions in one character.

Women's roles in noir films include man-eating femme fatales (Ava Gardner in *The Killers*); sexual predators/betrayers (Barbara Stanwyck in *Double Indemnity*); nurturers/good girls who are never sexual partners (Barbara Bel Geddes in *Vertigo*); vengeful victims (Ann Savage in *Detour*); seductive murderers who promise sex but never deliver (one of the twins played by Olivia De Havilland in *The Dark Mirror*); dead women who couldn't be saved and whose death haunts the hero (Cloris Leachman in *Kiss Me Deadly*); salvation incarnate (Ida Lupino in *The Man I Love* or in *On Dangerous Ground*); loyal, underappreciated, but uncompelling girlfriends (Virginia Huston in *Out of the Past*); women trapped by potentially dangerous men (Katharine Hepburn in *Undercurrent*); women in transition from one of these roles to another (Constance Towers in *The Naked Kiss*); and women who are practically all of the above (Rita Hayworth in *Gilda*).

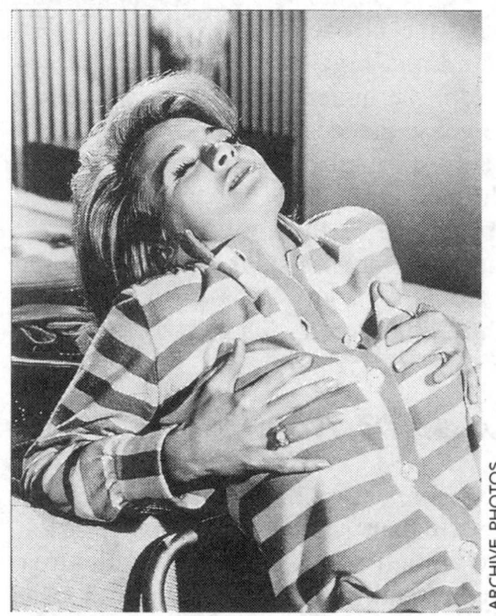

ARCHIVE PHOTOS

Angie Dickinson in *Point Blank*

Whether villainized or sainted, women in noir occupy central roles. They never stand on the sidelines. They are active participants in their own lives. Have women in cinema ever been depicted as being so powerful? Men in noir are often depicted as ''feminine''; they are passive, dependent on their women (John Dall in *Gun Crazy*), or so impassioned that they lose all common sense (Robert Mitchum in *Out of the Past*).

Women's power comes with a curse, however. A woman's ambition is seldom seen as a good thing. Any woman's seizing of power causes a man to suffer. Woe betide the man who trusts a woman, and when a woman proves trustworthy (Barbara Bel Geddes in *Caught*), she can't find a man who deserves her. A sexually active woman is automatically a betrayer, just as a sexually loyal woman is always an ineffectual helpmate, one who might provide a man solace, but no spark.

Women's nature serves as noir's most potent and recurring metaphor for the unpredictable, perverse mystery of life. Men cannot alter life to their aims, nor can they control the women in noir. Women, as fate, appear to grant favors, but those favors come with a hefty price. A man who loses himself in passionate, unthinking pursuit of a woman—or of any goal—(Robert Mitchum in *Out of the Past*) will succeed only as long as his unthinking faith lasts. The instant a man suffers confusion over a woman (Burt Lancaster in *Criss Cross*), she will turn on him. Women, like fate, honor strength.

• Modern Noir •

Classical noir sprang from several social factors. Among them are a terror of succumbing to the conformist pressure of society, an overwhelming sense of existential dread, alienation from others, a belief that an increasingly technocratic society is both controlling us and making it impossible for us to connect, and concern that a single individual means nothing to a brutal, expanding populace connected only by its mutual antipathy.

Our society today is, if anything, more conformist, more heedless of the individual, more dominated by technology, and more alienated than ever. The one big issue in the classical versus neo-noir debate is the modern demon of self-consciousness. Classical cycle noir directors were not consciously making noir. They were consciously exploiting a pulp storytelling format to address issues that other movies would not raise, but they remained unaware of working in a specific cinematic tradition. Nowadays we know too much and we cannot unlearn what we know. Any director attempting noir knows everything that has gone before.

Chinatown (1974) and *The Long Goodbye* (1973) reflect two different but archetypal neo-noir approaches. *Chinatown* delib-

ARCHIVE PHOTOS

erately evokes classic noir storytelling style, with old-style visuals and cutting. Polanski and screenwriter Robert Towne update the subculture even as they reference it, but address themes of character and politics that not even the most daring classic noir might attack. *The Long Goodbye* represents the other new-old school. Director Altman deliberately undercuts the noir form with his ironic approach, and constant jokey references to the long-ago movie-land from which his hero seems to have sprung.

But, both of these modern noir films transpose classic values to the new era. The protagonists of both pictures find themselves dealing with constant hopelessness in the face of an indifferent society. Both must hustle and break the law to get what they want. Both define themselves by their nonconformity, and both derive great amusement from their status as outsiders.

In a world with few credible private eyes, modern noir often celebrates a certain down-and-out sensibility. Standing in opposition to the repressive mainstream society are the heroic, eccentric outriders who triumph or fail (or both) on their wits and style (as does Elliott Gould in *The Long Goodbye*).

After Dark, My Sweet (1990) bears no superficial relationship to the noir films of old; it's shot in sunshine and in wide-screen, with none of the claustrophobia or shadow of the classic period. But in its characters' desperation, the existential pointlessness of their lives, and the doomed nature of their idiotic caper, *After Dark* is indistinguishable from classic noir.

A counterexample might be *Body Heat,* which for all its frantic co-opting of the superficial attributes of noir (a femme fatale, old-style hats, sexual betrayal, etc.) remains nothing more than a pastiche, a mock-noir. We are too much aware of the insincere hand of the director. Neither he nor his characters seem to suffer from the key sense of dread that motivates real noir. It lacks the profound subtext of noir, and has nothing to tell us beyond the actions of the characters.

• Noir 101—The Canon •

These are the noir films to see first. Each represents either a particular subgenre of noir, is exemplary of a noir director's best work, is of historical significance within the noir subculture, or is simply among the best noir films made.

The Asphalt Jungle. The ultimate caper movie, directed by John Huston in his signature clean, raw style. Suspenseful and bleak, but never self-conscious. Features a startling cameo by Marilyn Monroe.

Chinatown. Roman Polanski's masterpiece of structure; the core film of neo-noir. Polanski uses color rather than B/W, and wide-open horizontal lines (rather than entrapping verticals) to create his L.A. of the thirties. Jack Nicholson embellishes the noir private eyes of old, but creates a character all his own.

ARCHIVE PHOTOS

The Conversation. Francis Ford Coppola explores the classic noir theme of paranoia, but sets the story in contemporary culture. As Nicholson reinvented the private eye, so Gene Hackman updates noir's frightened little man, whose only desire is to go unnoticed.

Double Indemnity. Featuring Barbara Stanwyck as the first woman in movies to talk tough like a man, to pursue sex like a man, and to coldly betray like a man. Unforgettable repartee, fueled by director Billy Wilder's smooth style and cynical wit.

Force of Evil. The best of the political noir films, a saga of class war that erupts into astounding visual metaphors. Also notable for the contradictions between its realistic settings, poetic dialogue, and, in the end, completely fantastical visuals.

Gun Crazy. Incarnating the creative power of low-budget pictures and the poetic expressiveness of pulp, this quintessential tale of young, crazy lovers on the run features ground-breaking visual technique and surprisingly blatant sexuality.

Kiss Me Deadly. The most cynically violent and apocalyptic noir. Faced with the end of the world, director Robert Aldrich finds a hard-nosed visual complement for author Mickey Spillane's brutal, stripped-down prose.

La Femme Nikita. Director Luc Besson reinvents the wheel. Not only does he feature the first female action hero in noir, but he creates a modern visual equivalent for the cinematic language of classical noir. His blending of art movie, violent exploitation, and serious thematics provide the traditional foundation for a revolutionary modernist vision.

Laura. Like *Caught,* a good first choice for a woman interested in noir. Otto Preminger details how men construct the (fantasy) woman they desire, and then punish (real) women for being themselves. A telling dissection of men's self-made illusions and the treachery of the upper class.

Le Samourai. Nobody reflects America back to Americans like Jean-Pierre Melville, who creates a very Japanese ode to American movie heroes, to film noir, to the strict morality of the law-breaker, and to the enduring romance of the criminal. Sexy, religious, and cool.

M. Seminal prenoir by Fritz Lang, featuring the key noir themes of man at war with himself and the unspoken affinity between cops and crooks. A textbook of melding plot, visuals and characters.

The Maltese Falcon. John Huston's private eye picture changed everything with its tragic and moving ending. Huston proved that pulp could carry serious ideas, and that wit and charm could be as compelling as action.

The Man I Love. Key woman's melodrama, and proof that noir need not revolve around crime, capers, or murder. A tale of love's missed connections, set in a dark moral universe.

Night and the City. Pure hysteria. A searing portrait of American ambition abroad, featuring the least heroic of all noir heroes, the psychotically ambitious Richard Widmark. One of the nastiest and most thoroughly faithless movies ever made.

Out of the Past. The quintessential noir featuring every motif: Robert Mitchum as a gangster on the run from his own past; a femme fatale, voice-over narration, and flashbacks for a plot that makes no sense; shadowy, expressive camera work; and a deeply misanthropic finale.

BARSON COLLECTION/ARCHIVE PHOTOS

Touch of Evil. Anarchic virtuosity from Orson Welles, who decided to marry his own wreck of a physique to a wreck of a character. Bravura, death-defying camera work and untouched moral complexity put an end to the classic noir era.

Vertigo. The most perverse depiction of love ever made? The most tragic suspense film of all time? Hitchcock's obsessive poem to hopelessness remains his masterpiece. Career-best performances by Jimmy Stewart, Kim Novak, and Barbara Bel Geddes.

Noir began in 1941. It thrives today as a continuation of an American filmic tradition that lives to address classic American themes. For all its dark concerns, noir is seldom depressing. More often, it exhilarates and inspires, offering profound themes and sophisticated filmmaking. By reveling in the violence, paranoia, loss of faith, and fear of betrayal that marks its time and ours, noir grants us a powerful catharsis. And in its deliberate intelligence, noir provides a much-needed antidote to the mindlessness and empty flash of current American cinema.

Whether genre, style, motif, or subculture, noir remains a wolf in sheep's clothing, a secret voice whispering at midnight. Noir is the place where we go to discover the truth about ourselves.

• How to Use This Book •

[1] **Le Samouraï** [2](1967—FRANCE)

[3] 

[4]**Mood Guide: Dream-like Noir-Zen**

[5]*Director:* Jean-Pierre Melville; [6]*Camera:* Henri Decaë; [7]*Screenplay:* Jean-Pierre Melville, Georges Pellegrin

[8]*Cast:* Alain Delon, Cathy Rosier, François Périer, Nathalie Delon

[9]*In French w/English subtitles,* [10]*color*

[11]*Plot:* A silent, mysterious hit-man is ordered to kill the one witness to his earlier hit. Perhaps he will, perhaps he won't.

1 **Film Title**—Films are arranged alphabetically
2 **Year** of film's original commerical release and **country** of origin
3 **Icons** indicate the key noir elements that each film contains. Icons shown for this particular film represent:

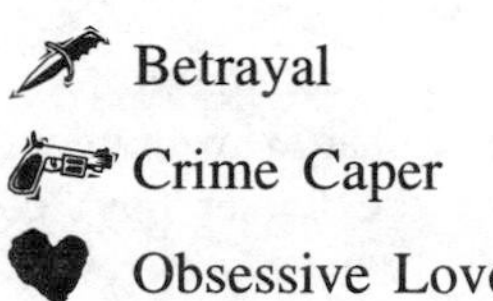
Betrayal
Crime Caper
Obsessive Love

 Suspense

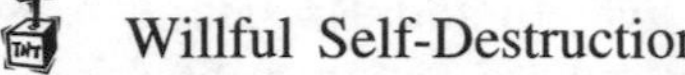 Willful Self-Destruction

Other icons include:

Deadly Self-Delusion

Femme Fatale

Secrets from the Past

Significant Dead Person

4 **Mood**—Describes the emotional atmosphere of the film
5 **Director**
6 **Cinematographer**
7 **Author(s)** of the Screenplay
8 **Cast**
9 **Language** of the film's dialogue
10 **Color**—Whether the film is shot in color or black-and-white (B/W)
11 **Plot**—A brief summary of the plot, designed to give a sense of the story but not to reveal any crucial details.

After Dark, My Sweet (1990—USA)

Mood Guide: Sunlit sensual doom

Director: James Foley; *Camera:* Mark Plummer; *Screenplay:* Robert Redlin, James Foley

Cast: Jason Patric, Rachel Ward, Bruce Dern, George Dickerson

In English, color

Plot: A former boxer stumbles into a child-kidnapping plot set up by a corrupt cop and a beautiful, alcoholic woman. Unwillingly drawn into the caper by the woman's charms, the fighter must contend with her, her psycho partner, and his own fatal demons. . . .

In Robert Stone's bleak novel *Dog Soldiers,* a character unintentionally sums up the entertainment value of noir: "It's nice to see a real loser really lose," he says. And that's *After Dark, My Sweet.* First we meet the losers, then we watch them lose. For connoisseurs of the emotional train wrecks that lie at the heart of noir, *After Dark* is an elegantly constructed demolition derby.

James Foley's (*At Close Range* [page 39] sense of mood is unmatched among contemporary directors. *After Dark*'s languid pacing, air of moral helplessness, and use of composition to underscore character relationships provide an emotional atmosphere as near to classical noir as a modern director could achieve. The only time Foley stumbles—postmodern guy that he is—he errs on the side of that postmodern blight, self-consciousness.

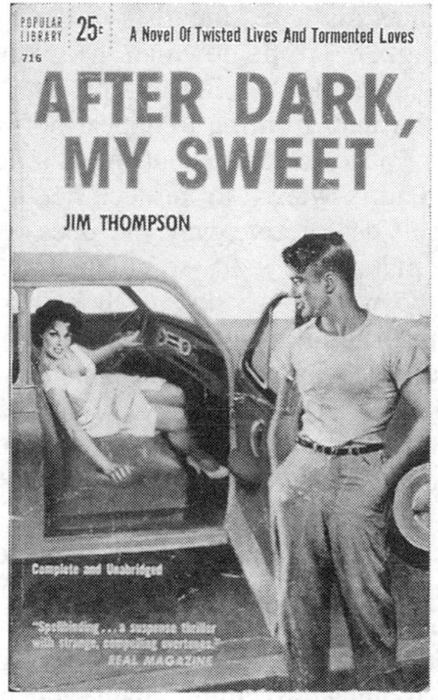

JON HAMMER/ARCHIVE PHOTOS

Shot for maximum melancholy in the pitiless sunshine of the country-club Southwest, the film wastes no time in establishing its characters' hopelessness. As the opening credits roll, Jason Patric stumbles from his hideout in a rock-strewn hill. At first, his voice-over tale of woe makes little sense. We learn that he's on the run and, through flashbacks, that he suffered gravely in a boxing match. The rest is a mystery. Patric sips a beer in a deserted roadhouse. A beautiful young woman comes in. When Patric talks to her, the bartender tries to throw him out. With one punch, Patric knocks the bartender unconscious.

The tale is launched: The beautiful woman—Rachel Ward, in a sexy, self-mocking, and multileveled performance—needs muscle for a harebrained kidnapping scheme. Patric, who falls hopelessly in love at the sight of her, seems a likely candidate. Bruce Dern plays Ward's coconspirator, the corrupt former policeman who dreamed up the crazy plan. Like Ward and Patric, Dern struggles to appear in control, but his weakness is manifest the instant he opens his loser mouth.

Dern is amazing. He tamps down all the overworked mannerisms he spent a career developing and presents a lucid portrait of a deeply twisted man fighting to appear normal. Dern's ineffectuality moves Patric to scorn, but Ward's helplessness triggers pity, and Patric wants to protect her. In Patric's own stumbling and self-destructive way, he does. And therein lies the tragedy that makes the story so compelling.

Foley keeps the wide blue sky in all his exterior compositions. It suggests the immense social and even cosmic weight pressing down on the characters. Once indoors, Foley fills the frame with close-ups. Thus he suggests that each character's personal mythology looms large, even if the outside world remains impervious to their desires. Where a B/W, classical cinematographer would drape the interiors in shadow, Mark Plummer drenches the characters in fluorescent blues and greens. His cinematography offers a rare combination of stark beauty and emotional narrative.

The screenplay, which hews closely to Jim Thompson's heartless novel, is unusually tight, spare, and well-constructed. The action develops the characters, and the characters' souls shape the action. Foley inverts the usual noir suspense device: The caper means nothing. All tension and energy derive from everyone's search for sanctuary, love, or peace of mind (no matter how perverse their fantasy of Nirvana or method of attainment). Foley finds compassion and poetry in this tale of fuck-ups fucking up, and so do we. Foley explains nothing, creates a pervasive air of sultry doom, and grants his characters no more sympathy than they deserve.

Hot love scenes, too.

Other recommended rentals directed by James Foley:
At Close Range (page 39)

The American Friend (1977—Germany)

Mood Guide: Arty angst

Director: Wim Wenders; *Camera:* Robby Müller; *Screenplay:* Wim Wenders

Cast: Dennis Hopper, Nicholas Ray, Bruno Ganz, Samuel Fuller, Lisa Kreuzer

Mostly in English, some German with English subtitles; color

Plot: In this convoluted, sophisticated tale of murder and art forgery, an art world con man convinces a craftsman that the craftsman's illness has worsened, leaving him only weeks to live. Offered a huge sum of money, the craftsman—in order to support his family from beyond the grave—becomes a hit-man for a French gangster. The con man and the craftsman become unlikely friends, and the con man comes to the craftsman's aid.

Wim Wenders's best movies are astonishing hybrids of American energy and European artiness. That's no easy trick: When Wenders indulges his arty side, the results can be torturously slow-paced. Here, for the only time in his career, Wenders renounced self-consciousness and devoted himself to plot, character, cinematography, and suspense.

On the one hand, there's Ripley (Dennis Hopper): a speed freak, a hustler; a stylish, rootless hustler with the attention span of a gnat, the arrogance of a vampire, and the aggressive instincts of a wolverine. On the other, there's Jonathan (Bruno Ganz): self-contained, stolid, an Old World craftsman, the good burgher whose safe universe contains his craft, his family, and the denial of everything else. Ripley confronts his dread by laying waste to whatever appears in his path. Jonathan hides from the certain knowledge of his own mortality by creating objects that endure. The two collide, and the tale begins.

In Wenders's adaptation of Patricia Highsmith's dark suspense novel *Ripley's Game,* Ganz and Hopper run the roundelay of adult male friendship: suspicion, insult, revenge, grudging admiration, teamwork, and, in the end, betrayal. Hopper gives the performance of his life. Wenders cast Hopper at the bottom of his career, when Hopper was regarded as not merely drug-addled and unhirable, but genuinely psychotic. Hopper's spontaneous, instinctive acting was as much an irritant to the controlled, overrehearsed Ganz as Hopper's character Ripley is to Ganz's Jonathan.

A famous drunken fistfight between Hopper and Ganz midway through shooting smoothed things between them, and mirrored offscreen the uneasy alliance forming between their characters.

To showcase this clash between the archetypal American and the ultimate European, Wenders successfully invented a new genre: the intersection of European art film and American noir. The hypnotic pace, solemn camera work, and unshakable air of profundity—plus a slew of famous film directors in cameo appearances—equals art film with a capital *A.* The suspense, tension, understated violence, and existential doom are hallmarks of noir.

Though the plot may not make a whole lot of sense the first time around—and the thick European accents of a couple of the major actors don't help—*The American Friend* is worth the effort. Few movies from any era or genre offer such rich characters, realistic human relationships, gripping action sequences, or sly humor.

Check out the gleeful, sadistic cameo by American director—and Wenders's mentor—Nicholas Ray (*Rebel Without a Cause, In a Lonely Place*) and the controlled moral rage of Lisa Kreuzer, Wenders's wife at the time of filming. Add to this the deep, oversaturated colors, the perfectly weird supporting cast, and the astounding music of Bernard Herrmann (he scored most of Hitchcock's films) and the result is a film you will rent again and again, and in which you'll discover a new pleasure every time.

Other recommended rentals directed by Wim Wenders:
Alice in the Cities
Lightning Over Water
Paris, Texas
The State of Things (page 230)
Wings of Desire

Angel Heart (1987—USA)

Mood Guide: Bloody supernatural suspense

Director: Alan Parker; *Camera:* Michael Seresin; *Screenplay:* Alan Parker

Cast: Mickey Rourke, Robert De Niro, Charlotte Rampling, Lisa Bonet, Brownie McGhee

In English; color

Plot: A private eye is hired by a creepy client to find a singer who reneged on a deal. He searches from Harlem to the voodoo-happy *haut monde* of New Orleans; wherever he goes, people get dead. The weirdo client appears repeatedly, reminding the P.I. of something he's trying very hard to forget. When he remembers, bad things happen.

A murky, amusing, and faithless faux noir starring Mickey Rourke in perhaps the quintessential noir plot. Mickey is hired to look for someone evil. As the story develops, that someone comes to closely resemble Mickey himself.

In the dog days of post–World War II New York, Rourke is approached by a sinister new client, Robert De Niro. They meet in a voodoo church in Harlem. A bloodstained chapel wall is the first hint of the godless universe awaiting Rourke. As

Rourke searches for a singer who apparently defrauded De Niro, he suffers recurring and unpleasant supernatural flashbacks. Also, everyone he talks to dies. When they do, director Parker takes the noir notion of a man lost to society, and to himself, one step beyond.

Here, Parker proves himself a bit grandiose. He pours four times as much blood as necessary over every violent or sexual scene, forcing the viewer to check out of the story and contemplate the director's foolishness. It's a shame, because the strongest lure of *Angel Heart* is Parker's ability to sustain a mood—a mood of groping, hopeless questing and palpable, building fear. Parker seems to react against his own skilled understatement; perhaps he found the mood too noir-subtle and felt he had to make the implicit explicit. After all, he did direct *Fame*.

When Rourke reaches the spooky world of old New Orleans, the hysteria increases. De Niro shows up as punctuation, as the satanic embodiment of what Rourke fears the most. Here folks not only get dead, but mutilated, too, including the erotically elusive Charlotte Rampling. You have to admire the sheer nastiness of a movie that would slaughter Charlotte Rampling without granting her (or us) a single love scene.

Nor does Parker cut much slack to American cultural icons. Blues guitar pioneer Brownie McGhee plays an irascible New Orleans hoodoo-man who fares no better than the rest. Most interesting among the icons is *The Cosby Show* veteran Lisa Bonet, who shows a rare gift for natural understatement and for taking off her clothes. She's hypnotically relaxed and quite convincing as the youthful future of voodoo priestess-hood. She's also incarnates Mickey's chickens coming home to roost.

Angel Heart's virtues are its creepy atmosphere, its bleak view of man's self-defeating attempts at transcendence, and a blood-chilling cameo by Robert De Niro. It's a convincing tale of a man lost in a universe without morals, a man who prides himself on his vicious cynicism but who discovers that he's an innocent lamb compared to his enemies. Only in noir does a hero learn a tragic lesson when it turns out he's nowhere near as corrupt as he thought. But, like all doomed noir protagonists, Mickey reaps no more than what he has sown.

Bonus features include evil New Orleans *mise-en-scène*; a

great soundtrack; a famous, bizarre, protracted love scene featuring Lisa Bonet; and an extremely cool, totally noir message for Mickey at the finale.

Graphically, needlessly bloody and violent. Especially the love scenes.

Ascenseur Pour L'Echafaud (Elevator to the Gallows and Lift to the Scaffold) (1957—France)

Mood Guide: French art-noir *avec* pretension

Director: Louis Malle; *Camera:* Henri Decaë; *Screenplay:* Ronald Nimier, Louis Malle

Cast: Maurice Ronet, Jeanne Moreau, Lino Ventura

In French, with English subtitles; B/W

Plot: Our hero, in love with his boss's wife, knocks off the boss, only to find himself trapped in an elevator. His girlfriend wanders the city searching for him, while two crazy French kids commit murder in our hero's car, using our hero's gun.

A slow, self-consciously arty, and pretentious murder-for-love antithriller. Louis Malle, overreaching in his film debut, attempts an art film, a noir that comments on noir, and a political broadside against France's ill-fated colonial efforts and the resultant *malaise* at home.

Jeanne Moreau, looking typically dreamy and postorgasmic, waits as her lover (Maurice Ronet) murders her husband (her lover's boss) and arranges the crime to look like a suicide. Ronet plays a robotic former paratrooper, a man supposedly stripped of emotion by his experiences in the hellpits of Indochina. After he kills his boss, Ronet finds himself stuck in an elevator—trapped by the corporate bourgeois machinery or some such metaphorical crap.

Meanwhile, his car is stolen by a young punk who commits a

murder with Ronet's gun. As Ronet struggles to free himself and the punk takes off, Moreau wanders the city, asking after Ronet in every bar and restaurant. Naturally, no one has seen him. When Ronet emerges from the elevator, he is immediately arrested for the crime he did not commit. Moreau's heartsick searching, meanwhile, has robbed Ronet of any potential alibi. Her love, in other words, has killed him. *Quel ironic, n'est-ce pas?*

Yet, boring.

Malle's soporific (read: anticommercial) pacing keeps the viewer distanced from the story, which never becomes more than the framework on which Malle hangs his formal, antinarrative concerns. Though much appreciated by film critics for those concerns, there is little drama and no convincing emotion.

A few worthwhile moments make this a decent rent for the serious film student or devout Louis Malle fan: Ronet sits down to breakfast at his favorite café, unaware that the morning paper features his face above the headline MURDERER. The other patrons read their papers and murmur as Ronet munches his croissant, oblivious. The redoubtable Lino Ventura weighs in as a tough cop, and there's plenty of cool 1950s Paris street atmosphere.

A seamy air of corruption, misplaced romanticism, and sexy violence help pass the endless minutes as Malle's camera creeps, at the pace of an *escargot,* to reveal one more expressionless face in weird, science-fiction close-up. The sole, saving grace is the improvised, boppy score by Miles Davis.

The Asphalt Jungle (1950—USA)

Mood Guide: Gritty, tough-minded caper

Director: John Huston; *Camera:* Harold Rosson; *Screenplay:* Ben Maddow, John Huston

Cast: Sterling Hayden, Louis Calhern, Jean Hagen, James Whitmore, Sam Jaffe, Marilyn Monroe

In English; B/W

Plot: A good-hearted criminal mastermind emerges from prison with a plan for a grand heist. Financed by a corrupt lawyer, the mastermind enlists a gang of experts. The gang attempts the robbery, but must deal with the double-crossing lawyer.

John Huston (*The Maltese Falcon*) directs in his usual classicist manner, with crystal-clear shots, hard-edged lighting, and a rhythmic, pulse-beat cadence to the editing, which is the best in the history of the subculture (even better than *Chinatown*). While the content—crime, corruption, a world without hope in which every effort comes to naught—may seem subversive, the style is pure Hollywood. It's Huston's commercial skills that provide the drum-tight structure and make the film so entertaining.

Marilyn Monroe and Don Haggerty in *The Asphalt Jungle*

Huston's sensibility is purely American. He makes no great metaphysical pronouncements. He's more interested in American evils, which he perceives as neither spiritual nor philosophical. They are: an insatiable desire for more, the inevitability of betrayal when a couple of bucks are at stake, and our inability to say no to one more illicit thrill.

Sam Jaffe shines as an intellectual hoodlum. He plans a big robbery, recruiting Sterling Hayden as a "hooligan," a guy who's tough as nails, if none too bright. Jaffe needs start-up capital and so gets involved with a slimy lawyer, played to perfection by Louis Calhern. The robbery goes awry, not from lack of courage or ability, but from a series of minor, unavoidable accidents, and from the general sliminess of mankind.

Huston presents the robbery as a straightforward Horatio Alger story: American men using their hard-earned skills to better their position in life. The robbery is among the best-staged heists in noir. The simple visual treatment, the precise movements of the actors, and the absence of music on the sound track raise the tension to the boiling point. Huston shoots in gritty, real-feeling urban locations and crams his characters way up in our faces, filling the forward edge of the frame. He blasts white-hot light from one side, casting harsh shadows on everyone. The tight shots create a claustrophobia that is entirely deliberate.

Though Hayden grabs the screen, it's the big-voiced, bald-pated Louis Calhern who gets the most close-ups. For Huston, Calhern incarnates the smooth-talking, avaricious hypocrites who run the world. Huston is unusually sympathetic to the petty crooks, lauding their in-group loyalty, toughness, and know-how. The downfall of each criminal is presented as a minor tragedy, but Huston shows Calhern no mercy.

Marilyn Monroe, looking impossibly fresh-faced and young—so untouched as to be almost unrecognizable—cameos as Calhern's sweet, near-virginal mistress. Even at this early stage, her star-power is incandescent; you cannot take your eyes off her. That doesn't mean she can act, however. Her struggle to deliver her lines is disconcertingly contrary to the spirit of the film, which honors taut, crisp execution above all.

But even Huston's best work includes moments of momentum-destroying cornball. The worst of these clankers is a self-righteous speech delivered by the goody-goody police commissioner at the film's conclusion. He rails against dirty cops and reminds us that without law and order we would be living in anarchy. Maybe the studio demanded this cant, maybe the censors put pressure on Huston. Or maybe the story turned out to be too bleak even for him.

Other recommended rentals directed by John Huston:
Fat City
The Maltese Falcon (page 173)
The Red Badge of Courage
The Treasure of the Sierra Madre

At Close Range (1984—USA)

Mood Guide: Oedipal crime in the heartland

Director: James Foley; *Camera:* Juan Ruiz Anchia; *Screenplay:* Nicholas Kazan

Cast: Sean Penn, Christopher Walken, Mary Stuart Masterson, Chris Penn

In English; color

Plot: Two brothers join their father's gang of farm equipment thieves. When the father fears informers, he starts murdering his own gang. When he fears his sons, he does even worse.

Based on the true story of a contemporary father-son gang of thieves, and of the father's betrayal of the son, this modern tragedy brings all the existential dread usually associated with rain-slicked, nighttime streets to the sunny farmlands of Pennsylvania.

Sean Penn's adolescent aimlessness has no criminal component until he reunites with the father who abandoned him, played to cunning, redneck perfection by Christopher Walken. Hoping to earn his dad's love, Penn becomes embroiled in his father's gang of tractor thieves. When Sean tries to leave the gang behind, he learns a hard lesson about the limits of paternal forgiveness.

Before Walken's much-deserved success turned his diabolical

menace into self-parody, he brought a complex amorality to his villains. Here his character thinks no one sees how dangerous he is; he believes he can charm the world. When Walken lets the evil emerge from behind the smile, it's terrifying. Walken plays the scariest guys on earth, and this guy is the scariest of all. Maybe because he's the ultimate, impossible-to-please daddy-figure, a daddy who confuses himself with the God of the Old Testament: a daddy of stern retribution and then some.

Nicholas Kazan, director of *Dream Lover,* wrote the screenplay. Modern noir specialist James Foley (*After Dark, My Sweet*) directs. Foley's understanding of the characters and their context make him a Scorsese of the heartland. Foley captures those endless empty rural nights and the pointless, unemployed days spent waiting for the nights. He shows the frustrations such a modern pastoral life produces and the violence that can provide the only relief.

The supporting cast—anchored by Tracey Walker as the psychotic Patch—includes Kiefer Sutherland, Candy Clark, David Strathairn, and even Crispin Glover(!). Mary Stuart Masterson debuts; her performance as a budding farm girl in love with Penn launched her career. Those familiar with her more lackadaisical performances in recent films may be surprised. She's never been so lusty, tough, or believable.

Since no picture from this period of Penn's career would be complete without an appearance by Madonna, she sings "Live to Tell" over the closing credits. The refrain from the song, sampled and elongated, serves as the backing sound track. The ballad is the most heartfelt and least contrived of Madonna's oeuvre.

There's plenty of heartbreaking violence and not one minute of it is gratuitous.

Other recommended rentals directed by James Foley:

After Dark, My Sweet (page 28)

The Big Clock (1948—USA)

Mood Guide: Loopy, farcical thriller-of-manners

Director: John Farrow; *Camera:* John Seitz; *Screenplay:* Jonathan Latimer

Cast: Ray Milland, Charles Laughton, Maureen O'Sullivan, George Macready

In English; B/W

Plot: A newspaper editor is trapped inside his own office, framed by his boss, an all-powerful media tycoon. The editor must avoid getting shot by the cops, convince his wife not to leave him, keep his job, and find the real killer. His only assets are his wits and a hilarious ensemble of New York wackos.

More screwball comedy than noir, *The Big Clock*'s big moments derive from snappy dialogue and over-the-top humor. Ray Milland, seeming weirdly distracted throughout, struggles to convey *savoir faire* as a magazine editor trapped in that old standby, a web of intrigue.

Milland's boss, a mega-publisher played with seductive and surprisingly contemporary malice by Charles Laughton, murders his mistress. Laughton pins the blame on Milland, and Milland doesn't dare produce his alibi. Why? Because it might *irritate his wife*—talk about upholding while subverting 1950s value systems! Milland allows himself to be pursued as a killer because he can't admit to his wife that he bought a (chaste) drink for another woman.

Such subversive Noel Coward humor provides the true motor of the picture. The filmmakers seem most to enjoy the funny stuff, because the suspense relies entirely on close-ups of Milland and he's not up to the job. The hard-bitten voice-over, delivered in Milland's urbane, overly articulate, and not at all hard-bitten manner, serves as the perfect metaphor for *The Big Clock*'s confused priorities.

PARAMOUNT PICTURES/ARCHIVE PHOTOS

Rita Johnson and Ray Milland in *The Big Clock*

Yet, *The Big Clock* remains consistently entertaining, insightful, and never camp. Laughton is masterful as a bullying, manipulative boss—hard as nails in the office, soft as taffy with his mistress. That softness proves the source of Laughton's murderous rage. Laughton, lisping and speaking in a slow rasp, shows the pain underlying his character's power. It's a riveting performance and provides the necessary anchor to this light fare. George Macready, with his pitted face and silky, resonant voice, plays Laughton's right-hand man, a smooth corporate assassin.

Macready and Laughton supply the dark cynicism at the story's core. Serving as symbols for the soulless corporate world, they will do anything to displace blame or advance themselves. In the face of their amorality and combined power, Milland finds himself unable to escape his suddenly oppressive workaday world. His once comfy office becomes a death trap. Thus *The Big Clock* makes its points about the pointlessness of pursuing conventional success. Milland's downfall, which is inseparable from his enlightenment about the corporate culture he has served so faithfully, is presented as simple moral progress.

Cinematographer John Seitz shoots the implacable world of big business in smooth grays, and the rapidly encircling dragnet in harsh-contrast B/W. He and director Farrow indulge in numerous astounding tracking shots of daunting length and complexity. The longest, talkiest scenes are performed in single, unbroken takes.

The snazziest of these feature Laughton and Macready crossing an enormous office, stepping into an elevator, chatting for several minutes, emerging at another floor, and stepping out. The complex shots compensate for the simple lighting schemes but do not intrude on the storytelling. Perhaps the cinematographer's virtuosity remains unintrusive because Laughton so dominates every scene in which he appears.

The funniest performance is turned in by Elsa Lancaster as a wacky bohemian painter. She serves as the counterweight to Laughton's self-serving pomposity. As amusing as Lancaster may be, the filmmakers don't endorse Bohemia, either. In this cynical world, the artists are just as money-hungry as the murdering executives.

The Big Combo (1955—USA)

Mood Guide: Failed morality tale

Director: Joseph Lewis; *Camera:* John Alton; *Screenplay:* Philip Yordan

Cast: Cornel Wilde, Richard Conte, Jean Wallace, Brian Donlevy, Lee Van Cleef

In English; B/W

Plot: A tough hood runs a mean, efficient mob. A simple cop falls for the hood's girl and tries to save her from the hood and from herself. People get hurt.

Though good cop Wilde and evil gangster Conte perform the requisite cop-criminal identity reversal (Wilde turns heartless and violent; Conte makes a failed, fatal attempt at trust), the story drags and the intended atmosphere of obsession seems forced. Coming late in the classical cycle and clearly an attempt to surpass the director's past accomplishments (the flawless *Gun Crazy*), Combo tries too hard to develop underlying profundity.

ARCHIVE PHOTOS

Lee Van Cleef, Jean Wallace, and Earl Holliman in *The Big Combo*

The screenplay compensates for a lack of cogency with a contrived (though occasionally erotic) undercurrent of sexual perversion. Conte's lover Jean Wallace is helpless before Conte's sadistic seduction; the more Cornel Wilde rejects show-girl Helen Walker, the more she craves him; Lee Van Cleef and Earl Holliman, a matched pair of thug-boys, appear to be lovers. Of all of these, the seldom-seen Wallace is the most interesting. With her breathy voice and unmistakably good breeding, she's a perverse blend of Marilyn Monroe and Grace Kelly. While Wallace is convincingly masochistic, everybody else's ornate sexual peccadilloes play like plot devices.

Cornel Wilde's the weak link, just as John Alton's poetic B/W cinematography is the saving grace. Wilde's a cop who must stifle his emotions in response to the cruelty of his foe (Conte). Unfortunately, Wilde never shows any emotion worth stifling. His cardboard face seems capable of only one expression: a sort of pained, quizzical befuddlement. As a hero he's disconcertingly passive, a bystander to every plot-advancing moment, including the climactic shoot-out. His disengagement leads to ours; it's hard to get involved when the lead character can't bring himself to act or to take action.

Conte is magnetic as usual, a ruthless lady's man who delivers his bullying lines with a *savoir faire* that makes him all the more frightening. The script hampers him with a couple of overwrought violent scenes, including one where he screams into the hearing aid of a suspected informer. After this campy form of torture, though, director Joseph Lewis turns the tables with a memorable image. Conte shuts off the volume on the stoolie's hearing aid just before the guy is executed. Lewis cuts to the victim's point of view, and we see silent machine guns spitting flames before the merciful fade to black. And that's the *Big Combo* experience in a nutshell: overdone, off-putting melodrama followed by extraordinary visual storytelling.

John Alton's camera work is definitive. He and Lewis concentrate on visuals at the expense of the story. The resulting frames are unforgettable: iron-hard shadows, figures in silhouette against a fog, hands and faces barely visible in an ocean of blackness, laserlike beams of light impaling someone like a lightning bolt of truth. The mood is dark. There's hardly a daylight exterior shot in the whole picture.

Wilde's and Wallace's silhouetted, hesitant walk toward one another through the fog and into a future of utter darkness is a noir touchstone. But Alton's genius of form cannot make up for Lewis's pedestrian content. When hit men machine-gun a moll through the back of an armchair, Lewis cuts to her hand lolling down, a cigarette falling from her fingers. Even the greatest noir cinematographer can't redeem such a hackneyed image.

Despite Lee Van Cleef's engaging turn as a laconic hit man, those looking for straight-up gangster kicks should rent something else. Students of noir might overlook the weak plot, hokey acting, and forced dialogue to enjoy extraordinary camera work, Jean Wallace's passive-aggressive sexuality, and Richard Conte's effortless, menacing star-power.

Other recommended rentals directed by Joseph Lewis:
Gun Crazy (page 123)

The Big Heat (1953—USA)

Mood Guide: Repressed saga of revenge

Director: Fritz Lang; *Camera:* Charles Lang; *Screenplay:* Sydney Boehm

Cast: Glenn Ford, Gloria Grahame, Lee Marvin, Jocelyn Brando

In English; B/W

Plot: A straight-arrow cop takes on a crime boss and the crooked policemen on his payroll. When the cop refuses to stop his investigation, his wife is murdered, and he's thrown off the force. Desperate for revenge, the cop enters a netherworld of dames and hit men, seeking to crush the corrupt empire around him.

Ford plays the toughest of tough cops, a man with an iron will and an unbending sense of right and wrong. While investigating a local mobster, Ford uncovers hints of unsavory connections between the mob, the mayor, the police commissioner, and other good citizens of Ford's little town. Enraged at being told to back off, he presses harder. Ford's wife is killed by a car bomb meant for him. Forced to turn in his badge, Ford pursues his wife's killers without the sanctifying overlay of the law. He tracks down his man, corrals him, and returns to cop life vindicated.

Glenn Ford's search for his wife's killers becomes an unknowing quest for his true self. He discovers, even if he can't admit it, a taste for sadism, rough sex, and self-righteous, hypocritical condemnation. Many die as a result of Ford's notions of right and wrong and his commitment thereto. Despite the high body count, Ford remains convinced of his own virtuous superiority.

For once, Lang's metronomic narrative progression and perfectly composed frames rob the story of any connective emotion. Ford, as a character and as an actor, possesses so little insight that he remains unsympathetic, unknowable, and preposterous. His unchanging, petulantly malevolent face and powerful antiglamour make him a black hole of screen energy: No light or spark emerges. Lee Marvin and Gloria Grahame, on the other hand, provide a salacious vibrance, and the picture picks up when they appear.

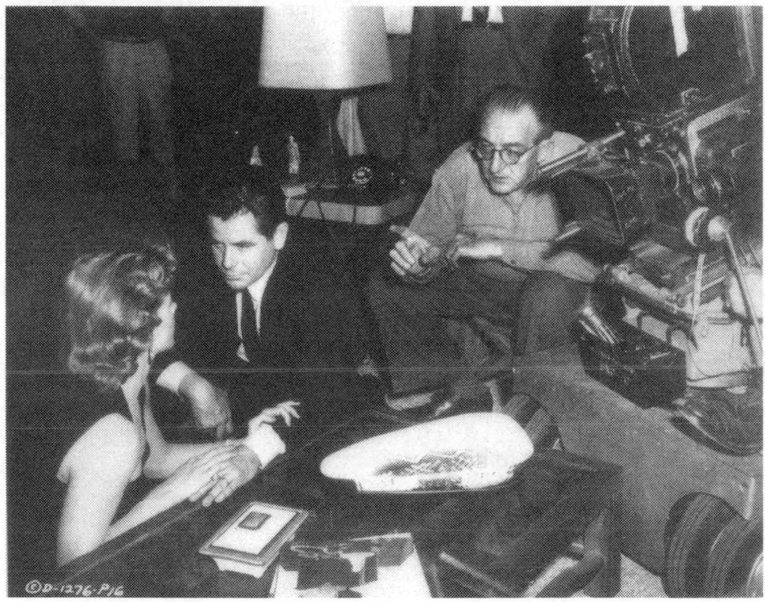

ARCHIVE PHOTOS

Fritz Lang directs Glenn Ford and Jocelyn Brando in *The Big Heat*

Grahame is a powerhouse of unrepressed conflicts. She's casually promiscuous and clearly aroused by Marvin's rough hands and rougher love. Posed as the defiant opposite to Ford's "good" wife, Grahame accepts the warring aspects of her nature and mocks Ford for being unable to do the same. Self-righteous creep that he is, Ford never understands Grahame; he sees her as trash, and exploits her cold-bloodedly. Ford remembers his wife as a saint, but regards other sexually active women as less-than-human whores. Ford, driven to distraction by his lust for Grahame, condemns her for her seductiveness.

And there the noir-ness comes through: The alleged protector of society is as violent, sex-mad, and exploitative as any hoodlum; the perverse whore possesses more sensitivity than the martyred wife; and Ford comes back to his community an honored man despite having blood on his hands up to his elbows. This is Lang's most coldhearted disavowal of society and, as such, seems overly formal, and lacks his harsh wit.

It's a bleak study, punctuated by some of the most famous set pieces in noir. Best known is Gloria Grahame's disfigurement at the hands of *über*-thug Lee Marvin, who flings hot coffee into her face. A loving (and overtly sexual) young wife gets blown to bits, a crippled woman is sacrificed to gangsters, a big bad criminal weeps like a baby after his girlfriend's violent revenge, and yet it all plays at a remove, somehow.

Despite Lang's powerful, functional composition, a wonderfully sparse screenplay, and remarkable work from Marvin and Grahame, the whole is never more than the sum of its parts. *The Big Heat* suffers long, dead spots and never overcomes the basic (and quite unpoetic) repugnance of its hero.

More fun for the noir enthusiast than the casual renter.

Other recommended rentals by Fritz Lang:

M (page 170)
Scarlet Street (page 222)
The Women in the Window (page 270)
You Only Live Once

The Big Knife (1955—USA)

Mood Guide: Hollywood indicts Hollywood

Director: Robert Aldrich; *Camera:* Ernest Laszlo; *Screenplay:* James Poe, from the play by Clifford Odets

Cast: Jack Palance, Ida Lupino, Rod Steiger, Wendell Corey, Shelley Winters, Everett Sloane

In English; B/W

Plot: A movie star faces the price he paid for success. His wife is leaving him, a scandal from the past threatens to engulf him, and the big moneymen from the studio demand his very soul.

Odetts overdoes it; that's his style. Where one bitter speech of recrimination between corrupt capitalists would serve for others, Odetts presents ten. It's galling and undercuts his best ideas, because in the rare event where his characters do talk like people rather than billboards, their struggles become urgently real.

Jack Palance, in an astonishing show of range, plays movie star Charlie Castle: self-obsessed, vain, childish, loyal, loving, sensual, paternal. The action takes place entirely in Charlie's fancy Hollywood home. Odets establishes his themes of power and corruption straightaway. In the opening sequence, Charlie kisses the ass of a powerful gossip columnist to no avail. She intends to dig up an old scandal: Charlie's publicist, it seems, killed someone in a hit-and-run.

Charlie's saintly wife, played by Ida Lupino, is leaving Charlie for his best friend, an incorruptible screenwriter who's giving up the movies to move Back East and write novels. (That Odets presumes to present Novel-Writing Back East as demonstrably more moral and less whorelike than Writing Screenplays Out West certainly reflects the contrast between his era and ours.)

Charlie's maniacal studio head, played by Rod Steiger as a menacing and unintentionally hilarious power-mad monster, demands that Charlie sign a new contract. It means giving up his

ARCHIVE PHOTOS

Robert Aldrich directs Jack Palance and Nick Dennis in the *The Big Knife*

soul, but Charlie signs. Turns out he was more involved in the hit-and-run scandal than he ever admitted, and the studio covered it up. That signing—the willful submission to corruption for money, stardom, and security—forces Charlie to face up to the sins of his past. He cannot, and therein lies his destruction.

Odets shifts maddeningly between pompous speeches and moments of closely observed and deeply moving clarity—moments that usually involve Palance displaying one side or another of his character's dangerously multifaceted personality. Those accustomed to Palance's usual one-note grunting will be amazed.

The smaller characters are stellar: Wendell Corey shines as Smiley, the studio's corporate hit man, the smoothie who can always deal. Jean Hagen appears as the masochistic sex-mad wife of one of Charlie's minions, but she also points up the limitations of the screenplay: Odets presents only two kinds of women—those who are unconditionally loving, loyal, and self-sacrificing, and those who are sexual and therefore destructive.

Granted, Odets is no kinder in his view of men, but he suggests men's lusts should be forgiven rather than condemned. Everett Sloane's portrayal of Charlie's cringing agent carries an awful lot of Shylock, but he's no less stereotyped than anybody else.

Aldrich's pacing is steady and assured. He never escapes the static, theatrical nature of the material, but then, he's stuck in one set for the whole picture. Ernest Laszlo, a key noir cinematographer, relieves or increases the claustrophobia as the moment requires, making his thematic points not with shadow but with simple tracking shots and dramatic framing. He shoots in wide-screen, high-contrast, B/W. The crisp cinematography provides a wealth of character detail. The difference in fabric of the two men's suits, for example, tells us everything we need to know about their relative places in the world. And that sort of distinction is *sooo* Hollywood.

Odetts might preach now and then, but he's a master of structure. As each character is introduced, we wonder how he or she fits into the larger drama and will change when confronted with Hollywood's almighty dollar. Nobody's predictable, everybody's articulate, and the cynicism is knee-deep.

This is Aldrich's first picture after the (complete and shameful) box office failure of his masterpiece, *Kiss Me Deadly* (page 151). If anyone had the right to vent about Hollywood and its machinations, Aldrich is the man. His hard-won credibility makes up for Odets's flights of rhetoric.

(NOTE: *The Big Knife* is available only on laser disc)

Other recommended rentals directed by Robert Aldrich:

The Dirty Dozen

Kiss Me Deadly (page 151)

The Big Sleep (1946—USA)

Mood Guide: Mystery as love-play

Director: Howard Hawks; *Camera:* Sid Hickox; *Screenplay:* Leigh Brackett, William Faulkner, Jules Furthman

Cast: Humphrey Bogart, Lauren Bacall, Martha Vickers, John Ridgeley, Charles Waldron, Elisha Cook, Jr., Dorothy Malone

In English; B/W

Plot: Blackmailers prey on a wealthy old man, threatening to reveal the sleazy secrets of one of his wild daughters. The old man hires Philip Marlowe to intercede. Marlowe discovers a web of gambling, vice, and murder. Does Marlowe dare trust one of the daughters enough to fall in love—even if she can save his life?

When Philip Marlowe, private eye, arrives to help General Sternwood, Sternwood's youngest daughter tries to seduce Marlowe at first sight. The levelheaded, oldest daughter, Lauren Bacall, finds Marlowe contemptible. Blackmailers and gambling debts hang over the family. Mobsters demand payment of various kinds. One daughter is having an illicit affair with possibly fatal consequences. Bogart must sort it out.

Bogie's budding dependence on Bacall, along with their heavy-duty flirting, remains the most charming and believable aspect of *The Big Sleep*. Their mutual attraction dominates the picture. It's surprisingly erotic, even inspirational, and deeply resistant to viewer cynicism. As Bacall's and Bogart's love-play becomes more confident and overt, the pointless machinations of the plot recede into insignificance.

This is a good thing, because the plot makes no sense. Any forward movement bogs down in irrelevant detail or digressions about who double-crossed whom and why. Early on, Hawks dispenses with cogent narrative to focus on what amuses him: a dark *mise-en-scène* that presents L.A. as a town not of sunlight but of shadow and hidden destructive impulses; the emerging love affair between Bogart and Bacall as played for maximum double entendre and sidelong glances; and the creation of Marlowe as a violent, lonely, but never (by his own notions) amoral man. Thus Hawks sets the stage for noirs to come, in which the story remains secondary to emotional and philosophical concerns.

ARCHIVE PHOTOS

However seminal it may be, *The Big Sleep* now plays like a self-aware commentary on private eye movies or a sex comedy with unconvincing violent interludes; it lacks the dark heart of noir. The nonsensical script does not suggest a world in which events and their sequence have no meaning (as does, say, the dark anarchy and narrative randomness of *Out of the Past*). Rather, it suggests literate, cynical, well-paid authors amusing themselves by stooping to genre. In search of self-entertainment, they sought to undermine gangster-genre conventions. Instead, they inadvertently created a template for a newly emerging tradition that would supersede the gangster picture: noir.

The Big Sleep is solid fun in the manner of, say, *Casablanca.* It's a classic of no particular passion, but so wittily self-amused and skillfully constructed as to charm audiences until the end of time. Students of noir will note that the archetypes created here do reappear in much more effective and brutal forms in later pictures; a few are even played by Bogart.

Other recommended rentals directed by Howard Hawks:

Bringing Up Baby
Only Angels Have Wings
Red River
Rio Bravo

The Black Angel (1946—USA)

Mood Guide: Fractured tale of doomed love

Director: Roy William Neill; *Camera:* Paul Ivano; *Screenplay:* Roy Chanslor

Cast: Dan Duryea, June Vincent, Peter Lorre, Broderick Crawford

In English; B/W

Plot: A selfish woman singer is murdered. An innocent sap gets framed and convicted. Searching for the real killer, the sap's wife teams up with the murdered woman's ex-husband, a drunken bum of a piano player. The sap gets convicted, but the search goes on.

June Vincent plays the sap's wife, and a strangely cold-blooded and unsympathetic love interest she makes, too. With her gigantic cheekbones and narrow, suspicious eyes, she's the picture of a frustrated, slightly aged actress desperate for more camera-time than her costars. She displays humanity only when onstage and singing. There, she's surprisingly touching.

She finds Duryea, the dead woman's estranged dipsomaniacal musician husband, and together they decide that crooked nightclub owner Peter Lorre is the real killer. Lorre's hilarious, as usual. They infiltrate Lorre's club as a piano and singer duo and begin their stakeout. There's almost no tension in this section, and the working out of the story seems unusually *pro forma.* No one's actions make any sense, since all the suspense depends on no one having ever read the papers, talked to the cops.

Duryea and Vincent fall in love (to the extent that Vincent is able to communicate such a thing), but Vincent refuses to give up on her condemned-to-die husband, even though he was cheating on her with Duryea's ex-wife. This willful self-destruction can be traced to the counterintuitive motivations that many Woolrich characters share, but it plays like an obvious plot device. Still, there is kinky thrill in watching the would-be lovers eye one another with barely suppressed desire as they pretend *not* to be rooting for the death of Vincent's now rather inconvenient husband.

The film is cheaply told, featuring dialogue painful in its crudity but tragic enough in the end to warrant the attention of those deeply vested in the subculture. Although there are moments of interesting camera work, the main attraction is the sneakily compelling plot derived from the Cornell Woolrich novel on which the screenplay is based.

Rent it for the tragic and moving grace with which Duryea tickles the ivories and for an early glimpse of Broderick (*Highway Patrol*) Crawford.

Blade Runner—The Director's Cut

(1982/1992—USA)

Mood Guide: Moody futurism

Director: Ridley Scott; *Camera:* Jordan Cronenweth; *Screenplay:* Hampton Fancher, David Webb Peoples

Cast: Harrison Ford, Sean Young, Edward James Olmos, Rutger Hauer, Daryl Hannah, Joseph Turkel

English; color

Plot: In the future, robots called "replicants" do man's dirty work in outer space. Six escape and return to Earth, wrecking havoc. A cop specializing in replicant destruction must find and kill the robots. Weary of his work and his life, the cop falls for a beautiful young replicant who believes she's human. Will she prove the cop's salvation or destruction? And can he find the replicants before they find him?

The least self-conscious and most emotionally credible sci-fi ever made, *Blade Runner* spawned an industry of cheapo copycats: the straight-to-video, postapocalypse, war-against- or war-between-robots genre. With their leather breastplates and Woo-like weaponry, all manage to miss the essence of the original. *Blade Runner*'s basic plot might be man versus robot, but the mood of *Blade Runner*—grand, romantic, hypnotic, laconic, doomed—is pure noir.

Harrison Ford, beaten down by a career of chasing and killing humanlike replicants, wants only to retire. His cynical boss forces him to take on one more assignment. Ford meets Sean Young, a replicant who believes herself to be human. Ford knows Young is unreal, but her emotional confusion affects him deeply. Their symbiosis is perfect: He can become vulnerable only to something that isn't human, while she feels emotion for the man she most fears.

Ford's performance is his most confused, his least self-confident, and, as a result, his best by far. His remarkable understatement hides a world of hurt. Sean Young is ravishing, cold, and strangely affecting; she has never equaled her work here. The supporting cast of M.

Emmet Walsh, Edward James Olmos, Rutger Hauer, and even Daryl Hannah never overstates or hits a false note. And all regard their world of flying cars, perpetual rain, and chaotic filth as no more remarkable than we regard our own. This adds a normality that makes the fantastic atmosphere seem even more real.

Among the numerous miracles that Ridley Scott achieves is his characterization of the replicants. Sociopathically violent, they remain somehow sympathetic, even childlike. In the end, even the worst of them proves capable of mercy. That mercy—more than any human offers—allows Ford his chance at redemption. Compromising that redemption is the tantalizing notion that Ford himself may not be human. Ford thus completes the classic noir search-cycle: In his relentless pursuit of something outside himself, he discovers the painful truth of his own essence. That discovery will grant him either ruin or transcendence.

ARCHIVE PHOTOS

Harrison Ford in *Blade Runner*

By eliminating the annoying voice-over that so violated the original—and much inferior—version, Scott forces our attention back where it belongs, on the interaction among the characters.

Because the voice-over offered explanations for Ford's every thought or action, nothing remained for the viewer to interpret. With all emotional ambiguity stripped away, the story was overwhelmed by Scott's detailed rendition of twenty-first century Los Angeles. In the director's cut, with no such explanation available, we watch the characters more carefully. Their tangled motivations acquire greater dramatic force than the costumes, the sets, or the fully formed futurist city.

Ridley Scott takes the rain-soaked nights of noir and turns them to his sci-fi purposes. His L.A. is a dark terrain of splashes and shadows. While there's technological splendor above—as cops and corporate powers zap through the restful night sky in their high-flying machines—below, the street remains a mire of despair. Scott sees the future through a very noir prism: Technology will liberate only those with the money or power to control it.

Great sci-fi, yes. But sci-fi is not the point. With its stunning visual style, its refusal to solve the moral ambiguities it raises, its repugnance for its own thrilling violence, its obsessive attention to lighting, framing, and shadow, and the romantic fatalism of its ending, *Blade Runner* is classic noir.

Other recommended rentals directed by Ridley Scott:
Alien

Blood Simple (1984—USA)

Mood Guide: Blood-soaked absurdism

Director: Joel Coen; *Camera:* Barry Sonnenfeld; *Screenplay:* Ethan Coen, Joel Coen

Cast: Frances McDormand, M. Emmet Walsh, Dan Hedaya, John Getz

In English; color

Plot: A jealous nightclub owner hires a hit-man to kill his philandering wife. The hit-man follows his own agenda instead. Trying to do a good deed, he unleashes a world of mistrust and murder, which he must clean up the only way he knows how.

A man stands in his doorway, absentmindedly gazing out his door, lost in thought. A newspaper sails into the frame in slow motion and strikes the screen door with a THWAP! of doom. It's one of the wittiest moments in noir and a perfect metaphor: The events of the day are paying our hero a visit, whether he wants them to or not.

It also encapsulates the mordant wit and understated filmmaking élan of the Coen brothers. Unlike other modern noir-makers (James Foley, Nick Kazan, Ridley Scott, William Friedkin, and even Wim Wenders), the Coen brothers refuse to present man's preference for bumbling, violent solutions to the most basic problems as proof of the breakdown of society or of the general existential godlessness of existence. No, the Coen brothers take a more Kubrickian view: They wallow in man's blood-drenched stupidity because they think it's really, really funny. The Coen brothers update noir in a singular manner: They infuse it with late-twentieth-century surrealism. Or, if you prefer, they comment on the surreality of late-twentieth-century life via the noir idiom.

The guy with the newspaper is a monosyllabic working man in love with the wife of a brooding club owner. The club owner hires a redneck hit man to kill his wife and her lover. Feeling merciful, the hit man fakes their deaths, instead. Somebody wacks the husband, but fails to dispose of his corpse. So, someone else has to finish the job. The boyfriend thinks the wife committed the murder; she thinks he did. Suspicious by nature, the hit man finds the whole happenstance too screwy and decides to hit the wife and her lover for real.

The plot is fueled by those eternal human attributes that late-twentieth-century life has ratcheted from the merely amusing to the potentially homicidal: willful misunderstanding, paranoia, lack of foresight, lack of brains, and an inappropriate urge to play the hero. This makes for very credible characters, and subsequent filmmaking history has revealed the casting of those characters to be extraordinary: a future Oscar winner (Frances McDormand), a future household name (TV's Dan Hedaya), a stalwart character actor (M. Emmet Walsh), and a guy who stars in trashy hard-R exploitation (John Getz).

The Coen style—deadpan, coldly intellectual, snotty, and unwelcoming—arrives full-blown in this, their first feature. As noir directors should, they turn a pale eye on human love or purpose, present existence as a series of pointless accidents, and believe in our capacity for violence above all other capacities. Their visual storytelling, as befits their budget, is clean and straightforward, but mixed with a cartoony love of cinematic sight gags. These, like most of the plot payoffs, will make you jump.

The camera tracks down a bar, rising slightly to clear a drunk passed out in a puddle of beer. A man buried before his death slowly raises one hand from his premature grave. A dying man lies under a sink staring upward where, to his horror, he can see a cold drop of water beading up on the pipes, ready to spatter him in the face.

Such mannered self-consciousness can be off-putting and admirable at the same time, but it's also shocking because the Coens bring an unabashed hipster's wit to the sexy bloodletting of noir. Their wit—a late-Twentieth-century American updating of Beckett's or Sartre's—is as brutal and hopeless as their violence. This makes *Blood Simple* not only subversive in the finest noir tradition, but also really scary.

Other recommended rentals directed by the Coen brothers:

Barton Fink
Fargo
The Hudsucker Proxy
Miller's Crossing
Raising Arizona

The Blue Dahlia (1946—USA)

Mood Guide: Alan Ladd vehicle

Director: George Marshall; *Camera:* Lionel Lindon; *Screenplay:* Raymond Chandler

Cast: Alan Ladd, Veronica Lake, William Bendix, Doris Dowling, Howard da Silva

In English; B/W

Plot: A returning serviceman is suspected in the murder of his unfaithful wife. Teaming up with the wife of the very man who cuckolded him, the serviceman searches for the real killer, whom he fears may be his shell-shocked best buddy.

Alan Ladd returns from the war with his platoon buddies. William Bendix plays one; he's an overwrought plot device with a steel plate in his head and a potentially lethal case of short-term amnesia. Ladd learns that his wife, the rather strange-looking Doris Dowling, has been unfaithful to him, primarily with nightclub owner Howard da Silva. Shortly after Ladd's return, Dowling is murdered. The script works hard to make Dowling unpleasant (so that her murder will feel like no great loss), begging the question as to why Ladd loved her in the first place. This is one of several ready-made script solutions that reduce the story's credibility and emotional pull.

Ladd meets Veronica Lake and, unaware that she is da Silva's wife, accepts her help in the unraveling of Dowling's murder. Naturally, Ladd is the prime suspect, with da Silver running a close second. Ladd is less concerned with his own wrongful arrest than with the possibility that his pal William Bendix might have murdered Dowling during a steel-plate-induced blackout. He and Lake scurry through the rainy nights and elegant nightclubs, searching out clues, punching guys in the face, and kissing like movie stars, with unmoving hair and lips welded shut.

Ladd's a commanding presence with his deadpan, chiseled mug and air of barely contained violence. Veronica Lake, to put it simply, has one of the two or three most compelling faces in

American movie history. Her physical stillness has an ironic edge that contrasts nicely with Ladd's repressed fury. Ladd and Lake side by side in close-up produce a hypnotic effect. No matter how silly the story, the camera loves these two, and watching them together is gratifying all out of proportion to the pull of the script.

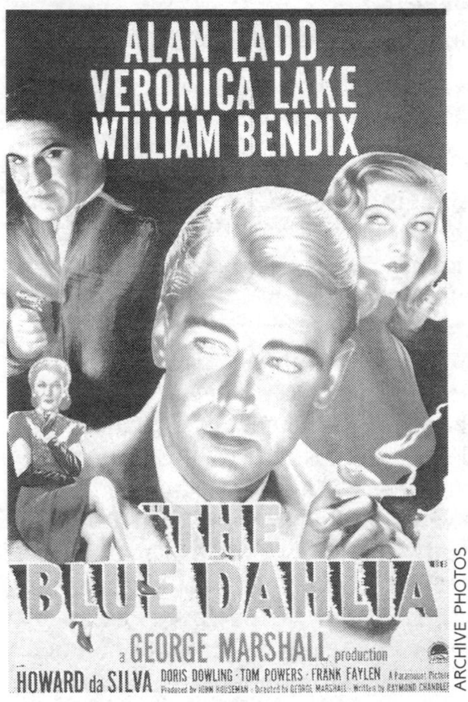

ARCHIVE PHOTOS

While other films make substantial atmospheric hay out of the themes of postwar confusion and coincidence, here everything seems deflatingly straightforward. Ladd and Lake meet because she pulls over in the rain to offer him (a stranger) a lift. This is only one of many unlikely occurrences that stems not from a larger cosmic design but from plot mechanics that lend the dialogue exchanges a dated, cartoonish air.

Further undermining the story is the meddling influence of the U.S. Navy. The most credible suspect is declared innocent because the Navy leaned hard on the production not to follow Chandler's original script, which delivered a much clearer message about the difficulties of assimilating millions of physically and emotionally scarred veterans. Following the Navy's dictates eviscerates the story, and takes much of the punch out of the unraveling of the clues. That is, the clues all point to a certain party. But, since the Navy won't let him be the murderer, another is invented rather late in the game, and some transparently hasty explanations paper over the resulting, gaping plot holes. The bastard conclusion is not only unsatisfying but embarrassing.

As is usual in a Chandler screenplay, figuring out who did what is secondary to the snappy dialogue and one or two moments of breathtaking amorality. Howard da Silva gets to deliver most of the cynical lines, and he's got the smarmy urbanity to pull them off.

Despite a screenplay from Raymond Chandler and competent, shadowy lighting and direction from George Marshall, the absence of any moral complexity makes this an uninvolving, dated, by-the-numbers star vehicle, saved by the chemistry of Ladd and Lake.

Bob le Flambeur (1955—France)

Mood Guide: Ironic French gangsters

Director: Jean-Pierre Melville; *Camera:* Henri Decaë; *Screenplay:* Jean-Pierre Melville, Auguste Le Breton

Cast: Robert Duchesne, Isabelle Corey, Guy Decomble

French, with English subtitles; B/W

Plot: Bob is a semiretired, much-respected gangster. He develops a scheme for robbing the Deauville Casino. To pull off the job, he enlists his protégé: an up-and-coming gangster in love with a wild young girl. Bob must deceive his good friend on the Paris police force, deal with betrayal, and find the right men for the job.

Auteur Jean-Pierre Melville wrote and directed deceptively simple noirs. His compact storytelling, cynical wit, hand-held camera, and use of street patois made him the forerunner of the French film movement known as *Cinéma de la Rue.* His hard-boiled dialogue and crisp visual language made him a mentor to a generation of young American film directors (Scorsese and Coppola among them), who sought out his work when no one in this country remembered it. Melville's influence was equally powerful among the young Turks of the French New Wave: Truffaut, Godard, Rivette, etc.—anyone who sought to shoot on the streets rather than in a studio, and who found in hand-held B/W the poetry of subversion. Melville wrote dialogue to match his visuals: spare, clipped, and functional.

Bob's opening shot—a slow, jerky pan of Montmartre at night—established Melville as a low-budget master. Melville's understated cinema delivers the following message: "I have no money. I know nothing of technique. I'm not a fancy guy. But I know my characters, I know my milieu, and I will not lie or manipulate. Here is my story, told with truth, please enjoy. And, remember, these gangsters, these mythic creatures, carry the good and evil in all of us. Look closely and you may recognize yourself."

Bob le Flambeur (Bob the Gambler) is one of cinema's enduring constructions, a completely modern (for the Fifties) heroic model for an entirely French sensibility. Cooler than James Bond, always relaxed and in charge, Bob drives a big American convertible slowly, slowly through the rain-slick, late-night, unbearably existential streets of Paris, holding the wheel casually with one hand while the other dangles stylishly out the window.

Bob, in his buckled overcoat or his oversized fedora (on him it looks good), both protects and falls for wayward angels of the Montmartre night. Cool as he is, Bob cannot resist the ennui of encroaching middle age. He gets a crackpot idea for one last big heist. So Bob plans and schemes with all his coolness intact, but you know about pesky old fate . . . and no director is more fatalistic than Melville.

While most noir films villainized women for their sexual hunger, Melville worships one of the most amoral femmes fatale in movie history. The magnificent, sixteen-year-old Isabelle Corey jumps in and out of beds, sating herself and breaking hearts without a backward glance. Melville not only does not condemn her, he congratulates her on her ability to rule her (admittedly tiny) world with no more powerful a weapon than her own carnality. Her casual, erotic nudity is a shocking surprise when *Bob* is compared to American films of the same era.

As Melville himself stated, *Bob* is not exactly a noir but a comedy of manners, in which the cops and crooks adhere to a rigorous, if unspoken, code of conduct. Melville is interested in atmosphere (not crime), in young lust and old folly, in style and its power.

The result is charming, light, and enjoyable. The story zips along agreeably, and it may only be afterward that you realize how skillfully Melville has created this imaginary, romantic world that for the previous ninety minutes seemed so real. A simple masterpiece, a triumph of wit and style.

Other recommended rentals directed by Jean-Pierre Melville:

Le Deuxième Soufflé (page 99)
Le Doulos (page 112)
Le Samourai (page 219)

Body and Soul (1947—USA)

Mood Guide: Boxing = class struggle

Director: Robert Rossen; *Camera:* James Wong Howe; *Screenplay:* Abraham Polonksy

Cast: John Garfield, Lilli Palmer, William Conrad, Canada Lee, Anne Revere, Lloyd Goff

In English; B/W

Plot: There's a charismatic young man with two strong fists and no moral compass. Despite the unconditional love of his devoted mother and loyal girlfriend, he corrupts his one natural gift—boxing—by falling in with a crooked fight promoter. Our hero races from fight to fight, leaving behind his mother, girlfriend, and best buddy. Just as his star is peaking, the crooked promoter insists that the fighter throw his championship bout. . . .

Garfield plays a greedy young man with no ideas and lots of ambition. His ineffectual immigrant parents want him to get an education, but he can't stand the thought of ending up like them. When his father is murdered, Garfield signs with a corrupt fight promoter. His excuse is that he has to support his mother. In truth, he's overcome with money-lust.

The promoter, played as the embodiment of the indifferent, exploitative boss(es) by Lloyd Goff, colludes in the death of Garfield's best friend. Garfield shrugs it off. The promoter heartlessly refuses to tell Garfield that an opponent suffers from a cerebral blood clot. Garfield nearly kills the man. Even after learning the truth, Garfield sticks with the promoter. In pursuit of filthy lucre, Garfield willingly sells his soul. Yet he remains charmingly immune to his own corruption. Garfield's lovability carries the film's weaker moments.

Opposing the boss in the war for Garfield's soul (and thence for the heart of the American working man) is Garfield's decent, hardworking mother and slavishly devoted girlfriend. Garfield's girlfriend is never explicitly described as Jewish (as are Garfield and his mom), but she's proud of her immigrant status, proud that her family "has always been nothing fancy." Garfield abandons her, preferring an overtly *shiksa* goddess. Garfield's lust for the tall, blond gold-digger is further proof of his distorted values.

Garfield hires the boxer he almost killed, a broken-down black fighter played by Canada Lee. Lee's performance of frustrated rage, fear, fealty, and trampled dignity is the most moving of the film. But Polonsky's message-making interferes. He presents Lee and Garfield as the hopeful bonding of Jews and African-Americans in opposition to the exploiter-class. There's also something of that horrible fifties concept, The Noble Negro, in Lee's character. Given that Lee had to play a man as well as a Concept, his performance is all the more astonishing.

It's a boxing picture, so there's plenty of boxing. Garfield never punches like a real fighter; he can look pretty silly. Cinematographer James Wong Howe forgoes his usual knife-edge and B/W for a muddier, grayer look, one that evokes the cigar-smoky arenas where Garfield plies his trade. The early fights are crude and quick, designed to showcase brutality. But the film's final bout, which goes on and on, is a hymn to the sport, to the rage and poetry with which the working man bashes his fellow for the amusement of the *über*-class.

A true message picture—one of the last and most annoyingly sincere examples of a Left-leaning, (self-consciously) Jewish social realism that drove Joseph McCarthy absolutely crazy. Just as the picture makes no bones about its sympathies—pro–working class, pro-immigrant, and anti-capitalist, McCarthy pulled no punches in his reaction to it. The film's three principals—director Rossen (*The Hustler*), screenwriter Polonsky (*Force of Evil* [page 117]), and star Garfield—had their lives and careers ruined by the House Un-American Activities Committee.

Body and Soul's noir-ness derives from the unyielding pessimism of its vision of work, brotherhood, greed, and sex. Despite its dated moments, the picture, like boxing itself, retains a visceral, glamorous power. How worthwhile you find it will depend entirely on how much you agree with its message.

Other recommended rentals directed by Robert Rossen:
The Hustler

Cape Fear (1961—USA)

Mood Guide: *Leave It to Beaver* goes to hell

Director: J. Lee Thompson; *Camera:* Samuel Leavitt; *Screenplay:* James R. Webb

Cast: Gregory Peck, Robert Mitchum, Polly Bergen, Martin Balsam

In English; B/W

Plot: A psychopath serves his time in prison and comes after the family of the lawyer who put him there. He stalks them, using one barely legal harassment after another until the family must cross the line to protect themselves.

A late-cycle metaphorical post-noir that accurately identifies the key fear of the post-noir audience: Would their *Leave It to Beaver* lifestyle be safe from dark forces within and without?

In this oppressive, creepy, and somewhat stilted defense of *Beaver*-dom, Robert Mitchum plays America's id, a vicious killer dedicated to making Gregory Peck's life a living hell.

Peck is the attorney who sent Mitchum to prison. Now free, Mitchum comes after Peck, and Peck's nauseatingly wholesome wife and child, with every semi-legal trick at his disposal. As Mitchum's harassment escalates from the merely annoying to the disturbingly pathological, Peck deliberately lures Mitchum into the bayou outback. There, aboard the family houseboat, Peck plays out his role as protector of the family while Mitchum proves himself predator incarnate.

Mitchum's performance is pure evil, and, in its way and for its day, is much more chilling than De Niro's performance in Martin Scorsese's Grand Guignol remake. The venomous force of Mitchum's hatred makes him a lot sexier than the constipated Peck, who plays a buttoned-down adult, as usual. Mitchum drops any notions of vanity or self-consciousness to deliver a villain of memorable complexity and neorealist psychosis. Mitchum's charisma generates great contradictions for *Cape Fear,* mainly because it's impossible to cheer for Peck and his family.

ARCHIVE PHOTOS

Robert Mitchum and Gregory Peck in *Cape Fear*

They're unbearably boring, repressed, and terrified of any expressed desire. Peck's marriage is so unneurotic, communicative, sexless, and perky that the desire to see it smashed to bits rises in the viewer unbidden. Polly Bergen plays the wife, and she ain't no feminist; she bursts into tears of paralysis when any crisis appears. Peck eventually learns to hate as virulently as Mitchum and allows himself to sink to Mitchum's level in order to fight, all the while refusing to relinquish any of his self-righteous claims to middle-class respectability.

And then there's the houseboat: all the comforts of home, all the vulnerability of a life at sea. Into the midst of this illusion of safety comes Mitchum, eager for blood. After all his failed attempts to make Peck and his suburban world admirable, director Thompson finally gets down to his real area of interest. Mitchum and Peck share one of the most unredeemed, sadistic, and graphic hand-to-hand fight scenes of any film of this era. And thus Thompson undermines everything about the American Dream he just spent two hours extolling.

Mitchum and Peck prove to have much in common. Each will murder, each is capable of brutality, each is driven to dominate. Though Peck is intended to represent the cherished (early sixties) American ideal that a threat of force must be met with an equal or greater threat, the enthusiasm he brings to the fight reads quite differently. It's a non-stop metaphor-fest, complete with a second-rate but still enjoyable Bernard Herrmann score and intense high-contrast B/W cinematography.

Intended or not, the clear message of *Cape Fear* is that in the heart of every suburban daddy burns a vicious, bloodthirsty demon. Peck finds transcendence in his righteous mayhem, and reconnects to the core of his supposedly neglected manhood.

A bit tedious, a bit obvious, but absolutely compelling as a window into the era of its production.

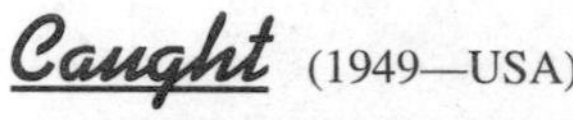 Caught (1949—USA)

Mood Guide: Suspenseful woman-in-peril romance

Director: Max Ophuls; *Camera:* Lee Garmes; *Screenplay:* Arthur Laurents

Cast: Barbara Bel Gedes, Robert Ryan, James Mason, Curt Bois

In English; B/W

Plot: A working girl dreams of a rich, idle life. She falls for a millionaire; he proves psychotic. Desperate for independence, she takes work as a secretary in a medical office and there meets a dashing young doctor. Torn between duty to her husband and the pull of her heart, she must choose before it's too late.

A harrowing study of dependence, exploitation, the deceptions of love, and the high price of redemption. With a vision as dark as any crime story, Max Ophuls makes an elegant, modern ''romance'' whose theme is not the elusiveness of love, but the abuse, confusion, and guilt that so often accompanies its pursuit. The only violence in this ''women's noir'' is psychological, as Barbara Bel Geddes confronts her conflicting needs for affection and financial ease.

Bel Geddes plays a naive working girl seeking both true love and an easier life. She falls for Robert Ryan, or is it his millions? Ryan's great wealth grants him a life of ease, but also the dubious privilege of abusing everyone around him. Ryan's psychiatrist tells him not to marry Bel Geddes, that he will destroy her. Ryan marries her just to prove his shrink wrong.

Once married, Ryan makes Bel Geddes's life a living hell. He orders her around, insults her in front of his friends, and abandons her for months at a time. Her only companion is Ryan's oily majordomo, played with languid, continental snottiness by Curt Bois. Unable to bear his teasing, Bel Geddes slaps Bois in the face. He laughs, reminding her that it's his job to take the punishment she wishes she could dish out to Ryan. As much as she loathes Ryan, Bel Geddes finds herself unable to run. This stems not from an addiction to Ryan's money, which

Robert Ryan and Barbara Bel Geddes in *Caught*

she sensibly begins to disdain, but from the classic paralysis of the abused spouse.

When she threatens to leave, Ryan taunts her, saying that she has no skills and is thus dependent on him and his money. To prove him wrong, Bel Geddes takes a job as a receptionist for an earnest, handsome doctor, played by James Mason. As her infatuation for Mason grows, Ryan appears and begs Bel Geddes to return. He pleads his love, but after several days of much-missed luxury, Bel Geddes learns that Ryan brought her back so she could make an appearance at a family vacation. She leaves again, but discovers that she is pregnant.

Ryan swears to Bel Geddes that he will break her, that he will hold her as his prisoner until her personality is destroyed. Ryan's performance is terrifying. There's not a spark of pity in him; his disgust for Bel Geddes stems from his own bottomless self-hatred.

While Ryan's a fearsome villain, and Mason a reluctant hero, Bel Geddes makes a curious femme fatale. She never really seduces anyone and she enforces her will on the world only with great difficulty, yet her honest confusion places her among the most fully drawn, most recognizable and empathetic women characters in all of noir.

Ophuls' genius is not limited to his shadowy cinematography and classic, stately pacing. He's a master at investing physical space with emotion. Ryan's vast house is sumptuous but oppressive; the objects within overpower those who live among them. Mason's spare doctor's office becomes the most comforting space imaginable because genuine affection unites those who work there. But even within that comfort, the bleakness of noir holds sway until a dissonant and jarring ending.

A keystone work, featuring complex characters, difficult questions of morality and freedom, a sophisticated European take on compulsive American naïveté, and an overriding sense of tragedy.

Other recommended rentals directed by Max Ophuls:
The Earrings of Madame de . . .
Lola Montes

Chinatown (1974—USA)

Mood Guide: Fable of love and corruption

Director: Roman Polanski; *Camera:* John A. Alonzo; *Screenplay:* Robert Towne

Cast: Jack Nicholson, Faye Dunaway, John Huston, John Hillerman, Burt Young, Diane Ladd

In English; color

Plot: A private eye with a tragic past is hired to shadow a philandering husband. The job turns phony, and the husband ends up dead. The P.I. falls into a web of intrigue as he falls in love with the dead guy's rich, smooth widow. Dealing with her sinister dad, the P.I. learns the conflicts of adult love and the high price of civic progress.

The perfect film?

Robert Towne's script is a puzzle-box of mystery and dread that slowly opens to reveal unsuspected, ever more disturbing, vistas. A mystery becomes a love story that unveils a murder that fuels a tale of urban piracy that becomes a treatise on the endurance of evil. Among the many perfections of the script are its steady, suspenseful pacing and the careful layering of clues that, on first viewing, are unrecognizable as such. Indeed, the viewer never fully grasps what the interlocking threads conceal until the story's climax. We then experience the same helpless understanding as the hero.

Nicholson plays a would-be tough-ass, a half-bright guy who reinvents himself after a devastating experience in "Chinatown," a physical and spiritual neighborhood of tragic ambiguity and futility. Bearing his smirking facade of world-

PARAMOUNT PICTURES/ARCHIVE PHOTOS

Roman Polanski, Jack Nicholson, and Roy Jensen in *Chinatown*

weariness like a shield, Nicholson considers himself a man who understands the city and his place therein. But his brittle shell of cynicism proves insufficient armor in the private clubs where the real power resides. Driven by memories of his previous failure, Nicholson finally abandons his pose, succumbs to sincerity, and acts from his heart. When he does, he's doomed.

Faye Dunaway at first appears to be a noir Black Widow. With her red lipstick, lace hat, and elegant cool, she seems the ultimate seducer-destroyer. In one of many superb twists, Towne reveals Dunaway to be an innocent, a victim. Her love scene with Nicholson suggests a woman more vulnerable and kind than Nicholson's cynical view of her.

Capable of kindness, yes, but in the end, far tougher than Nicholson. Just as her icy sophistication conceals her vulnerability, her vulnerability masks an iron will. When Dunaway finally reveals her secret, her contempt for Nicholson's shock and confusion is plain. Their roles reverse in an instant, and Nicholson finds her pity for him intolerable. Stung, he wrecks himself seeking her salvation.

The casting of John Huston—the director of *The Asphalt Jungle* and *The Maltese Falcon*—reflects Polanski's daring and his love of classic American movies. Huston's open-faced, garrulous malevolence symbolizes the city he rules. His smile equals the nonstop sunshine, and his sudden lurches into Lear-like dominance make him one of the scariest, most real and memorable villains in the subculture.

Polanski rejects the classic setting of looming cityscapes and rain-soaked streets. There isn't a single skyscraper, shadow, or dominant vertical line in the film. Polanski frames his story at eye level to remind us that the real menace lurks in the hearts and minds of the characters. Polanski's Los Angeles is a flat plain parched by drought and baked by the merciless sunshine. John A. Alonzo shoots the city in tones of browns and washed-out yellows, the colors of too much sun and not enough water. Light saturates every face, but only makes the truth harder to discern. The sunlight blinds us, as it blinds Nicholson, into thinking that this shadowless city could be understood at a glance.

A cinema structuralist par excellence, a self-proclaimed disciple of Orson Welles, Polanski understands America's invisible class warfare as only a foreigner can. His determinedly depressive aesthetic provided the completely downbeat ending. Towne preferred a different close, one that offered a glimmer of hope and a more literal sense of history. Polanski knew better.

Be sure to rent a Letter-Box version—the regular rental tapes cut Polanksi's exquisite framing in half.

Other recommended rentals directed by Roman Polanski:

Bitter Moon
Knife in the Water
Macbeth
Rosemary's Baby
Repulsion
Tess

City That Never Sleeps (1953—USA)

Mood Guide: Overwrought beautiful cop-saga

Director: John H. Auer; *Camera:* John L. Russell, Jr.; *Screenplay:* Steve Fisher

Cast: Gig Young, Marie Windsor, William Talman, Mala Powers, Chill Wills

In English; B/W

Plot: A disgruntled policeman wants to quit the force. His dad, a lifelong cop, urges him to stay. A crooked lawyer offers him a fancy way out. In his last night of duty, the cop finds out where he really stands.

In the opening shot, the camera pans across a dramatic, darkening cityscape as character actor Chill Wills (best known for his gravelly voice and cowboy roles) reads a laughable narration that purports to be the mystical voice of the city itself. "I am the city, etc." From that moment on, everything seems silly and little overdone.

Gig Young plays a cop in torment. He wants to sell his soul

ARCHIVE PHOTOS

William Talman in *City That Never Sleeps*

to a crooked lawyer. He wants to stay with his lovely wife, but he can't. She earns more money than he does, you see, and stays late at work. It's causing him to feel, as his dad puts it, "inferior." Hence his platonic but intense pursuit of a stripper in a nightclub. His wife decides to quit her job to spare Gig his torments. "We'll live on what he brings home," she declares with pride. The cop's dad not only keeps a straight face at this declaration, but nods with fatherly approval.

Chill Wills appears as a kind of *Twilight Zone* mystical cop-figure who may or may not ride around with Gig as his temporary partner. The film suggests that Wills is either a real and unbearably avuncular cop or the spirit of the city incarnated into cop-form for one night to help Gig.

What a convoluted mess of inequities this big city is. A pickpocket with big plans is set up by the sleazy lawyer (stolen whole from *The Asphalt Jungle* but badly duplicated). The lawyer doesn't know the pickpocket has seduced his wife, played by the always robotic and duplicitous Marie Windsor. The cop is supposed to arrest the pickpocket, but his dad ends up doing it instead. Because father and son have the same name, the pickpocket thinks the dad is breaking a prearranged deal. Panicked, the pickpocket shoots Dad dead, triggering an amazing chase through night-time Chicago that climaxes on the tracks of the elevated trains.

The picture wobbles between long stretches of unintentional hilarity and genuinely moving noir moments, all presented with consistently magnificent high-contrast, deep-focus cinematography. However overbaked its plot or flat its acting, *City* remains one of the best photographed films in noir. The night-for-night shooting of Gig Young's final chase of the pickpocket rivals the sewer chase scenes in *The Third Man* (page 251) for use of the cityscape to underscore a character's drama. In one mind-blowing sequence, pickpocket William Talman is caught standing on the tracks between trains moving in opposite directions. Seldom has the force, vitality, and inescapability of the city been so perfectly captured.

For noir buffs and students of cinematography. Watch with the sound off.

The Conformist (1971—Italy)

Mood Guide: Art movie of betrayal

Director: Bernardo Bertolucci; *Camera:* Vittorio Storaro; *Screenplay:* Bernardo Bertolucci

Cast: Jean-Louis Trintignant, Dominique Sanda, Pierre Clementi, Gastone Moschin, Enzo Tarascio

In Italian, with English subtitles; color

Plot: On assignment to murder his former mentor, a little man who thinks too much falls for his mentor's wife, who falls in turn for the little man's new bride. The little man must find the courage to either stop the killing or carry it out.

Unlike *The American Friend* (page 31), which is just as self-conscious about being a thriller as it is about being art, *The Conformist* plays like a straight-up European art film. Despite such art movie requisites as references to other movies, references to cinema itself, and some of the most dazzling and influential cinematography of the seventies, Bertolucci's political allegory hews tightly to a matched pair of key noir themes: character determines fate, and the sins of the past rule the future.

Free of the self-conscious, overanalytical thinking that slows much of his later work, Bertolucci presents his obsessions, and they turn out to be *tres* noir: alienation, sexual confusion, Oedipal rage, incredible risks taken to slake momentary lust, the anguishes and gratifications of betrayal, self-delusion, really nice clothes, exquisite interiors, styles of the 1930s, the looming architecture of Paris, and the allure/danger of women.

Providing plenty of allure and danger, Dominique Sanda lives out the classic bad-girl arc. At first she's a femme fatale, moving through the world seducing at will, protected from the consequences of her actions by her beauty and her husband's power. When his power wanes, her beauty will not protect her (does beauty protect a single woman in noir?), and she makes the near fun transition to victim.

Jean-Louis Trintignant is the classic anonymous man of noir. Desperate to squelch his inner confusion, he joins the Fascist Party in prewar Italy, seeking in mass identity a perfection to replace his own tragically flawed individuality. This cultured, repressed Everyman marries a passionate but idiotic woman in an attempt to become normal, to conform. Here Bertolucci inverts the noir convention: Rather than stay aloof from society's destructive conformist embrace, the Conformist races into its arms. Unlike the noir hero who battles heaven and earth to protect his personality, the Conformist hates himself so profoundly that he takes any path that might free him from himself.

At the Party's behest, he accepts the assignment of assassinating his former professor, but he falls in love with the professor's wife, played by Sanda. She might or might not love the Conformist, but she certainly desires his new bride. It's an amoral and sexually predatory universe, as the Conformist tries to pretend his wife is less sophisticated than she is, and that he is more so.

Intrigues follow, and the plot, with all its time shifting, may be difficult to follow on first viewing. Bertolucci jumps around constantly, flashbacking through the Conformist's life. The flashbacks—that is, the Conformist's memories—reveal the steady building of his self-hatred. Bertolucci takes a profoundly Freudian (and therefore noir) view of the Conformist's various inner terrors: He fears his own homosexuality, his lack of physical courage, and his muted sexual drive. The Conformist is a bully and never fails to smite the weak or cringe before the powerful. For Bertolucci, he's both hero (noir's little man trying to rise above) and villain (the psychologically twisted killer who acts out his rage in murder). Via this network of interlocking flashbacks, Bertolucci builds the Conformist's life brick by brick, so we understand—as does the Conformist—that he cannot escape his fate

Bertolucci uses architecture as a source of information about the characters, as frame-defining monuments and as a scale against which his characters measure themselves. When the Conformist visits the Facist headquarters, he's lost in the marble immensity of the hall; his father's lunatic asylum is a surreal outdoor theater in which his father plays a doomed Lear. This sense of impotence in the face of a dominating man-made landscape harkens to the towering ruins, Ferris wheels, and shadowy city blocks of *The Third Man.*

Bertolucci's sense of the cultural, sexual, and psychological mood of the early days of Italian Fascism seems preternaturally subtle and acute. Those days expand metaphorically to suggest any era when moral courage must be matched by physical bravery. The Conformist has neither and so must suffer the fate he dreads most: a life lived inside a self he despises but, as always in noir, he finds himself powerless to change.

Other recommended rentals directed by Bernardo Bertolucci:

The Last Emperor
Last Tango in Paris
The Sheltering Sky

The Conversation (1974—USA)

Mood Guide: Primer in modern paranoia

Director: Francis Ford Coppola; *Camera:* Bill Butler; *Screenplay:* Francis Ford Coppola

Cast: Gene Hackman, Robert Duvall, Harrison Ford, Frederic Forrest, Allen Garfield, Cindy Williams, John Cazale, Teri Garr

In English; color

Plot: The best professional eavesdropper in America bugs two young people for a sinister corporate client. Concerned by what he hears, the bugger wonders just what the assignment is all about. Attempting to atone for a fatal sin in the same profession, the eavesdropper asks questions that have no answers.

Gene Hackman shuffles across a busy street in San Francisco, a dour look on his face. He's supervising his crew of three as they electronically eavesdrop on the conversation of a couple strolling through a crowded park. Hackman's all business—for him the talk of others offers no real-world content. Their words are only sounds on tape, and the clearer, the better.

But, as Hackman orchestrates the reconstruction of this particular conversation, twiddling dials and filtering out background noise, something dangerous happens. Hackman begins to care about the couple, to worry about the possible consequences of what they say and of his eavesdropping. In pursuit of a worthy, but suicidally misguided impulse, Hackman destroys the life he worked so hard to build: a life of absolute anonymity based on absolute isolation.

Hackman distrusts emotion, especially his own. He prefers to experience the world via recording tape, where he can slow it down, speed it up, and parse it out at a safe distance. The control he so desires vanishes when he leaves his studio and enters the messy world of real-time: his mistress (Teri Garr, prestardom and showing unusual subtlety) grills him about his life when they're apart; his rival in the bugging business brings

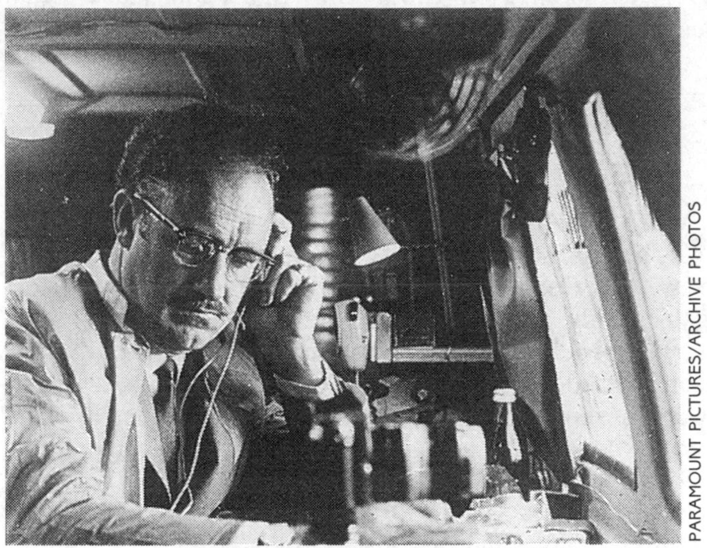
PARAMOUNT PICTURES/ARCHIVE PHOTOS

Gene Hackman in *The Conversation*

up a past tragedy; his assistant leaves him for the rival; and an appealing seductress turns about to be a spy.

Hackman's worst fears prove true. The standard currency of human interaction is betrayal. And, most heartbreakingly, Hackman's sincere attempt to do good—his desire to come down from his isolated roost—leaves him only more isolated.

Hackman is masterful. The repressed emotions and constant fear leak from behind his facade of control. Allen Garfield turns in one of his up-from-the-gutter, capitalist slime-molds, and Harrison Ford looking impossibly young, plays a menacing executive who regards Hackman's precautions and moral waffling as child's play.

Coppola proves frighteningly prescient about many aspects of our society: a growing, repressive corporate omnipotence; the sexiness of voyeurism; ruthless access to technology by those who don't understand its implications; the impossibility of remaining anonymous in a world of indelible electronic footprints; and the indestructibility of the elemental—though doomed—urge to connect. Coppola also confirms our paranoid notion—central to Hackman's character—that someone is always watching. Or could be if they wanted to.

The picture's tone is calm, distanced, and never ironic. As Hackman searches the conversation for clues, it's clear he's chasing himself through the fluttering, malevolent electronic tones. When Hackman commits a wholly self-destructive act of kindness, he thinks he's broken through to a climactic moment of clarity. But Coppola's merciless screenplay makes it clear he's gained only a deeper, more paralyzing confusion. Is this necessary payback for sins from years gone past, or the unavoidable breakdown of a system designed for failure? Hackman wants to engineer life as he does sound, but learns what he already knows: Life is engineered by those who embrace it. All he can do is watch.

From the same era as *Taxi Driver* (page 242), *The Conversation* proves a pivotal modern masterwork, one that seemed to focus on the concerns of its day but has been proven by the passage of time to be timeless. Deeply unsettling, suspenseful, and unforgettable.

Other recommended rentals directed by Francis Ford Coppola:

Apocalypse Now
The Godfather, Parts I & II
The Outsiders
Rumble Fish

Criss Cross (1949—USA)

Mood Guide: Obsessive love and armed robbery

Director: Robert Siodmak; *Camera:* Franz Planer; *Screenplay:* Daniel Fuchs

Cast: Burt Lancaster, Yvonne De Carlo, Dan Duryea

In English; B/W

Plot: While moping around in every sleazy joint in town, a drifter can't decide whether he really loves his former ex-wife. He *knows* he hates her current squeeze, a slimy gangster. Looking for a way out, the drifter cooks up a crazy heist. Is he man enough to do the job and steal the lady?

A tale of obsessive love and armed robbery, shot in rich, bleak shadows, and written with a knowing taste for the inescapable illogic of passion and greed.

Lancaster returns to L.A. after an absence of years. A passive sap with a quick temper and contrary personality, Lancaster seeks out his former wife, played by De Carlo. In a sustained, lewd, and surprisingly modern sequence, we meet De Carlo as she (dirty) dances to Esy Morales's rhumba band (and Esy *rocks!*). We're mesmerized, and so is Burt, until he learns that De Carlo's fallen for a low-rent gangster played with relentless smarm by Dan Duryea.

Lancaster's character victimizes himself by his spinelessness and ennui. Every time De Carlo or Duryea acts, he reacts, but never wisely or with sufficient commitment. Lancaster mistakes his own passivity for the machinations of destiny. He waits for things to happen to him, and sure enough, they do. Thus, director Siodmak (*The Killers*) inverts the noir convention of a man trapped by inexorable fate. Fate has nothing to do with Lancaster's problems. Typical of his loser's self-aggrandizement, Lancaster refuses to accept that his problems are his own fault. Because he's Burt Lancaster, this refusal does not make him unsympathetic.

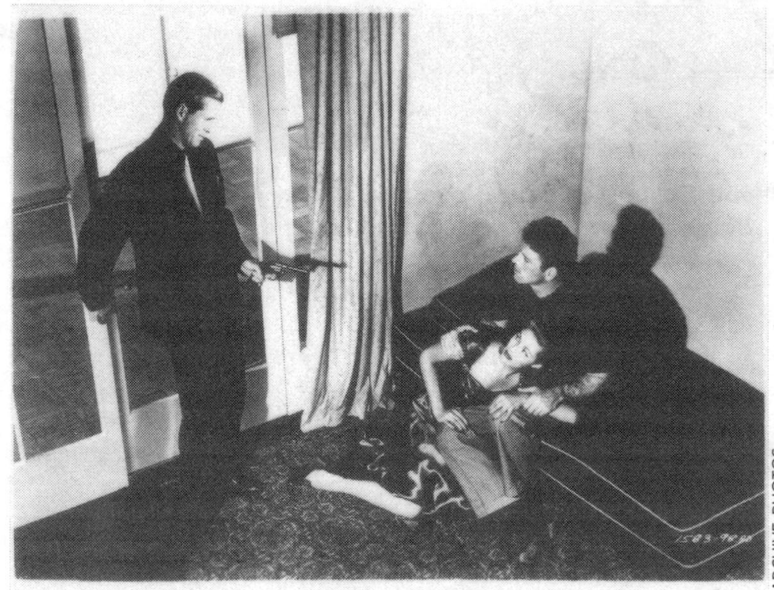

Dan Duryea, Yvonne De Carlo, and Burt Lancaster in *Criss Cross*

De Carlo plays a singularly straighforward femme fatale. Though she's a hot-blooded and potentially duplicitous noir harlot, De Carlo never exploits Lancaster's lunkheaded love. She freely admits to her lusts and never pretends to be what she is not. Lancaster confuses her. He demonstrates contempt for her desires even as he encourages them.

Lancaster's character is a regular Hamlet. He runs away from De Carlo when he needs her most and castigates her for unfaithfulness (to him) as he encourages her to cheat (on Duryea). Count on Burt to say the opposite of what he feels, no matter what the consequences.

Example: Burt sneaks into Duryea's house to meet De Carlo and gets caught. He claims he came to suggest a heist to Duryea: a harebrained scheme to rob the armored-car company where Lancaster works. Duryea likes the idea, or maybe he's amused by Lancaster's desperation and decides to call his bluff. Either way, the caper is on.

Lancaster's caught in the spirals of his own inept deception.

To get what he doesn't really want (De Carlo), he has to do something he doesn't really want to do (rob his friends). This is as lucid a portrait of postwar confusion as noir produced.

The armored-car heist generates considerable suspense and allows Siodmak to showcase his understated visual storytelling. After a dislocating, overhead shot of the armored car pulling into a depot, the robbery commences with a barrage of smoke grenades. Everyone lurches in and out of the man-made fog—some in gas masks, some with pistols, some grappling hand to hand with fearsome violence. The robbery plays as a fever dream, but its suspense is nothing compared to the nightmare that follows.

In today's Hollywood even a tough-guy schlumpf like Lancaster might find redemption and escape, but Siodmak shows no mercy. Lancaster's convoluted emotional paralysis leads to ruin, and that ruin feels like a genuine tragedy. The ending is a shocker.

Other recommended rentals directed by Robert Siodmak:

The Dark Mirror (page 88)
The Killers (page 146)

Crossfire (1947—USA)

Mood Guide: Well-intentioned message-making

Director: Edward Dmytryk; *Camera:* J. Roy Hunt; *Screenplay:* John Paxton

Cast: Robert Ryan, Robert Young, Robert Mitchum, Gloria Grahame, Sam Levene

In English; B/W

Plot: Three servicemen go on leave together. After a night of partying, one of them beats a man to death because the man is a Jew. The cops suspect the wrong guy and then use him as a decoy to trap his friend.

After an evening of drinking, chatting, and numerous sinister silences, Robert Ryan beats a middle-aged Jew to death. The

Jew strives to be harmless and inoffensive, but the mere sight of him drives Ryan into a rage. The man is weaker than Ryan; the man must die. Ryan's portrayal of a racist psychopath goes over the top, perhaps so the actor can, for once, separate himself from the loathsome urges of the character he plays. Mitchum seems to be in every shot, but proves a surprisingly passive Dutch uncle. Robert Young talks nonstop as the noble policeman who tracks down Ryan and turns Ryan's pals into stoolies.

By becoming a stoolie, Mitchum chooses the evil of informing on a friend over the evil of tacitly supporting anti-Semitism. It's weird how the taking of a life is not the moral lever applied to move Mitchum. It's almost as if the cops are saying, "Hey, any other murder we'd understand your reluctance, but this is a hate crime."

Dmytryk knew how to enliven his Poverty Row quickies, and he classes up his tale with sharp, Expressionist lighting, a haunting use of ambient sound, disjointed flashbacks, and self-conscious mirror shots. But Dmytryk cannot disguise the civics lesson lurking within, nor the absence of action. The picture moves slowly, the payoffs are few, and the climax is as limp as the plot leading up to it.

It's as if the earnest filmmakers dared not suggest violence in response to violence. By arresting the killer instead of exacting a personal revenge, Robert Young underlines that anti-Semitism is a crime against society and must be punished by society as a whole. But it also (unconsciously) suggests that Jew-killing is not heinous enough to warrant taking the law into one's own hands. If, say, Robert Young's wife had been murdered, his response would likely be very different.

The static narrative rules out thrills, though Ryan is compelling as usual. Young seems to be auditioning for *Father Knows Best,* and the rest of the cast, save Gloria Grahame, are ciphers.

Good intentions might ennoble the filmmakers, but they don't make the picture any easier to sit through.

Other recommended rentals directed by Edmund Dmytryk:
Murder, My Sweet (page 182)

Cutter and Bone (aka Cutter's Way)
1981–USA)

Mood Guide: Self-destruction in modern America

Director: Ivan Passer; *Camera:* Jordan Cronenwerth; *Screenplay:* Jeffrey Alan Fiskin, Newton Thornburg

Cast: John Heard, Jeff Bridges, Lisa Eichhorn

In English; color

Plot: Cutter, who isn't too stable, thinks he's witnessed a murder. Cutter's suspect: the richest man in the state. Cutter obsessively pursues his obsession while Cutter's wife and best friend try to dissuade him. To their regret, they get caught up in the chase.

The releasing studio, displeased with the minuscule first-week grosses, changed the title from *Cutter and Bone* (which they considered too depressing) to *Cutter's Way* (which sounds so much more lighthearted). Either way, no one went to see this singular thriller, and it vanished in a week, to be remembered as a benchmark of dark genius and inept marketing.

While providing astringent class-war commentary, this willfully ambivalent tale of self-destruction and anxiety follows Cutter—an alcoholic, terribly disfigured Vietnam vet—in his obsessive pursuit of a rich local landowner, whom Cutter believes has committed a murder. Bone, a going-nowhere, yacht-club party boy, is Cutter's best friend. He joins the hunt to amuse himself but becomes as fixated as (the possibly insane) Cutter. Cutter's neglected wife stays home and drinks. Cutter drinks with her, with Bone, and with anyone who will buy him a round. Cutter's wife and Bone may be in love; Cutter may be encouraging them to have an affair. Nobody is certain about anything, except Cutter: He's certainly pissed off.

Cutter's crippled body gives him reason to court despair, but his wife and Bone *choose* anomie; they've given up. Cutter's quest consumes him because he hopes a) to force someone to kill him since he lacks the courage to kill himself; and b) to infuse in his wife and in Bone the desire, however remote or ill-founded, to persevere.

Jeff Bridges plays Bone, John Heard is Cutter, and the seldom seen Lisa Eichhorn plays Cutter's wife. Their performances are unforgettable: low-key, neorealist, and in perfect sync with the quiet, foreboding rhythm of the screenplay. Everything in the film, from love to friendship to clues about the murder, is soaked in ambiguity. Credit the screenplay, which manages to be spellbinding, funny, hopeful, and tragic while never becoming self-important or manipulative.

Director Ivan Passer shoots in dark, somber tones. He begins the mystery in darkest night and lashing rain; he ends it in that heartless California sunshine that so encourages the blessed and so embarrasses the downtrodden. The savage story is redeemed by the honesty of its depiction, the razor-sharp dialogue, and Passer's accurate evocation of the lives of California's working poor and idle rich.

Passer trusts that his characters and a simple narrative style will reveal the profundity of his themes. He doesn't beat you over the head with the depth of his perception, and his picture loses none of its entertainment value for being such a downer. However memorable the characters, the murder mystery drives the plot, and its suspense never slackens.

The Dark Mirror (1946—USA)

Mood Guide: Which twin has the Toni?

Director: Robert Siodmak; *Camera:* Milton Krasner; *Screenplay:* Nunnally Johnson

Cast: Olivia De Havilland, Lew Ayres, Thomas Mitchell, Charles Evans

In English; B/W

Plot: The cops call a psychiatrist to solve a murder. They're stumped because the murderer is one of two identical twins and the cops can't tell them apart. The shrink discovers one to be good and the other bad, and he finds himself irresistibly drawn to, well, to which?

Siodmak brings his German Expressionist background to this hoary old chestnut—the *doppelgänger* plot device. His subjective camera and complex lighting provide the depth for a tricky, satisfying recounting of an oft-told tale.

Two identical twin sisters call the cops. One of them has murdered a guy she was dating. The sisters' legal strategy is simple: The one with the airtight alibi intends to confess. No jury will convict her because no jury can tell them apart. The pressures of Ayres' investigation—and a budding affection between Ayres and the good sister—drive the bad sister to a sinister plan. She intends to kill her twin and take her place.

De Havilland employs a rather English subtlety in her portrayal. Like Jeremy Irons in *Dead Ringers*, she makes the concept believable by creating only the smallest differences between the twins. De Havilland is too ladylike to be fully convincing as the "bad" sister. But her "good" sister, who's torn between attraction to Lew Ayres and her loyalty to her psycho twin, is a beautifully crafted piece of characterization.

Lew Ayres incarnates every fifties middlebrow notion of shrinkhood: he's a super-rationalist, ready to explain away deviant behavior. He brings "science" to the messy illogic of human interaction. The good versus bad woman concept presents the female psyche as fundamentally unknowable, and therefore untrustworthy. Lurking in every woman, the film makes clear, is an evil twin, ready to do emotional or physical violence, and ready to disguise herself as good only until she gains her ends. In other words, the inherent feminine mystery must inevitably lead to the destruction of man. How can a man trust or love when every woman carries the seed of duplicity?

The search for the bad sister serves one key function: to punish the seducer by identifying and banishing the cunning, nonsubmissive aspect of woman's nature. The suspense derives from our hero choosing correctly. He will be proven heroic if, with his superior mind and medical training, he avoids falling for the murderer, the castrator, the sexual betrayer, etc.

The film is careful to keep medicine jargonized and omnipotent so that any woman who can fool a (superior) medical man must be doubly powerful, doubly deceitful. Good women bow down to the holy knowledge of medicine, to the rational taming of the subconscious, and hence, the supernatural. In other words, if a man is man enough, he can unmask and dominate the witchy, inscrutable antirationality that is woman.

Siodmak's view is, as ever, quite dark. Under the guise of a suspense thriller, he presents the unavoidable manipulations of intimacy, the impossibility of really knowing another soul, and the violence always lurking in passion. Despite its allegories of sexual paranoia, the story remains gripping, beautifully shot, and lots of fun.

Other recommended rentals directed by Robert Siodmak:
Criss Cross (page 83)
The Killers (page 146)

Dark Passage (1947)

Mood Guide: Unprofound Bogart-Bacall vehicle

Director: Delmer Daves; *Camera:* Sid Hickox; *Screenplay:* Delmer Daves

Cast: Humphrey Bogart, Lauren Bacall, Agnes Moorehead, Clifton Young, Bruce Bennett

In English; B/W

Plot: A con escapes from prison, determined to undo the frame against him. A strangely friendly dame gives him a lift into town and helps him recover from plastic surgery. The con moves from clue to clue, dodging the cops, a wily blackmailer, and a dangerous woman who knows more than she lets on.

A convicted murderer escapes from prison. He moves in shadows and avoids the light. The director uses every cheap trick in the book to keep us from seeing the con's face. A cabbie recognizes him in the rearview mirror and offers to take him to a plastic surgeon. After the surgery, the con's face is hidden by bandages. When they come off, the con proves to be Humphrey Bogart. This proves a scant surprise, because we've listened to his inimatable voice at least half an hour.

By the time he's revealed as Bogie, Lauren Bacall has nursed him to health, and fallen in love with him. A convoluted plot point regarding Bacall's past convinces her that Bogie never committed the murder of his wife for which he claims he was framed. At the center of this plot point is a friend of Bogie's murdered wife. The friend is now also a pal of Bacall's.

The friend, played by Agnes Moorehead, is the only true noir element in what remains a mainstream Bogart vehicle. The story offers few credible moments, so its pleasures lie in Bogie, an upscale Hollywood attempt at gritty atmosphere, some shocking violence that seems especially graphic for the age, a parade of amusing, over-the-top character parts, and one of the least repentant female villains in cinema history.

Moorehead's character is mean-spirited, grasping, domineering, pushy, and coldhearted. She shouts orders at everyone and then whines that no one loves her. Moorehead's very nastiness, her lack of awareness of her nature, moves to compassion those she treats with the least consideration. She's a formidable monster, and Moorehead plays her for maximum monstrosity. The moral darkness at her core, and the depressing truth that it's hard to resist a determined bully, keep things compelling. Moorehead is never presented as either a sexual or inherently feminine evil. She's heartless and cowardly, pathologically jealous of the happiness of others, but holds little metaphorical significance.

In one particularly creepy scene, Bogart—with his new, unrecognizable face—attempts to seduce her. Moorehead's usually rigid features soften, her cold eyes light up with lust, and she turns oddly submissive. She and Bogart assume positions that emphatically suggest the immediate possibility of oral sex. Like Moorehead's sudden expression of horniness, it's deliciously unsettling and perverse. It's also proof that when he wanted to, director Daves could be subtle, adult, and noir.

Bogart moves around San Francisco, seeking clues to clear his name. In an effort to keep him wholly innocent, anyone who dies, no matter how villainous, does so by accident. The filmmakers want it both ways: for Bogart to bend the world to his needs, and to remain morally pure. In the noir universe, those goals are mutually exclusive.

In the end, it's clear the whole adventure is one big fairy tale. And you can't have a fairy tale without a wicked witch.

Dead Calm (1988—Australia)

Mood Guide: Harrowing sea-going woman-in-peril suspense

Director: Phillip Noyce; *Camera:* Dean Semler; *Screenplay:* Terry Hayes

Cast: Nicole Kidman, Sam Neill, Billy Zane

In English; color

Plot: Alone on a sailboat in the middle of nowhere, a married couple rescues a dangerous castaway. He tries to kill them. They resist.

The profoundly noir sensibility of director Phillip Noyce's early work (*Heatwave* [page 125]) makes his late-career descent into big-bucks hack-dom (*Sliver, Clear and Present Danger,* etc.) seem a tragic waste. Though *Dead Calm*'s premise couldn't be more basic, Noyce makes a terrifying, intelligent classic out of the simplest raw material. The suspense will kill you.

Nicole Kidman plays a grieving young woman on an extended sailboat cruise with her supportive, straight-arrow husband, Sam Neill. The cruise is an escape from the tragic death of their infant son, a tragedy for which Kidman blames herself. On a peaceful, sunlit day, Billy Zane appears in the middle of the motionless ocean, rowing like mad from a yacht barely visible on the horizon. Zane tells a tale of salmonella poisoning that he alone survived, of nightmarish days and nights trapped in a flooded cabin awash with corpses. Sam, straight-arrow that is he, rushes off in the dinghy to investigate, leaving Kidman

Billy Zane and Nicole Kidman in *Dead Calm*

alone with Zane. After a brief stab at polite conversation, Zane tries to kill Neill and make Kidman his new girlfriend.

Zane's pathological self-hatred/creepy vulnerability is particularly well-written and well-played, but its power stems from Noyce's noir vision. Zane's repellent killer possesses no small amount of seductive charm. Though she fears and despises him, Kidman recognizes that his wild glamour touches some perverse part of her.

Zane destroys Kidman's notions of sanctuary (the empty ocean), of home (the exquisite sailboat becomes a shattered battleground), of the sanctity of marriage, and of her own capacity for violence (considerable, vengeful, and relentless). While Neill's manly heroism is primal and old-fashioned—he mostly maintains discipline, refusing to give up no matter how tough the circumstances—Kidman's bravery is more complex.

She matches Neill for physical courage, but also calls upon her seductiveness and sexuality. Neill's struggles, which are entirely physical, do not require getting in touch with his anima.

Kidman, however, must connect to her masculine, aggressive side (and how). She plays a naive girl who comes into her own as a woman via the hard lessons her ordeal of survival. These lessons include Kidman discovering just how rooted in her dark side her womanhood will be. So, even though Kidman's clearly the victim, she's also the femme fatale.

This duality fuels Noyce's notions of noir, and makes Kidman's performance truly remarkable. It's the best, perhaps the only, real acting she's ever done. By picture's end, Kidman has grown up and possibly surpassed her husband, who watches her with a newfound, wary awe. Her evolution adds to *Dead Calm*'s weird appeal. With its explicit violence and sexual brutality, *Dead Calm* ain't exactly a date movie, but Kidman's journey makes it both accessible and compelling for women viewers who might normally avoid the trapped-on-a-boat-with-a-charismatic-psycho genre.

Noyce does wonders within some pretty severe formal limitations. He's got three people stuck on two boats—how visually compelling could that be? Watch the picture with an awareness of Noyce's problem, trying to figure out when he runs out of ideas, and you will be amazed: He never does. His camera swoops and dives, or holds rock-steady on the most unsettling scenes. Clocking in at around ninety minutes, *Dead Calm* is a tight little masterpiece; methamphetamine storytelling with no wasted shots, almost no back-story, and even less explanation. Once the narrative ball gets rolling, it's straight-up thrills until the big finish.

And by that time, you will be limp.

Other recommended rentals directed by Phillip Noyce:
Heatwave (page 125)

Deep Cover (1992—USA)

Mood Guide: Edgy articulate actioner

Director: Bill Duke; *Camera:* Bojan Bazelli; *Screenplay:* Michael Tolkin

Cast: Laurence Fishburne, Jeff Goldblum, Clarence Williams III

In English; color

Plot: An upright young black cop transforms himself into a drug dealer. Working for the CIA, he sells crack on the streets of L.A. There he meets a crooked lawyer with a greedy nature and little physical courage. Together, they take on the Colombians who supply them.

It's a classic B movie cop-crook thriller with a twist, set in the L.A. cocaine trade. The twist? The cop and the crook are the same guy: Laurence Fishburne starring as the smoothest man in America. The second-smoothest is Jeff Goldblum, all corruption-ambition, who becomes Fishburne's best friend and simultaneously the twisted mirror image of his conscience. Fishburne's the essence of reticence and hipster restraint. Goldblum's the overanxious middle-class kid grown up, desperate to convince the world he isn't as scared as everybody knows he is. Each serves as the other's fatal flaw: Who will crack first?

Fishburne plays an undercover cop recruited to infiltrate the world of high-level cocaine trafficking. He proves far too skilled at his new assignment, and unforeseen moral/career choices threaten to overwhelm him. As Fishburne sinks into a stylish mire of violence and money, he partners up with Goldblum, a lawyer with utopian dreams of dope-fulfilled riches and no shortage of trenchant insights. It's weird to see Goldblum shoot people, but with his beady eyes and newly hulking build, he makes a convincing, if unlikely, action toy.

Fishburne gets so deep into his new life that he forgets on which side of the legal fence he belongs. There to remind him is Clarence Williams III—Linc from TV's *Mod Squad*—playing the king of square-John policemen. Williams's subtle cameo is only one example of the charming hipness that runs throughout.

Director Bill Duke is a black actor best known for action roles in *Predator* and the like. He directs with seriousness (the performances are stellar) and witty noir references: B movie shadowy lighting; inspired, old-fashioned scene transitions: wipes, dissolves, fades, etc. His sense of pace is perfect; the story never lags.

The script—by Michael Tolkin, author of *The Player* and director of *The New Age*—features Tolkin's highly developed sense of irony. While Tolkin's knowing approach generates most of the lasting pleasure, it never interferes with the more immediately gratifying, traditional elements of classic cop action: shoot-outs, car chases, sex scenes, streetwise slang, and explicit violence. Tolkin's insistence that all his characters show both idiosyncrasy and intelligence makes this an action flick of unusual, if not literary, depth. Tolkin also creates the least stereotypical, most fully formed black characters in any film of recent memory.

It's not director Duke's visual references, but Tolkin's politics that move this cop-thriller into the realm of noir. In a mare's nest of conflicting missions, two honest men face off. Fishburne and Williams each represent two very different generations, two different paths of success for African-American men.

In pursuing the grail of duty, Williams let society make him a pauper. Fishburne doesn't start out seeing the big picture, but he learns from his so-called masters. As the upstart, he understands that he must accept the corruption within to fight corruption without. Tolkin closes the picture with the message that as Fishburne has grown up, so will he serve as a father figure to a boy who will learn from him.

On the other side of the class/race fence is Jeff Goldblum, who exemplifies the existential dread and self-loathing that marks modern noir. Though safe in a way Fishburne will never be, Goldblum believes his life of material pleasure has stolen his manhood. He seeks danger to prove himself, and sees in Fishburne the reflexive man of action his neurotic intellect prevents him from being. Goldblum is the white man who seeks from the black world the primal aspect he's surrendered. It's a subtle, easily denied form of racism, and Tolkin writes it with the complexity it warrants.

Enveloping the story, but never detracting from it or moving it toward propaganda, is a refreshingly straightforward summation of the big-time politics of the coke trade and the class war inherent therein.

Detour (1945—USA)

Mood Guide: Cheap thrills

Director: Edgar G. Ulmer; *Camera:* Benjamin H. Kline; *Screenplay:* Martin Goldsmith

Cast: Tom Neal, Ann Savage, Claudia Drake, Tim Ryan

In English; B/W

Plot: A guy hitchhikes Out West to meet his girl. The fellow who gives him a ride turns up dead. A femme fatale blackmails the hitchhiker even though he's innocent, maybe. He tries to escape the dame, but fate holds all the cards.

A Hobbesian journey into hard-boiled noir, where the hero's life and the film itself are nasty, brutish, and short. One of the quickest and most cheaply made films in noir (the low-tech back-projections will crack you up), it's a touchstone for its monosyllabic visual language and absolute faith in both the cruelty of fate and the hopelessness of postwar America.

A down-and-outer, played by squeaky-voiced Tom Neal, hitchhikes cross-country to chase his girlfriend, who leaves him after one of the most petulant, badly acted, and clumsily written parting sequences in movie history. The guy who gives Neal a ride falls out of his car and dies. Neal fears that no one will believe the guy died by accident, so he dumps the corpse by the roadside and assumes the dead man's identity. Heading west in the dead man's car, carrying his wallet, and wearing his suit, Neal plans to ditch the car when he reaches his sweetheart. He picks up the predatory and well-named Ann Savage, who, unfortunately for Neal, also recently rode with the deceased. She forces Neal to take her to L.A. and there tries to engage him in a crackpot scheme.

ARCHIVE PHOTOS

Ulmer's dazzingly low-rent cinema so distances the viewer from the narrative that only the (classic noir) message remains: God has one mean sense of humor. The protagonist deserves to be the butt of this humor, the film suggests, because he lacks the guts to take responsibility for his own actions. No existential crisis here, Ulmer makes plain, only the harsh fate due a coward.

But Neal's a coward who knows the score. The dead man is rich, Neal's a nobody. His terror of engaging the supposedly helpful mechanisms of society—the cops, the courts, attorneys—reflects the new social reality. Each class looks out for it own, and Neal had better fend for himself. That he does so poorly marks him as a victim of the postwar order. And remember, these low-budget quickies played in low-rent movie houses packed with guys just like Neal.

Ulmer has neither the time nor money to play around with metaphors. Ann Savage is the prototypical vicious femme fatale; the only power available to her is sexual, and as a long-exploited being, she does not hesitate to exploit when for once the power-balance shifts her way. Savage as Savage may be, Neal's such a sap that you hardly blame her for wrecking his every dream of happiness.

Although *Detour* is cheap, easily mocked, and comically bad, its virtues overwhelm its faults. Like great rock and roll, the film remains moving and expressive because of its crudeness, not in spite of it. It's the simplest, most direct and Kafkaesque of all the cruel-fate noirs. Both unintentionally hilarious and deeply moving, *Detour* is an inspirational monument to the (quintessentially American) practical and spiritual ingenuity of the Poverty Row filmmakers.

In theme, narrative, character, and style, *Detour* is a powerful influence on every noir that followed.

Le Deuxième Souffle (Second Breath)

(1966—France)

(?)

Mood Guide: Honor among thieves

Director: Jean-Pierre Melville; *Camera:* Marcel Combes; *Screenplay:* Jean-Pierre Melville

Cast: Lino Ventura, Paul Meurisse, Raymond Pellegrin

In French, with English subtitles; B/W

Plot: A tough con escapes from prison and with his old mates pulls off an extraordinary highway robbery. The con seeks only to escape with the loot and his lifelong love, but the heartless police Inspector cares not about loyalty or honor. And the Inspector always gets his man.

Le Deuxième Souffle bears little resemblance to the bemused charm of *Bob le Flambeur* (page 63). *Souffle* is proto-Melville:

a cynical, unsentimental but visually lyrical study of cops and their gangster counterparts. The most American of all French directors, Melville's hard-boiled sensibility and poetic, reductive intellect make him *the* noir master. His B-movie story lines deliver both cinematic thrills and deeper philosophic content. The pacing is smooth, if a little slow, and Melville's sense of humor is as deadpan as his detached narrative style. If the film occasionally seems dated, it's only when Melville makes too big a deal of an already melodramatic moment.

Three men hide behind a wall in an impenetrable gray fog. They climb down a fence, run through the rain, and struggle onto a moving freight train. Only after ten minutes of silent nonstop action do we understand that we're watching a jailbreak.

Once free, noir star Lino Ventura—a former pro wrestler discovered by Melville—finds his loyal sweetheart and prepares to escape France. Lino also hooks up with some old pals. Together they plan and pull off an armored car heist. Lino's nemesis, the police Inspector, tracks down the gang, one by one. With his craggy, impenetrable, yet somehow repentant face, Lino is the toughest

ARCHIVE PHOTOS/ARCHIVE FRANCE

Lino Ventura, stoned-face in the milieu, in *Le Deuxième Souffle* guy around, a man who kills if he must, yet remains incapable of betrayal. He might get caught, but he'll never crack.

The armored car heist that forms the center of the story has to be seen to be believed. Since he had limited funds, Melville shoots events simply, though he's not above flinging a prop car off a thousand-foot cliff. Melville presents even the most brutal violence with a romantic languor, dreamily switching from mountain vista wide-shots to knife-edge closeups. Melville likes to frame his characters against vast landscapes and he likes to put his camera right up their noses.

Melville's cynicism is pragmatic, never condemning. He understands that cops and criminals live by similarly rigorous, if inverted, moral codes. Melville's world illustrates Bob Dylan's words: "To live outside the law you must be honest." With no legal niceties to modulate their world, Melville's hoods choose to behave honorably (at least toward one another). Their illegal skills become the standard by which they judge themselves. Melville finds in this world of hoodlums both morality and commitment to excellence.

His view of cops is less charitable. While they match the crooks in determination, cops live a life of reaction. The crooks steal, then the cops chase. Being at such a disadvantage, the cops can't afford the luxury of honor. The Inspector doesn't care that he makes men do things they find repugnant. He neither enjoys nor sentimentalizes the corruption he inflicts: The Inspector cares only about results. The criminal's preference of style (means) over success (ends), make them the seductive antibourgeois heroes they are.

By presenting their doomed embrace of morally correct behavior with such admiration, Melville delivers the noir message that to conform—to join the mainstream of society—is to accept spiritual death. The crooks choose to die rather than embrace that fate. The Inspector, whom Melville admires for his cynicism, suffers for having the death of such fine men on his conscience.

Warning: Avoid the 102-minute English-language version. Search out the subtitled 130- or 150-minute French originals.

Other recommended rentals directed by Jean-Pierre Melville:

Bob le Flambeur (page 63)
Le Doulos (page 112)
Le Samourai (page 219)

Les Diaboliques (1954—France)

Mood Guide: Perverse nastiness, in French

Director: Henri-Georges Clouzot; *Camera:* Armand Thirard; *Screenplay:* Henri-Georges Clouzot, Jérôme Géromino, Frédéric Grendel, René Masson

Cast: Simone Signoret, Vera Clouzot, Paul Meurisse, Charles Vanel

In French, with English subtitles; B/W

Plot: A sadistic schoolteacher is murdered by the unholy duo of his long-suffering wife and his tough-ass mistress. Once dead, he continues to cause problems. His body vanishes, and the women drive themselves to a frenzy searching for it. When a grizzled cop with a nose for murder shows up, something's got to give.

Half-horror film, half-psychological terror, Henri-Georges Clouzot's *Les Diaboliques* prefigures Hitchcock in theme,

ARCHIVE PHOTOS

Verna Clouzot and Simone Signoret prepare an *aperitiff* in *Les Diaboliques*

presentation, and morality, even as it honors and subverts him.- The similarities to Hitch are unsurprising; Clouzot adapted *Les Diaboliques* from a French novel by the same authors who wrote the book on which Hitchcock's *Vertigo* (page 267) was based. *Les Diaboliques*'s audience was begged, like Hitchcock's audience for *Psycho,* not to give away the shock ending.

Clouzot shows little of Hitch's gentility, however, or preference for hinting at the sexual. His vision of falsehood, fate, the (cheap) value of life, and the (enduring) tyranny of bullies is expressed with malign, multileveled, Gallic subtlety. Clouzot wanted to make a commercial blockbuster (which he did), and so bludgeons us with the commercial staples of sex, violence, and bourgeois hypocrisy.

The film begins with two women presented as victims, despite their disparate personalities. Simone Signoret is tough as nails, Vera Clouzot wouldn't hurt a fly, and together, they murder. Unlike most victims of murder in noir, Vera's husband, played without a trace of sympathetic qualities by Paul Meurisse, deserves his grisly death.

Set in a run-down boarding school (symbol of the amoral universe), where the sky is always gray, the water in the swimming pool always filthy, the teachers drunk, and the students punished for telling the truth, little in the story is what it seems. Vera Clouzot—in real life the director's wife—plays the long-suffering wife of a vicious headmaster. When he's not slapping her around or forcing her to have sex, he's off with his mistress, Signoret, another teacher at the school.

Though Vera Clouzot murders right beside Signoret, her (Catholic) guilt and compassionate nature make her sympathetic. She forms the more classically female side of the partnership: She's sincere, vulnerable, and kind. In Clouzot's universe, add those qualities together and they spell: V-I-C-T-I-M. With her high heels, jutting sweater, and ever-present cigarette, Signoret's the femme fatale: overtly sexual, hard-assed, and motivated solely by self-interest. Her vibe is not particularly hetero, but that only adds to her scary allure. That and her gigantic black shades.

Signoret and Vera Clouzot's murderous scheme is foiled when Meurisse's body disappears. Slowly cracking up from guilt, and from the stress of keeping all her lies in order, Vera searches for her husband's corpse. Her hysteria leads her to the police, who join in her search. She and Signoret have a falling out, as murderers will.

In her relationship with Vera Clouzot, Signoret assumes the man's dominant role (automatically making her the transgressive villainess) and orders Vera about. Vera shows the same impotent frustration at Signoret's intransigence as she did at her husband's bullying. This further underlines the unspoken sexual aspect of their relationship. Vera's character suggests a need to be slapped around, an unacknowledged desire to be punished. This makes her desperate to confess. Signoret grows desperate that she does not.

Clouzot pulls the Hitchcockian trick of making the audience root for the murderers and builds the suspense on whether they will get caught. The critics of the time savaged Clouzot for his amorality, but today his approval seems a calm acceptance of human nature. Folks behave as we expect them to. That is, horribly.

Clouzot runs out of ideas at about the three-quarter mark, and treads water for an unnecessary ten minutes. But his dispassionate camera and measured pacing so add to the relentless suspense of the first ninety minutes that this little break is a welcome relief.

About as mean-spirited and unredeemed as it gets. The suspense will make your hair fall out.

(Avoid the modern remake with Sharon Stone and Isabelle Adjani.)

Other recommended rentals directed by Henri-Georges Clouzot:

La Salaire de la Peur (Wages of Fear) (page 228)

Monsieur Hire

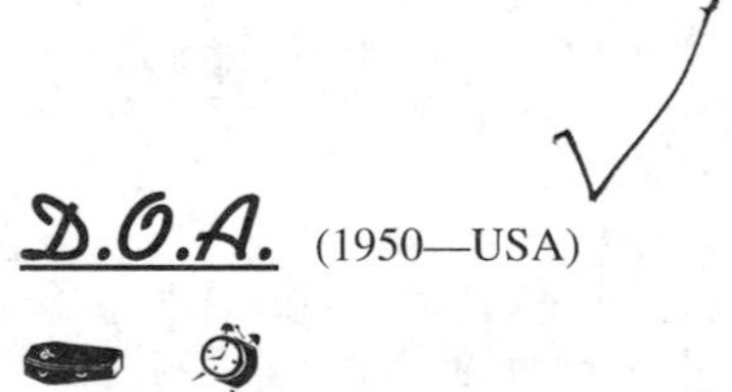

D.O.A. (1950—USA)

Mood Guide: Mystery Science Theater 2000—noir style

Director: Rudolph Maté; *Camera:* Ernest Laszlo; *Screenplay:* Russell Rouse, Clarence Green

Cast: Edmond O'Brien, Pamela Britton, William Ching, Luther Adler
In English; B/W
Plot: A man staggers into a police station and announces his own murder. Twenty-four hours earlier, he was poisoned. In flashback, he recounts his day, from a spat with his girlfriend to a wild night in a San Francisco jazz club to the discovery of his predicament to his frantic search to find the reasons behind his random killing.

Director Rudolph Maté wastes the single most brilliant idea in noir. The first three minutes are riveting, as O'Brien strides down the endless corridors of a police station, the world shrinking around him. We never see his face, only his exhausted back and determined stride. With what is clearly his dying strength, O'Brien lurches into the Homicide Bureau. He sinks into a chair. "I want to report a murder," he tells the head cop. "Who's been murdered?" the cop asks. Maté cuts to a full-face close-up of the haggard O'Brien. "I have," he says.

And it's all downhill from there.

UNITED ARTISTS/ARCHIVE PHOTOS

Edmond O'Brien is *D.O.A.*

In its own sophomoric, rushed fashion, *D.O.A.* does carry the noir flag. It presents a man who throws off every trace of civilization to stay alive, a pervasive underworld of dirty dealers, and a moral universe where a man's life can be snuffed out to protect the lusts and follies of others. There's even one or two bravura visual moments, built around the moving camera of Ernest Laszlo.

The two best sequences are the most hysterical. In a shoot-out in a drugstore, the camera follows the druggist as he creeps up on a hoodlum. The druggist hurls a bottle at the hood and it shatters right on his face. The hood turns to shoot the druggist, but a cop blasts the hood first. Those fifteen seconds are so violent and real, it's hard to believe director Maté had anything to do with them. No other sequence in the picture is as powerful.

The other captivating moment is less well executed. It's a rapid-fire montage set to the wild rhythms of a jazz band in an underground club. Maté may have wanted to show the seductive carnality of the music, but he keeps intercutting the musicians with embarrassing renditions of Hollywood beatniks who say things like: "Dig that crazy jive."

The acting is laughable, especially Pamela Britton as O'Brien's love interest. She speaks with a pathetic earnestness that compels the viewer to hurl wisecracks back at the screen. O'Brien shows the patience of Job in his scenes with her and manages to deliver passable line readings in response.

Maté turns the most serious moments into high camp. O'Brien suffers from "luminous poisoning." So, a doctor comes in with a test tube of fluid taken from O'Brien, never mind how. The doctor turns off the light, and the tube glows like a nuclear reactor. O'Brien recoils with his eyes bugged out like the good citizens fleeing gorilla-aliens in *Plan 9 from Outer Space.*

Naturally, one wants to know *why* O'Brien was poisoned, and his search for the killer is the source of all suspense. The explanation, when it does come, is buried in a hail of dialogue and makes absolutely no sense. This is the most piercing of *D.O.A.*'s disappointments.

Noir fanatics should rent this for the first three minutes, and then fast-forward with the sound off to enjoy Laszlo's hambone tracking shots of O'Brien running through the San Francisco night, with his mouth gaping and his tie askew. Along the sidewalk, citizens packed three-deep celebrate the moviemaking process by staring solemnly into the camera as it races by.

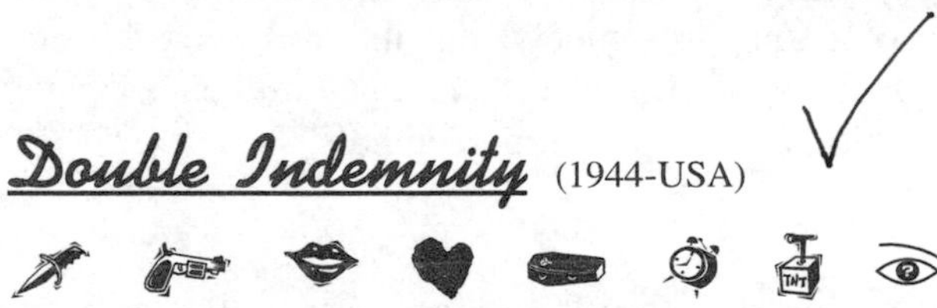

Mood Guide: Obsessive love and snappy repartee

Director: Billy Wilder; *Camera:* John F. Seitz; *Screenplay:* Raymond Chandler, Billy Wilder

Cast: Barbara Stanwyck, Fred MacMurray, Edward G. Robinson, Porter Hall, Jean Heathe

In English; B/W

Plot: A levelheaded insurance man meets a dangerous babe. He falls in love, and they plot to murder her husband. Everything goes like clockwork until the insurance man finds love's course running less than smooth. His boss suspects him. He fears he's being played for a sap. There seems to be only one way out, but that solution is nothing but murder.

Wilder's mainstream, entertainment-oriented approach to moral emptiness substitutes nasty wit and slick storytelling for the bleaker sensibility of the more ruthless, guttersnipe noirs. Though based on the novel by noir-god James M. Cain and considered by many to be *the* American classic, *Double Indemnity* suffers from a big-studio slickness and sexually punchless stars.

Lumbering super-clod Fred MacMurray, insurance salesman extraordinaire, meets Barbara Stanwyck, lets the little head do the thinking for the big head, and winds up enslaved by passion. Fred and Barb exchange Raymond Chandler's snappy dialogue, which is intended to connote steamy sexual intent but instead showcases Fred MacMurray as the cinematic asexual dumbass of all time. Or maybe Fred's supposed to be a boob, to make an easier mark for Stanwyck. Either way, he's no Valentino.

As the temperature on their flirtation rises, Fred directly addresses what both are thinking: He tells Stanwyck he cannot murder her husband. She throws him out of the house. Later, she appears at his dingy bachelor pad, they embrace and commit to the job. The plot unspools nicely, but its credibility cannot withstand the education in forensic techniques audiences have gained from five decades of police procedurals.

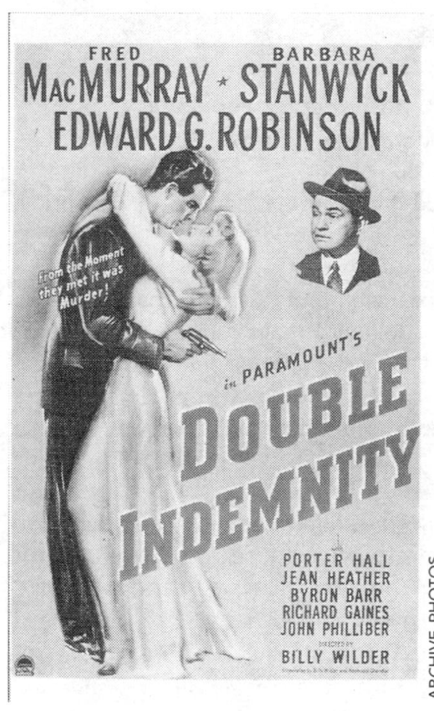

ARCHIVE PHOTOS

As passionate as Fred claims to be about Barbara, the object of his true affection seems to be his wily boss, played with slobby abandon by Edward G. Robinson. Robinson gives an acerbic, motormouth performance, racing through the funniest lines in the picture. When he leaves the screen and Stanwyck returns, the energy level drops palpably. While MacMurray stands around with his hands in his pockets and unrolls his lines in that avuncular

Son of Flubber/My Three Sons manner, Robinson rants and raves. He's the old-fashioned conscience of the world of absolute morality, a world going to hell right before his eyes. Straitlaced, tiresome, sarcastic, and preachy, Robinson's character is the most fully realized.

But *Double Indemnity*'s not a classic for nothing. There's plenty of fine and enduring weirdo subtexts: The innocent daughter Lola moves her mouth around her lines like a thousand-dollar hooker. She's the real seducer; it seems unlikely Fred could do all that riding around with her and not take a tumble. Similarly, the unmistakable love between MacMurray and Robinson gives their interchange an amusing sheen of perversity, especially since MacMurray delivers the last line of the picture not to Stanwyck, but to Edward G. "I love you, too," MacMurray says.

Though remarkable for being among the first American films to identify with, and even root for, murderers, *Double Indemnity* remains more admirable than moving. It's a shiny, impenetrable artifice, gleaming and lovely, a tribute to its own slickness rather than an enveloping drama.

Still, it remains the best starting place for those who prefer their noir more Hollywood and less dismal.

Other recommended rentals directed by Billy Wilder:
The Big Carnival (aka *Ace in the Hole*)
Sunset Boulevard (page 234)

A Double Life (1948—USA)

Mood Guide: Backstage psychological melodrama

Director: George Cukor; *Camera:* Milton Krasner; *Screenplay:* Garson Kanin, Ruth Gordon

Cast: Ronald Colman, Signe Hasso, Edmond O'Brien, Shelley Winters

In English; B/W

Plot: A successful but unstable actor performs *Othello* on the Broadway stage. His identity drifts as he merges with the Moor. The actor becomes violent, jealous, and loses himself. Like Othello, he murders.

Ronald Colman, showing a light touch and self-effacing wit, plays an actor venturing way too deeply into the character of Othello. His long-suffering costar and ex-wife—Signe Hasso—recognizes that Colman is changing for the worse. She urges him to leave the play, but he's already possessed. A secret affair with a young (and svelte) Shelley Winters turns violent, and there's no way out for Colman. He takes Othello's fate as his own, and the cycle of tragedy is complete.

Colman's fun to watch. His Othello is unconvincing, but maybe his character is supposed to be a Broadway blowhard who's not quite up to the classics. He shines in the scenes of backstage repartee, and his descent into madness is so convincing that Colman won the Oscar for Best Actor. Signe Hasso is the perfect foil to Colman's tortured neurotic. She displays the casual, articulate self-possession that seems the birthright of actresses in Cukor pictures. Shelley Winters plays the sluttiest waitress in New York, and those accustomed to her scenery-chewing in *Lolita* or *The Poseidon Adventure* will be surprised to see her underplay skillfully.

Another in the series of recently rereleased "Martin Scorsese Presents" classics, *A Double Life* uses dark and light to suggest the tortured soul of its protagonists. Because Scorsese helped restore this film, the rental prints are flawless and showcase Milton Krasner's artful, deep-shadow cinematography. Colman's psychological meltdown is represented by Cukor's brilliant visual mirroring. As Scorsese says in his introduction to the film, every element—from the lighting, to the set design, to the placement of actors in the frame—provides a visual metaphor for the emotional state of Colman's character.

Cukor doesn't really have a noir sensibility. He's more interested in the demons faced by the upper classes, where any problem that can't be solved by charm proves unsolvable and must therefore be ignored. Since Colman's character's already an egomaniac, his friends perceive his encroaching madness merely as self-indulgent eccentricity. He gets more obnoxious as he gets crazier, and his friends flee.

Cukor so loves Othello, and the processes of stagecraft, that he spends half the film on Colman and Hasso performing the play's final scene again and again. Each rendition presents Colman in a different mental state. Each is designed to raise the level of suspense. It gets a little oppressive, like the boxing noirs that use endless fight sequences to teach us about character.

But then there are those Cukor moments . . . in one scene between Hasso and Colman, Cukor moves the camera forward for no apparent reason. But somehow, magically, that tiny camera movement changes the emotional dynamic of the scene. Everything becomes more intense, more desperate. Though at first the film is hypnotic, the pace proves slow; the plot machinations feel forced, and since we know what's going to happen from the get-go, the payoff seems a long time a'coming.

Still, if you have the slightest interest in Othello or the backstage world, this film must be seen. The relentlessly stark B/W cinematography sets the tone. There is no gray, no middle ground, and no escape for Colman. Krasner's ferocious shadows suggest an ever-expanding maze of psychological desperation. Long after the nuances of Colman's performance are forgotten, the foreboding atmosphere, sumptuous locations, and Cukor's genius of craft will linger.

A good first noir for viewers who are not all that compelled by the heavy plotting of crime-noir.

Other recommended rentals directed by George Cukor:

Adam's Rib
Gaslight
Gone With the Wind
My Fair Lady
The Philadelphia Story
A Star Is Born

Le Doulos (The Finger Man) (1962—France)

Mood Guide: French thriller of manners

Director: Jean-Pierre Melville; *Camera:* Nicolas Hayer; *Screenplay:* Jean-Pierre Melville

Cast: Jean-Paul Belmondo, Serge Reggiani, Monique Hennessy, Michel Piccoli

In French, with English subtitles; B/W

Plot: A hood gets out of jail and plans a heist. The cops seem aware of every move. Is the most likely informer the informer? And if he is, should he be killed?

Melville must have been in a good mood. No matter how seriously he regards the themes of honor and betrayal among those who live outside the law, he maintains a light touch, and even the most serious scenes have an amused charm. Credit the presence of Belmondo, whose insouciance masks the profundity of his character's moral struggles.

Belmondo suffers from a (possibly unfair) reputation as a professional informer. Even so, he's simultaneously best pals with the head cop and a tough hood newly returned to the streets. The hood plans a big caper and, despite the warnings of other hoods, accepts Belmondo's promise of loyalty. As the hood moves through the Paris underworld, recruiting experts, gathering gear, and making plans, the cops thwart him at every turn. The hood suspects Belmondo, and so do we, until the complicated but credible solution. The French critics of the time were never sure about the resolution, and even now Belmondo's exculpation seems a little fanciful.

When the caper crashes, the surviving hoods go looking for Belmondo. But since Belmondo's the only one not preoccupied with whether Belmondo is a traitor, he's free to seek out the true villain. Belmondo provides the rough justice expected in the criminal milieu, and all's right once more. Or so it seems. . . .

Bob le Flambeur is a comedy of manners. *Le Doulos* is no less obsessed with the habits and proprieties of the underworld, but takes a much bleaker view of the consequences when those manners fail. Crooks don't talk their morality, they walk it. A white lie or reneged responsibility in the middle-class world causes little damage. But Melville takes pains (and three-quarters of the movie) to show how the intricate pyramid of trust and professional commitment that forms a single underworld caper can be brought crashing down if a single brick is out of place.

ARCHIVE PHOTOS/ARCHIVE FRANCE

Is Jean-Paul Belmondo *Le Doulos?*

Melville's diagrammatic sense of the various criminal hierarchies, conflicting loyalties, and professional snobberies provide the necessary aesthetic and moral background to the foreground tale of multiple identities. Is Belmondo crook, cop, or some bastard in between? Is he afraid to face the consequences of the commitment required to live in the underworld, or does he face it more bravely than any of his fellows? Is he really an informer, or punished because he seems insufficiently concerned with the good opinion of his fellows?

The camera work is self-consciously dazzling, with more movement and editing than in other Melville pictures. But there's a certain needless complexity, with a million characters running around and everyone telling different versions of the same event. It's hard not to credit the discursive influence of Godard's *A Bout de Souffle (Breathless)*, which also stars Belmondo racing around Paris being charming and talking a mile a minute.

It's as if Melville decided to show Godard how to remake *Breathless* as a real noir, instead of a commentary on it. So, like Godard, Melville proves how much he loves Paris (great shots of streets, cafés, French style, etc.), and uses witty dialogue and jump cuts: all that *Nouvelle Vague* stuff.

In Melville's world, even crooks don't much care for nonconformists, who must be braver and smarter by far to survive. Despite the heavy thematics, it's still Melville, which means the robberies are more compelling than the moral conversations, and the suspense never lags.

Other recommended rentals directed by Jean-Pierre Melville:
Bob le Flambeur (page 63)
Le Deuxième Souffle (page 99)
Le Samourai (page 219)

The Driver (1979—USA)

Mood Guide: Car chases, mock-profound silence, car chases

Director: Walter Hill; *Camera:* Phillip H. Lathrop; *Screenplay:* Walter Hill

Cast: Ryan O'Neal, Isabelle Adjani, Bruce Dern, Matt Clark, Ronee Blakley

In English; color

Plot: An obsessed cop, desperate to capture a master-driver who hires out as a wheelman for armed robberies, colludes with two vicious hoods to set up a sting. The cop chases the driver, who might be chasing a femme fatale.

To paraphrase British film critic and author Chris Petit, this is an American version of a Jean-Pierre Melville film, only without the brains. Walter Hill conceals his directorial shortcomings in the monosyllabic, deadpan style of Melville's French gangster thrillers of the sixties.

Ryan O'Neal is the best wheelman in the city. Robbers hire him to drive their get-away cars. Bruce Dern is a psycho cop determined to catch O'Neal. Isabelle Adjani might be O'Neal's sweetheart or just a girl in trouble. Dern sets a trap for O'Neal using Adjani. Everybody speaks in monosyllables.

Ryan O'Neal lies on his bed in an anonymous hotel room, staring at nothing, as does Alain Delon in Melville's masterpiece *Le Samourai* (page 219). When Delon stares at nothing, it's

ARCHIVE PHOTOS

Is the glass half-full or half-empty? Ryan O'Neal as *The Driver* conceivable that he's actually thinking. In O'Neal's case, that seems unlikely. O'Neal's supposed to represent a man so deep into his work (driving) that he comes alive only behind the wheel. Problem is, O'Neal's every bit as deadpan and apparently brain-dead behind the wheel as he is lying on his bed in mock-profound silence.

Walter Hill attempts to convey a world of blank, seductive surfaces that hint at another, deeper world. But his own methods undermine him. Hill cast the least profound, most superficial actors available. As if O'Neal didn't raise the glass half-full or half-empty question all by himself, Hills adds the literal-minded Bruce Dern and Isabelle Adjani, who demonstrates the emotional range of a frozen carp. Give these actors well-written characters and they can create at least an illusion of depth. Here, all they do is pose, which gives one plenty of time to reflect on Ryan O'Neal's blank, puppy face. As the picture goes on, O'Neal's mock-profound posturing becomes extremely annoying.

While depth isn't Hill's thing, screeching tires are. The car chases last forever; they involve numerous stunt cars weaving in lethal choreography; O'Neal apparently does much of his own driving; each sequence climaxes with an ornate crash (or crashes); and there are some very nice cars, especially O'Neal's cut-down, white-mag-wheeled, flame-red pickup truck. No cheesy music a la *Starsky and Hutch* underscores the urban-driving action. The only sound is tires, shifting gears, revving engines, cop sirens, and cars slamming into things. The chase sequences are so artful, and the technique used to present them so subdued, that in spite of Hill's irritating groping after profundity, they become profound.

While the cars are racing around, we believe what Hill wants us to believe: that O'Neal is a samurai who lives only for his craft, that O'Neal needs driving as his (and our) only source of exhilaration, that car chases can be poetic cinema; and that cars (and the mediated exhilaration they provide) serve as a metaphor for our current state of divorcement from our emotions. When the tires stop screeching, all those propositions seem as silly as they probably are.

Watching *The Driver* generates a weird sense of dislocation. You might find yourself rooting for Hill's concepts to work. You might nod in satisfied recognition at an occasional good line or slick camera move. But the picture's cold, distanced style ultimately rebuffs any attempts at connection.

Unless you love car chases. If so, then think of *The Driver* as the noir equivalent of a surf movie: dumb characters and just enough plot to keep things moving until the next action sequence. And every action sequence is worth waiting for if you truly love cars.

MGM/ARCHIVE PHOTOS

The class struggle in action: *Force of Evil*

Force of Evil (1948—USA)

Mood Guide: Morality play in a gangster universe

Director: Abraham Polonsky; *Camera:* George Barnes; *Screenplay:* Abraham Polonksy, Ira Wolfert

Cast: John Garfield, Thomas Gomez, Beatrice Pearson, Marie Windsor

In English; B/W

Plot: A crooked lawyer tries to save his brother from the Mob, but his efforts only estrange his brother. Falling for an innocent young girl, the lawyer confronts his own corrupt nature. Trying to do good too late, the lawyer wrecks his life and everyone else's.

Force of Evil is quintessential noir. Its director and star had their careers curtailed by the blacklist; the plot delivers great action sequences and suspense while underlying themes offer astute social commentary; every character demonstrates both villainy and heroism; the visual storytelling relies on strange camera angles and a dominating cityscape; and the film packs an emotional punch not usually associated with simple crime dramas.

Martin Scorsese championed the rediscovery of this classic. Scorsese's name appears on the display box of the beautiful new rental print that he helped restore.

John Garfield stars as an ambitious lawyer working for a mob boss. Garfield and the boss enact a complex scheme to control the city's illegal numbers traffic. Garfield's estranged older brother, played with morose fatalism by Thomas Gomez, is a low-end numbers "banker." Garfield affects a reunion and tells Gomez that the mob boss intends to bankrupt every small numbers bank in the city, Gomez's among them. Garfield promises to protect Gomez and make him rich.

Gomez wants none of this corrupt capitalism. Polonsky, a Marxist, presents Gomez as the little man ground down by a lifetime of fighting the pitiless, Darwinian market. Hopeless but defiant, Gomez urges Garfield to give up the rackets, to realize that money cannot save him. Garfield refuses to listen. He believes he can grow rich without losing his soul. With painstaking inevitability, Garfield gets proven wrong.

Garfield and his brother argue in dialogue so crude, and yet so sophisticated, that Scorsese calls it "blank verse." Phrases are repeated in a rhythmic cadence, and characters hesitate as they speak, giving every scene a contradictory, powerful sense of both the street-real and the theatrical. Their poetic speech draws attention from the rather conventional story and underlines the moral questions concealed within. When two head gangsters meet to carve up the city, they decide the fate of thousands in a terse, blunt interchange. Their brief words are made all the more powerful by what goes unsaid. Polonsky underscores this savage minimalism by staging his most violent sequences in a brutally unadorned style.

Polonksy shoots simply, relying on tight close-ups in which one character dominates another, until the final sequence. Then, Garfield runs down a series of never-ending stone steps, shot from a greater and greater distance, so that he appears smaller and smaller in comparison. As Garfield races deeper into the hell he has made, Polonsky breaks loose, shooting the Williamsburg Bridge like a golden path to heaven that Garfield will never tread. Garfield's path leads instead ever downward. Buildings and walls loom over him to suggest the trap the city has become. The heavy stone steps down which he flees represent the unbearable weight of Garfield's newly found conscience.

Beatrice Pearson makes her screen debut as the good girl who falls for Garfield. Her innocence features a luscious, seductive edge. As much as she abhors moral corruption, she silently begs Garfield to teach her the joys of physical abandon. Her ripe, quivering mouth serves as the film's sole erotic element. Pearson incarnates a cinematic femininity that seldom appears in noir: the Virgin Whore. Marie Windsor, all overdone black lace and high heels, appears briefly as a stereotypical femme fatale. She's the film's one sop to convention, and her scenes form its only weak moments.

As in *Night and the City,* Polonsky's bleak, enclosed world of crooked cops, politicians, lawyers, and gangsters offers no alternatives, no choice but to knuckle under to corruption or be destroyed. Polonksy intertwines Marxism with existentialism, so his characters are trapped by the wearying choices they've made. There is no future, only consequence.

Force of Evil is a deliberately poetic, watershed noir: a fast-paced, violent thriller with a brutal philosophical and moral parable underneath.

ARCHIVE PHOTOS

 (1946—USA)

Mood Guide: Sick obsession, unrequited love, fear of women

Director: Charles Vidor; *Camera:* Rudolph Maté; *Screenplay:* Marion Parsonnet, adapted by Jo Eisinjer

Cast: Glenn Ford, George Macready, Rita Hayworth, Steven Geray

In English; B/W

Plot: An itinerant gambler takes a job from a casino owner. Their friendship is threatened by the owner's new wife. When the owner dies, the gambler and the wife have to decide—are they bound by love or hate?

Glenn Ford and George Macready meet and instantly fall in love. Not that they're going to admit it—to the censors or to each other. But their innuendo-laden conversation carries a clear declaration of affection and lust. To consummate their bond, casino owner Macready shows Ford a sword hidden inside his cane. Sexual power concealed within a symbol of bourgeois respectability, that's Macready's character, all right. At the unveiling of the blade, Macready and Ford share a meaningful glance.

What Ford lacks in style (slick and evil Macready's metier) he makes up for in competent hardheadedness. Between the two of them, they make a whole man. Ford manages Macready's casino and his devotion to Macready is absolute. Imagine Ford's shock, then, when Macready returns home and announces his marriage. Ford's hurt because Macready never told him his plans, and doubly so when he discovers that Macready's new bride is Ford's old flame, Rita Hayworth.

Making perhaps the best-known entrance in movie history, Hayworth tosses her hair back from her face (she is heart-stoppingly, unbearably beautiful) and says only: "Me?"

And here appears the central problem: Hayworth cannot act. Her clumsy line readings and petulant air of self-consciousness shatter the illusion of every scene. They force us to remember we're watching a lovely woman trying to fill a role she cannot understand. Her famous dance sequences, while carrying great thematic weight, prove desperate and embarrassing. They seem a sop to her rising stardom, the kind of solo scene a studio might enforce on a production no matter its irrelevance to the story. When Rita dances and sings, the plot stops dead. When she stops, the plot returns.

The contradictions engendered by her performance, however infuriating, prove hypnotic, and lie at the heart of *Gilda*'s enduring power. Hayworth is dressed like a movie star and lit like a movie star, while Ford and Macready are dressed and lit like supporting characters. Hayworth is an enigma in a spotlight, and whether her presentation stems from studio policies or a desire to show woman as "other" just doesn't matter. She exists both within the story and without: as a poorly performed character, as a completely objectified woman (both for the characters in the story and the film's audience), and as a complex, problematic commentary on objectification precisely because Hayworth's allure makes her such an irresistible object.

Hayworth sings "Put the Blame on Mame," and the dissonance between her performance and what the song represents is overpowering. The song's lyrics make plain that Gilda understands the power of her role as an object of lust. She celebrates the very seductive, manipulative elements of femininity that most terrify Ford and Macready (and every other man on the planet). Her unabashed connection to her sexual power makes her invulnerable. At the same time, she's dressed and lit to appear deeply vulnerable, and to suggest that her sexual machinations spring from her search for meaningful love.

Men hate and desire Gilda for her sexual charms. They hate and desire her for her vulnerability because her easily bruised emotions prove that she prefers love to power. Men further hate and desire her because they cannot completely possess her; Gilda never equates the granting of sexual favors with the sharing of her soul.

Ford chooses the most perverse solution to this conundrum: he refuses even to try to possess her, preferring the obsessive frustrations of having nothing to the deeper frustrations of having less than everything.

Back to the plot: Once he learns of Ford and Hayworth's shared past, Macready appoints Ford as Gilda's sexual guardian. Ford turns passive-aggressive. He will neither report Hayworth's various infidelities (out of loyalty to her) nor will he make a pass at her (out of loyalty to Macready). When Macready appears to die in an airplane accident, Ford marries Hayworth, but their marriage does not lack for tragic complications.

Whew—what a journey. As a bonus for those who prefer to watch movies instead of thinking too much about them, the mystery within the love story really works, the contrasty cinematography offers a few lovely moments (a plane exploding over the ocean is particularly dreamlike and lovely), and Ford's performance of simian brutality and clumsy romance is the best work of his career.

As for Hayworth, you can't take your eyes off her.

ARCHIVE PHOTOS

Peggy Cummins in *Gun Crazy*

Gun Crazy (aka Deadly Is the Female)

(1950—USA)

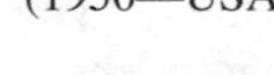

Mood Guide: Amour fou

Director: Joseph Lewis; *Camera:* Russell Harlan; *Screenplay:* MacKinlay Kantor, Millard Kaufman, Dalton Trumbo

Cast: Peggy Cummins, John Dall, Berry Kroeger, Anabel Shaw

In English; B/W

Plot: A gun-obsessed, innocent guy falls for a violent, manipulative young woman. They steal cars, rob banks, and terrorize the heartland. While their passion burns deep, these two crazy kids can only run so far.

The ultimate tale of crazy love on the run, shot with low-budget vitality and genuine cinematic wit. A hundred other violent-lovers-against-the-world movies sprang from this low-budget, adrenaline masterpiece—*Bonnie and Clyde, Natural Born Killers,* and even *Badlands,* among them. But none come close to capturing the murderous innocence and all-consuming passion of this pair of crazy kids.

Our puppylike hero, played by John Dall, loves guns. Boy, does he love guns. He meets his soulmate, played by Peggy Cummins, at a carnival. She's a trick shot. The sight of her shooting—especially when she bends over and fires between her legs—awakens something deep within him. He challenges her, and they shoot at a crown of matches on one another's heads. (Credit the brilliance of the screenplay to blacklisted, future Academy Award–winner Dalton Trumbo.) He holds still as she fires. She sends five matches into flames. Now it's her turn: she stands as his target. He ignites six. Their eyes meet. So much for foreplay.

They hit the road. Niagara Falls crashes down. Old Faithful spews up. The sexually loaded visual metaphors may be perfectly camouflaged as the cornball honeymoon clichés of the era, but there is no mistaking the look of orgasmic satisfaction on Peggy Cummins's face. John Dall dreams of a bucolic little cottage, but she's got bigger plans. While slowly pulling on a pair of silk stockings, Cummins tells him it's her way or the highway. He can't live without her, and acquiesces. According to her wishes, they rob folks. Robbing folks raises their desire to a fever pitch and forces them to hide from the world. Their universe soon consists of nothing but sex, kicks, and the road.

Their mutual sexual magnetism is palpable; so is the sledgehammer gender-bending. It's not so much that she wears the pants, but that she pulls the trigger. He's a better shot but cannot kill. Which of them, then, is more potent? Some scholars paint her as a vicious seducer, but he's a big boy. Once she shows him the highway to hell, it's his foot that holds the petal to the metal.

Director Lewis has a Scorsese-like flair for functional, awe-inspiring camera tricks that drive the plot, and express the characters' emotions without a word of dialogue. Lewis moves the camera like an artist, and Trumbo plots like a B-movie pro. The action rips along without a moment of silly exposition or bogus sentimentality.

Few movies, high or low budget, match the economical visual storytelling. In one sequence, Lewis tucks his camera down in the backseat of a car. In one unbroken take, the kids drive through a small town and pull up in front of a bank. John Dall goes in to rob the place. A cop strolls up to the car. Peggy Cummins steps out to chat with him and clouts him unconscious when the alarm goes off. Back in the car, we ride with the couple as they race out of town. Dall asks Cummins to check behind, and she looks back into the camera, her eyes ablaze with lust. Fade to black.

No film (and no other single shot in all of cinema) so convincingly unites youthful restlessness, sex, violence, and automobiles. *Gun Crazy* revels in the glamour of this combination. Lewis and Trumbo make clear how much fun it is to be young, doomed, and living outside the law. Lewis and Trumbo's obsessive treatment of their heroes' obsessions, coupled with the take-no-prisoners pacing, make *Gun Crazy* one of the all-time greats.

Heatwave (1983—Australia)

Mood Guide: Sweaty urban terror

Director: Phillip Noyce; *Camera:* Vincent Monton; *Screenplay:* Phillip Noyce, Charles Rosenberg

Cast: Judy Davis, Richard Moir, Chris Haywood, Bill Hunter

In English; color

Plot: A corporate architect in charge of demolishing a run-down city block gets seduced by a feisty activist. He has second thoughts about his huge project and learns how the big boys play hardball. The activist becomes his lover, his teacher, and perhaps his only salvation.

A crappy old housing project in Sydney must come down to make way for a shiny new office block. When the project's residents protest, the corporation opposing them sets fires and sends goons to gang-stomp the protesters. Nobody else in the sweltering city pays much attention.

The mild-mannered architect in charge of the project—Richard Moir, in a spacey, self-contained performance—doesn't perceive any big moral struggles. To him, it's simple urban progress. His bosses seem unusually anxious about this particular deal, but he doesn't notice. He prefers not to notice anything, ever.

But Moir's in for a life-change. He meets a tough-minded, hot-blooded community activist, played by Judy Davis, who introduces him to the seamier side of construction politics, big-city hardball, juggernaut capitalism, and even himself. He wakes up, joins the opposition and learns how much friendship and loyalty matter in the real world: that is, not at all. His fiancée is appalled and his colleagues react with instant hostility.

This sweaty thriller uses the hotbox of a Sydney Christmas to underscore the money pressures cracking down on everyone. Here the burning sun stands in for the dark night of most noir—since the sun is always out, the real secrets must be hidden away inside, in the cool dark of corporation hallways. There, things prove to be other than they seem. The architect's sleek, expensive office is built on a tottering shell game of rotating loans. The architect's betrothed encourages him to sell out with a smile on his face. The architect can't understand why he's so attracted to Judy Davis.

She's anarchy in the flesh, everything his repressed bourgeois self has been yearning for. He just didn't know that releasing his id meant losing everything he had worked so hard to gain. This is no socialist fable; the architect doesn't want to lose everything. He wants to keep on making money and feeling righteous. Only, the moral imperatives of noir won't let him. The architect must commit, but he's lost in a swamp of moral ambiguity. Both sides are pushy and self-righteous, both are greedy in their own way. Neither mind beating the shit out of their enemies. But only one of them murders.

Moir makes an interesting protagonist. He's a tall, handsome variant on the little-man-crushed-by-capitalism trope. If he buckles under and conforms, then riches and approbation will be his. If he stands up for his beliefs (never a safe or smart thing to do in noir), his enemies will crush him like a grape.

And so he ponders and waits, afraid to jump in either direction. His own passion scares him, the thought of losing all his money scares him, goon squads kidnapping activists scare him, Judy Davis scares him, but finally, the thought of living his life as a gutless wonder scares him the most.

And, once he plays the big hero, he learns more hard lessons: Love does not redeem, being morally right does not produce results; the sword is mightier than the pen; and happy endings are hard to come by.

Talk about selling out—Phillip Noyce never should have gone to Hollywood. His gift is for the compact, self-contained thriller; for simple camera work and for drawing stellar performances from his talent. As in *Dead Calm* (page 92), the protagonist is a calm, manly man and the femme fatale/victim is a high-strung woman with a matter-of-fact connection to her sexuality that entices and intimidates the man. His strength, he learns, is no match for hers. And if he loses her, where can he turn?

Noyce's unsentimental grasp of urban politics and his refusal to believe in the salvation of love supply all the nihilism any modern noir requires. The sparse camera work and inescapable sunshine provide the rest.

Other recommended rentals directed by Phillip Noyce:
Dead Calm (page 92)

He Walked By Night (1949—USA)

Mood Guide: Creepy, compelling police procedural

Director: Alfred Werker/Anthony Mann; *Camera:* John Alton; *Screenplay:* John C. Higgins, Crane Wilbur
Cast: Richard Basehart, Scott Brady, Roy Roberts, Jack Webb
In English; B/W

Plot: A cop is murdered by an expert thief and marksman. He flees, and an enormous manhunt is launched. The mysterious killer cannot be found, and we enter the world of investigative method as the cops slowly but surely hunt down their man.

A cop on routine patrol interrupts a man picking a lock. The guy shoots the cop and flees. In a twist that sounds far too familiar nowadays, the suspect's car turns out to conceal an arsenal of weapons and electronic gear. The cop dies, and L.A. launches its biggest manhunt in history. The story cuts back and forth from the cops to the suspect, from the hunters to the prey. The cops are colorless, placid, indomitable. Their prey is high-strung, inscrutable, and eerily compelling.

EAGLE FILMS/ARCHIVE PHOTOS

Richard Basehart plays the role model for all subsequent cinematic creepy weirdos. An electronics expert, silent and withdrawn, Basehart moves through sunny L.A. like a shadow. None of his neighbors or coworkers remember what he looks like; none of his classmates recall a single thing about him. He's modern society's Lost Man: skilled, obsessed, and alone.

The story runs on two parallel tracks. The cops build evidence and Basehart runs, heading ever more underground. He pops up now and then to commit another "senseless" crime, thus reminding the audience that anarchy lies everywhere unseen, ready to erupt and dislodge their well-ordered lives. Director Mann suggests that the overly rational, step-by-step methodology of the cops is the only alternative to the intuitive but destructive fixations of the unpredictable nonconformists represented by Basehart.

The story moves slowly, and the acting—Basehart's aside—is barely discernible. The film grinds to a halt in the second act as a room full of good citizens help the police construct an image of Basehart's face. Mann's fascination for this dull interlude might be his commentary on America becoming a nation of informers. Or, he might be killing time until the plot reappears. Worse yet, it might be Mann showing an unwarranted faith in the precise telling of the true story on which the film is based.

John Alton's extraordinary cinematography saves the day. As the noose tightens around Basehart, Alton traps him in a world of increasing shadow and blackness. Alton's masterpiece is an extended chase sequence through L.A.'s underground storm-drain system. The cops charge forward with their piercing, stark-white lights, and Basehart retreats into the hostile, enveloping darkness. After seventy-five minutes of groping for a hook, the picture wakes up and becomes a genuine nightmare. Longer and splashier than a similar, more famous sewer chase sequence in *The Third Man* (page 251), Alton's intercutting of light and dark (good and evil) save *He Walked* from being just another police procedural.

Jack Webb's tiny role apparently launched an enduring chapter in TV history. From the opening shot of a map of L.A. (complete with pins), to the booming voice-over, to the presentation of cops as tough-minded saints of the rational method, *He Walked* is the very model not only of Webb's show *Dragnet* but of *Highway Patrol* and every other TV cop show of the 1950s.

Noir scholars maintain that Mann's films are either weirdly flat or strangely overwrought because Mann's real interest is in a passionate presentation of emotional and philosophical subtexts. For the noir buff, that subtext offers several poetic moments. Everyone else should fast-forward to Alton's storm-drain chase sequence and never mind the rest.

The Hit (1984—UK)

Mood Guide: Languid gangster road movie

Director: Stephen Frears; *Camera:* Mike Molloy; *Screenplay:* Peter Puinct

Cast: Terence Stamp, John Hurt, Tim Roth, Bill Hunter, Fernando Rey

In English; color

Plot: A snitch gets nabbed by a hit-man ten years after he ratted out the hit-man's boss. They drive across Spain, en route to the snitch's date with destiny. He doesn't seem too concerned, but the assassin has to contend with his own stupid assistant, a tough Spanish whore, and an Australian mobster who doesn't know when to keep his mouth shut.

A contrary English suspense thriller with a snitch for a hero, a hit-man for an antihero, the hallmarks of a road movie—lovely, full-frame landscapes coupled with a solemn sense of the passing of time—and a very nasty sense of humor.

Terence Stamp, looking impossibly beatific, plays a gangster-turned-informer hiding in Spain ten years after he ratted out his mobster boss. John Hurt, appearing nerve-racked and satanic, plays a hit man assigned to kidnap Stamp to Paris for the mobster's revenge. Hurt's assistant is Tim Roth as a bungling, impulsive assassin-in-training. Once kidnapped, Stamp doesn't seem too worried. He's been doing a lot of reading about the nature of death, he says, and has no fear of The End. The hit man, having seen (many) others in similar situations, remains unconvinced. "Wait till it really happens," Hurt says, "and see how you react." So we do.

Hurt and Roth stagger around Spain with Stamp in tow, lurching from misadventure to screwup to disaster. These misadventures, though unusual for a noir, seem real enough to anyone who has ever had a important errand and finds that events just won't cooperate. Even the most exotic jobs (like that of hit man) run afoul of mundane problems.

Director Frears (*Dangerous Liaisons*) revels in the big frame of the movies after years spent directing television. He fills the screen from top to bottom with the blue Spanish sky and the vast Spanish plains, across which the tiny car containing the three men flies. Frears uses the same big-screen approach inside the car, blasting close-ups like Sergio Leone. And, like Leone, Frears cuts from wide-open landscape shots to huge full-face reactions. It's a powerful technique.

It's not that the picture resembles a Western so much as the characters behave as if they were living through one, especially Tim Roth. Hurt just wants to do his job, but Roth and Stamp are too aware of their mythic, highly charged situation (killer and victim in close proximity) and both keep trying to be larger than life. Hurt, like a (deadly) mother hen, wearily reminds them of the dreariness of their circumstances. Even though Roth is going to shoot Stamp, they become secret allies, almost pals. Hurt notes this breach of hit-man decorum with understated alarm.

Underplaying is John Hurt's métier, and he makes the most of his opportunities to do or say nothing. His stillness carries considerable import; it's sinister as hell. Hurt finds trouble only when he succumbs to a merciful urge. Stamp has problems when The End comes sooner than he expects. Roth learns that perhaps he should try another profession.

The thrills are in the acting, the hilarious arguments, and the constant shifting tensions between the men. Those shifts are caused by a young Spanish beauty whom they snatch as a hostage, and by Stamp's increasingly irritating serenity in the face of certain death. Hurt argues with Roth, Roth chases the girl while befriending Stamp, and Stamp watches it all unfold, smirking like a Zen monk. When the big moment comes, will he crack?

Witty, graphically violent, and featuring a distinctive visual style, an elegant sound track by Eric Clapton, and a simple moving tribute to John Lennon.

Other recommended rentals directed by Stephen Frears:
Bloody Kids
The Grifters

Homicide (1990—USA)

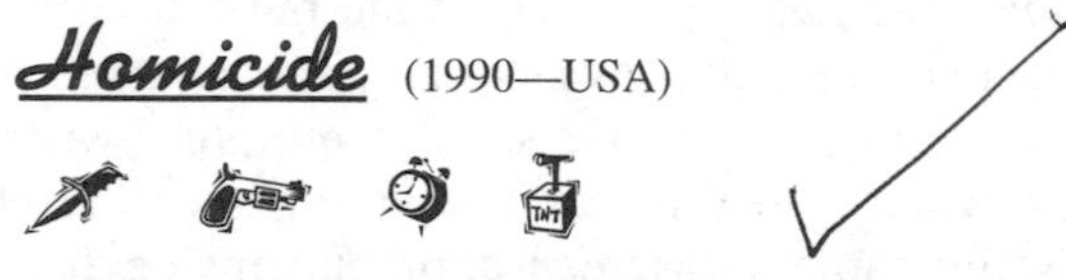

Mood Guide: Intellectual cop movie

Director: David Mamet; *Camera:* Roger Deakins; *Screenplay:* David Mamet
Cast: Joe Mantegna, William H. Macy, Ving Rhames
In English; color
Plot: While tracking a killer, a tough cop learns he's not who he thinks he is. His search for identity merges with his struggle to solve the crime. The cop must find his place in the world, and his place in the world of cops. These prove to be two very different places.

David Mamet's finest film is a two-headed beast of daunting emotional/intellectual complexity and power: half-cop movie, half-brutal journey of self-discovery. It remains the most accurate film on race relations in America yet made, and a thorough exploration of the theme of achieved identity. It's also a totally satisfying *policier,* with villains, suspense, and violent cop movie action.

Though a cynical, well-executed thriller in dialogue, plot, and attitude, *Homicide* is after bigger game. Mamet—award-winning playwright of *Speed-the-Plow* and *Oleanna*—uses the world of cops to explore the themes that intrigue him: What gives us our sense of belonging? To what or to whom do we owe loyalty? Is it possible to render change in life without suffering tragic, crippling loss? How do Americans deal with the overlapping, contradictory identities of class, race, profession, and religion?

Mamet regular Joe Mantegna plays a man who considers himself all cop until he's forced to choose between cop loyalty and what he perceives as loyalty to his true, long-hidden self. It's the classic noir dilemma in a thoroughly modern noir.

Homicide's protagonist is a misunderstood man who lives by his own moral code that forms the core of a self-invented identity. When this code breaks down, our hero, like all noir protagonists, must take his fate into his own hands and blaze his own trail for good or ill.

Mamet delivers his existential message undiluted: We make our own moral choices and for those choices, large and small, moral dues must be paid. The price our hero pays will mark him for the rest of his life. And our hero's insights regarding the difference between who he thinks he is and who he is revealed to be will be neither pleasant nor life-affirming.

Mamet's hypernaturalist dialogue—all stops and starts and weird fragmented phrases—is intended to remind us how difficult is any communication; how different in-groups create their own speech—both to protect their identity from outsiders and to reinforce their bond within the group; and to demonstrate how, in the "world of men" (Mamet's phrase) obliqueness is all. None of Mamet's characters ever say anything as direct as: "I love you," though they may say, "Remember that girl that time?" and mean "I love you." His characters' determination never to say what they mean forces the viewer to pay strict attention to every nuance. This adds to the considerable suspense.

Mamet's actors seldom use wild gestures: They speak slowly and clearly; they move with deliberation. Their performances, like Mamet's camera work, are understated to the point of invisibility. You may find this style slightly off-putting at first, but after a few minutes it becomes remarkably familiar.

A harrowing, suspenseful mixture of cop stuff and philosophy, one of the ten best films of 1990 and one of the sadly neglected films of the last ten years.

Other recommended rentals directed by David Mamet:
House of Games
The Untouchables (screenwriter only)

Gloria Grahame and Glenn Ford in *Human Desire*

Human Desire (1954—USA)

Mood Guide: Sex, obsession, jealousy

Director: Fritz Lang; *Camera:* Burnett Guffey; *Screenplay:* Alfred Hayes, from the novel *La Bête Humaine,* by Émile Zola

Cast: Glenn Ford, Gloria Grahame, Broderick Crawford, Kathleen Case

In English; B/W

Plot: A returning vet, a jealous railroad man, an innocent girl, and a femme fatale meet on the wrong side of the tracks. Murder, true love, revenge and seduction follow.

Scholars complain that Gloria Grahame's sexual perversity is but a pale shadow of the freakiness presented by her character in the French film version (of the same title) directed by Jean Renoir. That may be, but Grahame's blithe bed-hopping, the pleasure she derives from confessing her own sinfulness, and the supposedly unknowing masochism with which she snares Glenn Ford combine for more frank sex-talk and display than in any American film of this period.

Ford comes home after the Korean War, happy to return to his job as a locomotive engineer. As such, Ford wears a funny hat, but it grows less absurd with each passing minute. Lang enthralls as usual with a masterful opening montage of trains switching tracks, sliding into tunnels, and roaring across the landscape. If one remembers how, at that time, trains represented a certain romantic freedom of movement and the life-renewing potential of new places, then this montage serves as a strong metaphor for the unstoppable momentum of fate, as Ford is about to discover.

He travels with his old pal and takes up lodging once more in his old pal's home. A big surprise awaits; the young daughter of Ford's old pal has grown up to be the va-va-voomish Kathleen Case, and she has eyes only for Ford. She's the incarnation of ripening young lust, but Ford seems oddly unmoved.

Meanwhile, surly Broderick Crawford's been fired from his job at the railroad. He forces his wife, Gloria Grahame, to beg a big shot of her former acquaintance to rehire Crawford. It appears Grahame slept with the guy, and Crawford—who's a bit of a jealous psycho—arranges to kill him. He does so in a train compartment while Grahame looks on, sloe-eyed and apparently uncaring. In one of Lang's resonant, memorable moments, Crawford casually wipes the blood from his knife-blade onto his topcoat.

Ford sees Grahame in the railroad car but refuses to identify her at an inquest. They begin an affair. Crawford sinks into drunkenness because Grahame will no longer touch him. Crawford's only leverage over Grahame is the note he forced her to write the dead man. She dares not leave Crawford until she retrieves the note. It's difficult to tell if she's playing Ford for a sucker; she seems genuinely afraid of Crawford and insists to both men that the dead rich guy forced himself on her when she was only sixteen. Still, Grahame keeps Ford on a leash, switching from innocent to corrupted as his erotic appetites require.

Grahame's seduction of Ford shows her cunning. She lowers her dress off one silky shoulder to reveal bruises left by Crawford's rough touch. She looks up at Ford as if to say; "You could do that, too, if you wanted, but I know you're too kind to even think of it." Ford appears dumbstruck by an avalanche of dirty thoughts. He's a goner.

Lang's unsentimental insight strikes once more: Ford could have the lush, innocent flower who really loves him, but he prefers the corrupted ersatz. Like most of Lang's character's, Ford rejects the worthwhile and utilitarian in pursuit of the elusive, the ruinous, and the perverse.

It's a cold, uncaring world, though Lang does suggest the potential for redemption for those not wholly corrupted. Each carefully composed frame advances Lang's relentless narrative movement and supports the elegant visual construction that no one in noir—and damn few directors, period—can match. His visual foreshadowing is so simple, and plays with such profound effect, that you may find yourself rewinding to catch a certain edit or perfect instant of lighting.

Adult, casually sophisticated, riveting from start to finish, and worthy of repeat viewings.

Other recommended rentals directed by Fritz Lang:

The Big Heat (page 46)
M (page 170)
Scarlet Street (page 222)
The Woman in the Window (page 270)
You Only Live Once

Made for each other: Gloria Grahame and Humphrey Bogart *In a Lonely Place*

In a Lonely Place (1950—USA)

Mood Guide: Damn smart, heartbreaking suspense

Director: Nicholas Ray; *Camera:* Burnett Guffey; *Screenplay:* Edmund H. North, Andrew Solt

Cast: Humphrey Bogart, Gloria Grahame, Frank Lovejoy

In English; B/W

Plot: Maybe a screenwriter's a murderer. Maybe the actress who falls for him shouldn't have given him that alibi. Maybe their newfound love can save them both. Or maybe they're just two screwed-up, lonely people who can't escape the traps they've set for themselves.

Humphrey Bogart plays a screenwriter with a dangerous, perhaps murderous, temper. Acting on a whim, Gloria Grahame, who plays an actress, provides him with an alibi when he's charged with murder. They try to fall in love, but Bogart's jealous insecurity conflicts with Grahame's sincere, if matter-of-fact, method of demonstrating her affection. In the mode of classic tragedy, Bogart's growing need for Grahame only makes him doubt her fidelity all the more. His jealousy fuels his temper, and as Grahame sees the extent of Bogart's inner rage, she begins to doubt his innocence. Grahame seeks to withdraw, and Bogart becomes more convinced that she'll betray him. In perfect synchronicity, the two avidly construct the walls of their own doomed fortresses, as only adults can.

All this is played out under the constant, looming cloud of Hollywood's unrelenting, polarity of soaring success or crushing failure. Accordingly, when Bogart's and Grahame's characters act against their heart's best interests, director Ray is careful to portray their mistakes in career terms as well, since in the movie business it's often impossible to separate the two. The result is the most accurate treatise on emotional self-destruction and the social patterns of Hollywood—two closely related subjects—ever made.

The unobtrusive B/W camera work grows increasingly claustrophobic, presenting each player as trapped in the world he or she has made. This visual sense of the walls closing in contributes to the potent suspense that fuels the second half of the film. Bogart and Grahame turn to love to escape the unpleasant patterns of their lives, but force of habit proves too much for both of them. Bogart's habit of suspicion and Grahame's of forgiveness should dovetail perfectly, but instead they cancel each another out. It's almost too real.

As are the easy humor, the accurate barroom banter, the deep silences of both affection and (later) hostility between Grahame and Bogart. Bogart underplays to perfection, and his rages spring to the surface with a terrifying and entirely believable energy. Grahame seems, as ever, completely insane. Her singular combination of vulnerability, bullet-proof toughness, and resigned willingness to accept the demons in herself and in others could only have been drawn from her by a director of uncommon sensitivity: Grahame and Nicholas Ray were husband and wife as this film was made. If Ray couldn't understand her, who could? This is Grahame's finest hour; the performance that solidified her legend.

And throughout, the underlying psychological tension of the love story only heightens the suspense of the murder mystery. Each subplot makes the other stronger because among the many virtues of this purely American existential landmark is the flawless structure of the Solt's screenplay. He and Nicholas Ray build a modern tragedy out of modern materials: alienation, self-created distrust, and a willful refusal to believe in the unscheduled arrival of good news.

Other recommended rentals directed by Nicholas Ray:
Bigger Than Life
Johnny Guitar
They Live By Night (page 245)

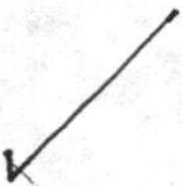

Invasion of the Body Snatchers (1954—USA)

Mood Guide: Epic of paranoia

Director: Don Siegel; *Camera:* Ellsworth Fredericks; *Screenplay:* Daniel Mainwaring

Cast: Kevin McCarthy, Dana Wynter, Larry Gates, Carolyn Jones, Sam Peckinpah

In English; B/W

Plot: A doctor returns home from a convention to discover his small town in disarray. A son thinks his mother is not his mother. An older woman believes her uncle has undergone some sort of transformation. The doctor learns that these worried souls are right, and then some. He and his lady love try to flee with their heart and soul intact.

Don Siegel is no poet. He's the most literal-minded, prose-oriented director of the classical era. That's why his cop-thrillers don't quite make it as noir—they're gritty and street, but lack underlying dread, philosophic subtext, or visual storytelling.

When Siegel shows a man walking through a door, there's no commentary, just description. His absence of frills does comprise a style, though; a visual equivalent of the stripped-down prose of the hard-boiled novel. Siegel's spare approach is, by way of contrast, perfect for this lurid tale.

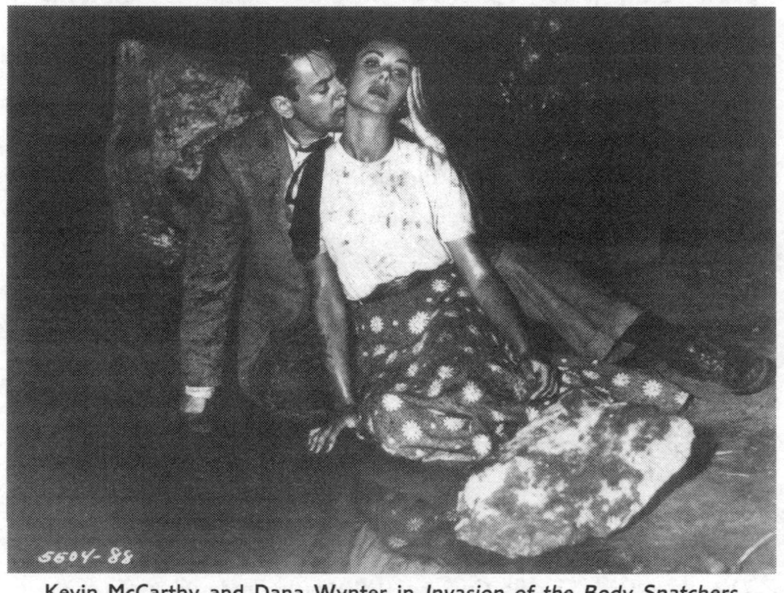

ARCHIVE PHOTOS

Kevin McCarthy and Dana Wynter in *Invasion of the Body Snatchers*

Kevin McCarthy, a small-town doctor, comes home from a convention. A little boy runs screaming in front of his car. The boy is convinced his mother is not his mother. Kevin reunites with a recently divorced old flame, Dana Wynter. A friend of Wynter's believes her uncle to be possessed by another, colder personality. Ever the proper rationalist, McCarthy makes an appointment for her with a shrink. But he sees other, disquieting signs: No one goes out to eat; everyone is weirdly calm. And, the day after they complain, those who were hysterical now say everything is just swell.

In the opening act, Siegel sticks to his literal style. McCarthy makes a credible heroic figure, and Dana Wynter is the picture of elegant sensuality. Even in her preposterous fifties summer sundress, she's an island of cool remove with a hint of heat lurking behind her smooth facade.

A friend calls McCarthy in a panic. There's a dead body on his pool table (Siegel revels in the symbolic comforts of suburbia and takes great pleasure in demonstrating how none of them provide the slightest sanctuary), a body that's starting to look a lot like him. McCarthy races to his girlfriend's house and discovers a similar changeling. Soon, McCarthy, Wynter, and their friends uncover weird seed-pods in the greenhouse. These pods—with all the credibility-shattering of really cheap 1950s special effects—are growing likenesses of everyone. When people sleep, the pods replace them with perfect replicas. The soulless pod-people obey some mysterious central command.

When McCarthy smashes the pods and notifies the (already pod-corrupted) cops, the chase is on. McCarthy is determined to get out of town and warn the world. The pod-people intend to make him one of their own. If he sleeps, they will.

As the pod-people close in on McCarthy and Wynter, Siegel's style becomes, in his own controlled manner, positively lyrical. McCarthy's world becomes a cramped series of barred closets; long, narrow hallways; dead-end alleys; and muddy mine shafts. The chase becomes increasingly harrowing, frenzied, and hopeless. You might be shocked at how powerful such a simple, supposedly cheesy, concept can be. Siegel's quotidian style makes McCarthy's living nightmare all the more real.

The film's terror comes not only from Siegel's enclosing visuals, nor from the lynch-mob violence of the pod-people horde, but from simpler, more frightening, moments. McCarthy and Wynter spend the night hiding in his office. At dawn, they peer fearfully out the window, their faces aghast with terror. When the camera finally shows us their view, we do not see the apocalypse we anticipate, but instead a sleepy little town on a quiet Saturday morning. The normality of it all is horrifying, as horrifying as the look on McCarthy's face when his loved ones betray him.

Touted by some as a Red Scare picture, wherein the pod-people stand for the Commie menace, *Invasion* is instead the very portrait of justifiable paranoia. In normality and conformity Siegel finds, as did many noir directors, the absolute death of the soul. For Siegel and screenwriter Mainwaring (who wrote *Out of the Past*), normal American life is the most frightening thing in the world. And if you let your reason sleep, the pod-people—vile creeping ordinariness—will get you.

(The remake, starring Donald Sutherland, Brooke Adams, and Jeff Goldblum, offers more sophisticated settings and characters, more believable special effects, and a nice mood of fear. But its literal-mindedness as regards the pod-people, and its dependence on chase sequences, prevent it from rising above spooky sci-fi. Nice cameo by Leonard Nimoy, though.)

Other recommended rentals directed by Don Siegel:
The Lineup
Dirty Harry
Hell Is for Heroes

I Wake Up Screaming (1942—USA)

Mood Guide: Unconvincing mystery

Director: H. Bruce Humberstone; *Camera:* Edward Cronjager; *Screenplay:* Dwight Taylor

Cast: Betty Grable, Victor Mature, Carole Landis, Laird Cregar, Elisha Cook, Jr.

In English; B/W

Plot: A promoter teaches a pretty young waitress how to behave in high society. Shortly after ditching him to try out for the movies, she turns up murdered. The promoter is the main suspect; he is relentlessly pursued by a creepy cop. The dead girl's straight-arrow sister falls for the promoter. The cops follow him, and he tries to keep his head above water.

A script so dumb, it could be made today.

Perhaps this was the first version of a much-repeated story:

A strong-willed girl falls for the man accused of murdering her sister. All the clues point to him, but . . .

There's a plethora of creeps around, any one of whom could be the killer: a weird cop, a concierge with a crush on the girl, two supposed friends who might turn out to be enemies. The girl helps Mature avoid the law and search for the real killer. Ho hum, you say? It gets worse.

The plot, dialogue, and use of sound track are so silly as to make the picture unwatchable. Yet, *I Wake* has utility. It's a prime example of the shortcomings of some noir scholarship. This second-rate picture is often recommended by noir scholars because it bears many of the visual hallmarks of the noir style: strange-angle two-shots; the shadows of window blinds slanting across a face; long, foreboding shadows; and cinematography that places one cast member in shadow and another in dazzling light.

Moreover, because *I Wake* comes early in the noir cycle (1942), these noir stylistic trademarks seem remarkably unselfconscious and laden with sincere emotion. Those with great curiosity, a great love for Betty Grable, or even an irresistible compulsion toward Victor Mature should rent it, if only to complete your noir lexicon. Try watching with the sound off. You'll see the noir visual style created before your eyes, the hallmarks of which include the Fox studio preference for natural locations—there's a clumsy sequence at a public swimming pool—and sinister lighting.

Without the sound, you'll miss only Betty Grable's screechy voice (it matches her strangely petulant countenance) and the most perverse use of "Somewhere over the Rainbow" in movie history. Though *The Wizard of Oz* came out only three years before, *I Wake* uses a tinny symphonic version to express Grable's longing for Mature. It's quite odd and gives the picture a confusingly camp subtext.

Laird Cregar is creepy and terrific as a weird cop in pursuit of Mature. A very young Elisha Cook, Jr., is equally unsettling, but neither make up for the hackneyed script.

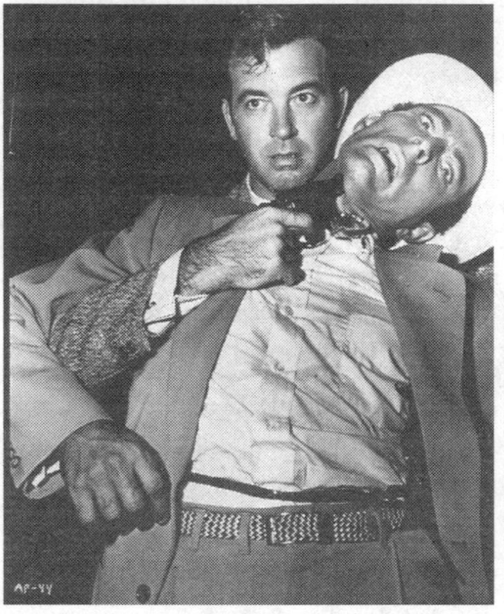

UNITED ARTISTS/ARCHIVE PHOTOS

John Payne reasons with Jack Elam in *Kansas City Confidential*

Kansas City Confidential (1952—USA)

Mood Guide: Crude, violent gem in the rough

Director: Phil Karlson; *Camera:* George Diskant; *Screenplay:* George Bruce, Harry Essex

Cast: John Payne, Coleen Gray, Preston Foster, Jack Elam, Lee Van Cleef

In English; B/W

Plot: Four hoods rob an armored car. They escape in a floral delivery van. The (innocent) driver of an identical van gets arrested for being in on the job. Once free, he tracks the gang to Mexico.

> There, he falls in love with a retired cop's daughter. When everyone comes together for the big payoff, roles change and identities alter as fast as slugs from a snub-nosed .38.

This is what got the French so excited: Unrepressed American brutality merged with poetic, low-budget visuals and a passionate, if slightly stupid, presentation of the existential dilemma. Bringing all the hysteria associated with the late classical noir cycle, *Kansas City Confidential* looks and sounds laughably cheap, but presents its philosophy with admirable economy.

If the budget permitted camera movement, it might be the work of Samuel Fuller. With its overheated exchanges, claustrophobic close-ups, and sexually tinged violence, *Confidential*'s style seems a key influence on Martin Scorsese. Even so, it remains a connoisseur's delight: a cheesy, tawdry B movie whose charms won't be apparent unless you've seen at least twenty other noirs.

John Payne, an ex-con, gets arrested in the aftermath of a clever heist. All the heisters wear masks—their identities remain a mystery even to one another. They split up, agreeing to wait for telegrams signaling their reunion and a split of the loot. Payne's an inadvertent fall guy. The robbers meant him no harm, he just happens to get in the way. When the cops finally let Payne go, his anger at fate's dirty tricks compels him, for once, to forge his own destiny.

Psychotic with frustration, Payne tracks the hoods to Mexico. In Tijuana he disputes his assertions of innocence by proving himself as violent as the worst criminal. Assuming the identity of one of the hoods, Payne meets the rest of the gang and falls for the only unalloyed innocent in the picture. Acting out of love for her, Payne commits an uncharacteristic act of generosity, which generates an unexpected outcome. Though the ending might appear a reversal of the noir outlook, it's founded on murder, lies, and dirty money.

Director Phil Karlson cut his teeth in the B-movie studios of World War II. He prided himself on working quickly and on "screwy camera angles." Telling his tale in bizarro super-close-ups of one sweaty face after another, Karlson has little use for establishing shots. When he goes to a rare long shot, a lone voyeur stands in the foreground, visually dominating the object of his attention, who invariably appears as a distant and powerless figure.

Karlson's employs a limited visual vocabulary, but it builds suspense and carries the story. Every two-shot displays power relationships; somebody is always looming over somebody else. Another effective trick—much copied by Scorsese—is Karlson's cut to a super-close-up of a big meaty fist smashing down toward the camera. Sadly, the available rental prints are awful, with muddy sound and poor contrast. Several key visual plot-points are almost indecipherable in the murk of grainy videotape.

Payne's big-featured face rules the screen, but Karlson gives his costars plenty of close-ups. Like Jean Wallace in *The Big Combo* (page 43), Coleen Gray is another long-lost, heart-stopping noir beauty. Her innocence shines in her lovely eyes, and her skin glows. She's like a creature from another planet, redemption reaching out to Payne in exquisite form. Jack Elam and an inhumanly sinister Lee Van Cleef are so scary that Payne seems a babe by comparison.

Kansas City Confidential is a gem in the rough, a condensed roller-coaster of vengeance, betrayal, deception, the fluidity of identity, the microscopic line between guilt and innocence, and the power of luck, both good and bad.

The Killers (1946—USA)

Mood Guide: Tragic mystery, told in flashbacks

Director: Robert Siodmak; *Camera:* Woody Bredell; *Screenplay:* Anthony Veiller

Cast: Burt Lancaster, Edmond O'Brien, Ava Gardner, William Conrad, Albert Dekker

In English; B/W

Plot: Two hired killers show up in a small town. Their intended victim doesn't even try to run. After his death, a curious insurance man re-creates the dead man's life. It's a tale of prison, armed robbery, and fatally betrayed love.

Two killers (including roly-poly future TV star William Conrad) saunter into a diner in some jerkwater town. They ask for "the Swede" and assure the awestruck yokels that they've come to kill him. Lying paralyzed with spiritual fatigue in his flea-bag hotel room, Burt Lancaster waits. Pretty soon, Conrad kicks open Burt's door and fills him full of lead. Conrad and his pal are only doing a job Lancaster hasn't the heart to do himself.

ARCHIVE PHOTOS

Ava Gardner in *The Killers*

Edmond O'Brien's an insurance investigator. He thinks something's screwy about the Swede's death and investigates. He learns of the Swede's past as a prize-fighter, of a two-year rap the Swede took for a beautiful dame (Ava Gardner) who stole a necklace, of the Swede's mix-up in a fatal bank robbery, and of the double-cross that crushed the Swede's will to live.

O'Brien becomes a player in the Swede's story, and deals with a potentially fatal double-cross himself.

At the heart of those betrayals is Ava Gardner, who plays the quietest, most selfish, and least sympathetic femme fatale in noir. As her husband dies in her arms, she begs him to lie with his last breath and declare her innocent. As a young girl looking for kicks, Gardener is overwhelmingly horny, gorgeous, and larger than life. It would take some man to deal with her dark side, and Lancaster ain't up to the task. He barely can acknowledge his own.

As in *Criss Cross* (page 83), however, Siodmak refuses to condemn Gardner. Lancaster must share the blame for his pathetic fate. With his simpleton's romantic streak, Lancaster expects Gardner to change just because he loves her. She won't. With her sloe eyes, slithery movements, and passive/aggressive silences, Gardner's the most powerful figure in the story. As Frank Sinatra said of her: "She's a real broad."

It's a compelling tale, told in a flashback structure that plays with logic and clarity. The screenplay combines the tension of a mystery that unfolds one clue at a time, underscored by the more basic suspense of whether the narrator is going to live long enough to tell us what he's learned. The perfection of the construction is marred slightly by occasionally overdone dialogue. The only scene that tries too hard to be hard-boiled is the opening interchange between the gunsels in the café. Ironically, their dialogue was lifted verbatim from the Hemingway short story on which the film is based.

The multiple flashbacks rend time into nonsense. A strange suspense accrues as we hang between events that have and have not yet occurred. Sorting through the confusion, O'Brien ignores the (emotional) complications of the unfolding saga by throwing himself into a (hopeless) search for meaning. O'Brien's determination to choose facts over emotions equals Siodmak's view of our progress through life: We conflate events with a deeper purpose to distract ourselves from our (inevitably) disappointing interaction with others, from the pointlessness of trust, ambition, desire, or love.

Between Gardner's appeal and the interwoven flashbacks, director Siodmak makes a compelling case for his favorite proposition (as also presented in *Criss Cross* [page 83] and in *The Dark Mirror* [page 88]): The sins of yesterday rule tomorrow.

Other recommended rentals directed by Robert Siodmak:
Criss Cross (page 83)
The Dark Mirror (page 88)

ARCHIVE PHOTOS

Elisha Cook, Jr. and Marie Windsor in *The Killing*

The Killing (1956—USA)

Mood Guide: Classic suspenseful heist picture

Director: Stanley Kubrick; *Camera:* Lucien Ballard; *Screenplay:* Stanley Kubrick, Jim Thompson

Cast: Sterling Hayden, Elisha Cook, Jr., Vince Edwards, Timothy Carey, Marie Windsor

In English; B/W

Plot: A tough, smart crook assembles a gang of cronies for the ultimate racetrack heist. Too bad he didn't realize that the wife of one of his guys is a deadly two-timer. All the planning in the world makes no difference when betrayal is an inside job.

To pull off a big racetrack heist, Sterling Hayden enlists an eccentric but quintessential gang: a crooked cop, a henpecked track clerk, a debt-ridden barkeep, a psychotic rifleman, and a chess-playing, philosophizing wrestler. The plan goes like clockwork, but is undone by the greed and deception of the track clerk's wife. When all the desperate planning, sweaty effort, and hard-earned trust lies ruined by betrayal, murder, and fate's dirty tricks, all Hayden can say in response is: "What's the difference?"

Marie Windsor plays the track clerk's scheming wife. Given the restraint that Kubrick usually imposes on his actors, her over-the-top performance suggests that Kubrick endorses her stereotype of vicious feminine sexuality. He presents Windsor's lust as an expression of greed, her every tenderness as tactical, and her innate loyalty as nil. While men struggle honorably, willing to trust and to lay their lives on the line, women hang back, ready to support the victor only after the outcome is settled. It's not a pretty portrait.

Windsor's sexual aggression and hostility seem to express Kubrick's terror of any raw emotion, or his contempt for the power of the sexual urge. Windsor's such an unredeemed villain, it's hard to take her seriously. It's a puzzlement what psychological agenda she represents for the director, or perhaps for his screenwriting collaborator, the hard-boiled (and way-misogynist) avatar himself, Jim Thompson.

Kubrick plays with time like no other noir director. He slices events into fragments and pastes them together in flashbacks, flash-forwards, and—to show different events occurring simultaneously—in meticulous cross-cutting. This manipulation of space and time serves two functions: It raises suspense to an almost unbearable degree, and it underscores Kubrick's recurring theme of man at the mercy of fate. It also makes a fairly straightforward caper that much more complex, exciting, and commanding.

Kubrick's time-slicing must have been mind-blowing forty years ago, and if it seems a little overdone now, it does not muddle the storytelling. The constant, overbearing voice-over that announces the day and time of every new flashback ("Earlier that Tuesday, at 11:08 P.M., Johnny entered a seedy café.") both dates the picture and becomes increasingly intrusive. But it does serve as the voice of the merciless god that Kubrick imitates with his obsessive control over every filmmaking element.

Weirdly, it's Kubrick's mania for control that allows this picture to retain its wallop. Kubrick brings a certain gravity to every exchange of dialogue, and because his actors speak in natural, conversational tone, each speech is fraught with hidden meaning.

Think of it as a gripping, beautifully photographed—and, at times, suprisingly modern—collection of noir's Greatest Hits: the deadly femme fatale, the complex heist, the poetically bizarre characters (Timothy Carey's "performance" of psychopathy has to be seen to be believed), the harsh lighting, the mumbled dialogue, the brutal, pointless violence, and, of course, the bitter twist of fate.

Other recommended rentals directed by Stanley Kubrick:
- *Barry Lyndon*
- *A Clockwork Orange*
- *Dr. Strangelove or: How I Learned to Stop Worrying and Love the Bomb*
- *Full Metal Jacket*
- *Lolita*
- *2001: A Space Odyssey*

Kiss Me Deadly (1955—USA)

Mood Guide: Nihilistic apocalyptic thriller

Director: Robert Aldrich; *Camera:* Ernest Laszlo; *Screenplay:* A. I. Bezzerides

Cast: Ralph Meeker, Gaby Rodgers, Albert Dekker, Maxine Cooper, Cloris Leachman, Jack Elam, Marian Carr

In English; B/W

Plot: A nasty private eye almost gets killed helping a helpless dame. He obsesses over her memory and tracks down her killers as they track him. Everybody's searching for a mysterious item of great power. When they find it, nobody's going to be happy.

Mike Hammer, as portrayed by Ralph Meeker, is noir's ultimate blunt object. For Mike, thinking causes confusion, but action provides a solution, no matter how destructive. Robert Aldrich's direction and A. I. Bezzerides's screenplay brings Mickey Spillane's private eye to the screen as brutal, simple-minded, heedless, and amoral, driven by an American's adolescent fixation with girls, gizmos, and guns. Mike enjoys himself, but his antics exact a high price: the end of the world.

BARSON COLLECTION/ARCHIVE PHOTOS

Careening home in his sports car one night, Hammer almost mows down a desperate hitchhiker. She's escaped from a nearby asylum, but not for long. Her pursuers run Mike's car off the road and leave him to die in the wreckage. The hitchhiker is tortured to death. With the help of his dedicated, if somewhat masochistic, secretary Velma, Mike tracks down the killers. Unknown gangsters plant bombs in his car; strange women offer themselves; a sinister secret is somehow contained in a warm, glowing, leather-bound box: the "Great Whatsit" that everyone kills to attain (and the inspiration for the glowing briefcase in *Pulp Fiction*). Aldrich distracts us, and Hammer, from his violent quest with really cool cars, sharp suits, bachelor-pad oddities (like a primitive answering machine), and stellar babes.

Hammer's an amoral pig, which he freely admits. His contempt for the world is genuine and crippling. His personality makes him unfit for any profession other than private eye. That is, he's lazy, sadistic, likes spying on people, and feels morally superior. And in this universe, Hammer's the hero.

The charming destructive energy that fuels Hammer is reflected in the world around him. Everyone grabs what they want, with no sense of consequences. Because Aldrich, like Hammer, is neither a poet nor a deep thinker (like Hammer, he's a hard-ass, if occasionally discursive, problem-solver), *Kiss Me* is unusually satisfying both as a tough-minded, cautionary sleigh ride of thrills and as a coldhearted metaphor for the breakdown of society.

With her androgynous haircut, languorous sexuality, little-girl voice, and constantly shifting loyalties, Gaby Rodgers provides a fitting coda to fifteen years of duplicitous femmes fatales. She incarnates a dissolute, randomly lustful and utterly relaxed ruthlessness. Her identity changes according to the company she keeps, her social role alters as her ambition takes root, her ambitions grow as she learns the extent of her sexual power, and her sexual power breeds suicidal megalomania. If Rodgers was in fact neither insane nor distracted to the point of schizophrenia, then her performance is one for the ages.

This is a very different entertainment than the A-picture, Hollywood slickness of *Double Indemnity* or *The Killers*. In most noir films, the hero's loss of innocence is represented as a loss of faith, a calamitous acquiring of cynicism springing from tragic death or broken hearts or dashed expectations. Hammer never had any faith to begin with; he's just a nasty guy. His comeuppance consists of learning just how ruthless, brutal, greedy, and destructive his enemies can be. (And all this time he thought he was the toughest monkey in the urban jungle.)

It's an alienated, debased portrait, and a visceral prophecy. Aldrich's nihilism is boundless; he's determined to bring an end to the romanticization of cynicism, violence, and self-made morality that comprises noir. He succeeds as Peckinpah did with *The Wild Bunch,* by so raising the stakes that no one could possibly follow.

Other recommended rentals directed by Robert Aldrich:
The Big Knife (page 49)
The Dirty Dozen

Kiss of Death (original version) (1947—USA)

Mood Guide: Flat, Hollywoodish thriller

Director: Henry Hathaway; *Camera:* Norbert Brodine; *Screenplay:* Ben Hecht, Charles Lederer

Cast: Victor Mature, Richard Widmark, Brian Donlevy, Coleen Gray, Karl Malden

In English; B/W

Plot: A family man robs a jewelry store, is caught, and given a long sentence because he refuses to turn informer. After his wife's suicide, the con changes his mind and rats out his associates. Released from prison, he pals around with the fearsome hit-man on whom he also informs. When a jury fails to convict the hit-man, he comes looking for revenge.

Properly remembered for the scene in which Richard Widmark flings a helpless, wheelchair-bound granny down a flight of stairs, *Kiss of Death* offers few other charms.

Mature, convicted of a not very competent armed robbery, refuses to name his accomplices. This refusal is good, in crook-morality terms, and marks Mature as a criminal of integrity. He describes himself as such to the cops repeatedly. They all shake their heads at Mature's fortitude, filled with a mixture of pity and admiration.

When his wife dies, Mature changes his mind. He informs on his pals in order to get out of prison and raise his children himself. His wife's offscreen suicide serves as plot justification for a moral turnaround that makes Mature a difficult hero to admire. To accommodate this turnaround, everyone from the arresting officer to the prison warden to Mature's kids' baby-sitter, remarks constantly on Mature's upstanding character. This seems at odds with Mature's apparently lifelong profession as a holdup man.

Mature convinces a mob lawyer that a former associate is the real informer. This associate, Mature believes, failed to look after Mature's wife as promised. Richard Widmark is dispatched to eliminate the guy. The script would have us now admire Mature even more; he saved himself by informing *and* he incited others to do his dirty work.

This murder, like Mature's wife's suicide, takes place off-screen. Although it celebrates the bourgeois ideal of hard work and a dirty conscience as the best cures for criminality, *Kiss of Death* suffers from a hypocritical bourgeois delicacy regarding matters of bloodshed. The film seems sincere about praising family life and abjuring violence as a problem-solver. Real noirs tend toward the opposite perspective, which is a lot more fun.

Mature's character never seems quite credible. As a result, his many lingering close-ups provide time to reflect on the extraordinary *size* of his chin, nose, and cheekbones. Since Widmark performs with an excess of zeal, his close-ups provide the opportunity to ponder why none of the performances are believable. There's a cinematic slickness, a disruptive falseness that just won't go away.

The script seeks to admire Mature as a crook, even though he's not very skilled at crookery, and to admire him as an upstanding member of the community even though he achieves that status via betrayal. Perhaps the confusion stems from screenwriter Ben Hecht's apparent personal distaste for squealers colliding with the plot necessity of Mature becoming one. Or perhaps, with clouds of repression looming on the horizon, the climate of the times demanded a paean to the spiritual suffering of those who inform.

(The modern remake starring David Caruso and Nicolas Cage offers a higher-adrenaline, more Nineties sort of dumbness, with lots of violence, car chases, and half-naked women.)

Kiss Tomorrow Goodbye (1950—USA)

Mood Guide: Surprisingly vicious gangster saga

Director: Gordon Douglas; *Camera:* J. Peverell Marley; *Screenplay:* Harry Brown

Cast: James Cagney, Barbara Payton, Helena Carter, Ward Bond, Barton MacLane

In English; B/W

Plot: A con busts out of prison, determined to rule the world. He takes over a corrupt town: Officials compete for his graft, women fall at this feet, cops commit murder for bags of money. But nothing lasts, especially when the con double-crosses the wrong dame.

An unrelentingly cynical, action-packed tale of a psychopathic gangster on the ascend, played with old-time, big-star charisma by Jimmy Cagney as an adult version of the demonic punks he played as a younger man.

The world bends to Cagney's will: The scarier and more selfish he becomes, the more desperately others seek to do his bidding. And in this misanthropic, amoral universe, Cagney's women are as perverse as he. One (Barbara Payton) hurls every dish on the table at Cagney in a fit of jealousy, and moments later laughs at her own rage and kisses him frantically. Another (Helena Carter), a spoiled rich girl with a daddy complex, surrenders to Cagney after he bosses her around in the presence of her dominating father. These women's willful self-destructiveness represents neither the usual noir feminine cunning nor weakness; they serve only as the womanly embodiment of the corrupt world here portrayed.

AMERICAN STOCK/ARCHIVE PHOTOS

Barbara Payton, Jimmy Cagney, and Helena Carter in *Kiss Tomorrow Goodbye*

Everybody's got an agenda, and Cagney's only too happy to serve, as long he gets served in return. Society is a sick place, apparently, and capitalism makes it so. The almighty dollar corrupts . . . but, in the end, Cagney pays. Not to the forces of justice (which do not exist), but because he transgressed against his girlfriend and she takes revenge.

Cagney is id unchained. He leaps from whim to whim as he builds a gang and tries to take over a city. He and the rich girl elope on a moment's notice and are discovered when her father flings open the door to their bedroom. Their marriage appears oddly unconsummated, if the twin beds in which they sleep on their wedding night are any clue.

Those beds—and the awkward, frantic prison-break sequence of the first five minutes—are the only indication that this picture was released half a century ago. The dialogue is remarkably sophisticated, Freudian, and grim. It's both the engine that drives the story and our window into the amusingly diseased souls of all concerned.

There's no moral, no happy ending, and no hope, save that of judicial vengeance. There is seldom a pause between the nonstop lurid thrills. Each is photographed with increasing attention to the irresistible lure of psychosexual violence. When Cagney assaults someone, it's clear he's sexually aroused. When he seduces one of his babes, it's clear that savagery fuels his passion. When Cagney charges the camera, jagged champagne bottleneck in his hand and homicide in his heart, his rage is terrifying.

Perhaps to soften the enjoyment everyone finds in their own awfulness, the story is told through the device of a prosecutor recounting the tale as he seeks to convict every wicked soul involved. He grows tiresome with his recitation of "evil," but maybe the censors made him do it. The sheer audacity of Cagney's lust for blood, money, power, and "dames," and the glee with which he indulges himself, makes *Kiss* the most crazed, believable, and sexy of Cagney's gangster performances.

The Lady from Shanghai (1948—USA)

Mood Guide: Anarchic tale of a fool for love

Director: Orson Welles; *Camera:* Charles Lawton, Jr.; *Screenplay:* Orson Welles

Cast: Orson Welles, Rita Hayworth, Everett Sloane, Glenn Anders

In English; B/W

Plot: A down-and-out boat bum falls for an expensively kept dame. She finagles him into captaining her husband's sailboat. The husband's up to something, and so is the husband's crony. The sailor

> can feel the noose tightening around him, but has no idea who's holding the rope.

Welles plays an idealistic, itinerant sailor who rescues Rita Hayworth from a robbery attempt. She inveigles her billionaire husband into hiring Welles for a cruise on their sailing yacht. The husband, a crippled, mastermind attorney, brings his sinister henchman along for the ride. Welles knows a plot is brewing against somebody, but can't figure out who. We can't figure out a damn thing, at least on first viewing.

ARCHIVE PHOTOS

As if his Blarney Stone accent wasn't sufficiently off-putting, Welles employs a deliberately chaotic narrative style. The story is relatively simple, as double-crosses go, but seems to make no sense. Events occur without apparent purpose; events follow one another with no evident connection. Welles's visual style matches the harum-scarum narrative. Needless establishing shots are interspersed between some of the most jarring, weird-angle close-ups or exquisitely imaginative sequences in movie history. Every moment is compelling, hallucinatory, transcendent (except for the establishing shots). Such constant inspiration makes for an unsettling and, at times, wearying viewing experience.

The acting, like Welles's accent, constantly shatters the Fourth Wall. The players' shift between neo-realist (or super-theatrical) intensity, and contentless, big-studio placidity. Rita Hayworth floats through the picture serene, unmussed, and inexpressibly beautiful; a star's star. Glenn Anders, meanwhile, playing the evil henchman, sweats bullets every minute, and speaks in the voice of a psychotic robot; he's a hideous, too-real lowlife. Hayworth and Anders hardly belong in the same picture.

Welles's voice-over provides the unifying thread. His character tells us the story from memory. Accordingly, the transitions, areas of emphasis, and shifts in emotional temperature occur with as little narrative logic as memory itself. Or, with every bit as much: The unfolding of Welles's story may not make much rational sense, but its emotional pitch is perfect. The story follows the heart, and the heart remembers very differently than the mind.

Lady is the clearest proof of the argument that noir makes its most important points not by storytelling, but by style. The style here is of a fever-dream. Exchanges between characters are pointlessly overheated or weirdly emotionless. In the most famous sequence—the bravura gunfight in the Funhouse mirror-room—the shifting, myriad reflections make clear that everyone carries multiple identities, contradictory motivations, and self-destructive, self-canceling desires. ("Of course, killing you means killing myself," says one of the characters just before pulling the trigger.)

No one in the story could possibly have and hold all that he or she wants, except Welles, and he wants very little. For his modesty (his absence of the fatal hubris that marks the others), Welles is doomed not only to fail, but to be haunted by failure. The others, more ruthless by far, never suffer the luxury of conscience.

Welles gets burned by love, and Hayworth—at the time the reigning beauty/sex queen in Hollywood and, not coincidentally, Welles's wife—plays a base femme fatale, a former whore who married the attorney for his money and pretends to love Welles only to make him her dupe. Yet Hayworth's sins remain entirely offscreen. We see the consequences of her actions, but never enough of their genesis to convict Hayworth of the wrongdoing we know she's committed. Again, is this the voice of Welles's memory—he who loves too much to construct a clear portrait of his beloved's betrayal? Or did she really love him, and ignore her love to satisfy her greed?

Lady bears at least two viewings. The first time, some of the slower sequences might seem self-indulgent and some of the faster sequences, baffling. But on a second viewing, the path through the labyrinthine story shines clearly, and Welles's daring genius will guide (or fling) you over any remaining rough spots.

Other recommended rentals directed by Orson Welles:

Citizen Kane
The Magnificent Ambersons
Touch of Evil (page 258)

Lady in the Lake (1947—USA)

Mood Guide: High-concept amateurish mystery

Director: Robert Montgomery; *Camera:* Paul C. Vogel; *Screenplay:* Steve Fisher

Cast: Robert Montgomery, Audrey Totter, Leon Ames, Lloyd Nolan, Jayne Meadows

In English; B/W

Plot: Marlowe's hired to protect a shady dame. The cops don't like it; they think she's a murderer. Marlowe thinks so, too, only he won't admit it to them or to himself. The only way to clear her is to find the real triggerman, and he doesn't like being looked for.

An annoying one-trick pony starring the least convincing and most grating of all the screen Marlowes. Robert Montgomery, who plays Marlowe, directs without a clue to the potential character nuances of Raymond Chandler's private eye. What makes this picture memorable—though not worthwhile—is that the whole film is shot from Marlowe's point of view.

Audrey Totter, Robert Montgomery, and Lloyd Nolan in *Lady in the Lake*

This means every shot—every damn shot—purports to show only what Marlowe sees. The camera turns to follow a pretty girl walking across an office. A pair of lips rise to close-up for a kiss. A fist flies toward the lens.

So that we may occasionally be reminded of Marlowe's presence, Montgomery stares at his own reflection in a mirror. He gazes at himself with considerably more approval than he grants his annoying costar, Audrey Totter. Her adenoidal voice rises to a screech as she orders Marlowe: "Don't fall in love with me!" He does, anyway. Their love-talk, in fact their every shared scene, seems as false as the smirk that never leaves Montgomery's face.

Lloyd Nolan shines as a nasty, suspicious cop. He seems determined not to be dragged down by his director/co-star. Jayne Meadows's sultry sex-bomb of a performance steals every scene she's in. The story makes little sense, and the action remains trapped in a few drab sets. It's a cheesy little picture, the victim of its own tiny ambitions. Perhaps a gifted director might make art of the tedious POV approach, but not Montgomery.

La Femme Nikita (1990—France)

Mood Guide: Quintessential modern noir

Director: Luc Besson; *Camera:* Thierry Arbogast; *Screenplay:* Luc Besson

Cast: Anne Parillaud, Jean-Hugues Anglade, Tchéky Karyo, Jeanne Moreau, Jean Reno

In French, with English subtitles; color

Plot: Nikita's a vicious street thug scheduled for execution. Instead, a shadowy government agency trains her to be a killing machine. Despite her training, she falls in love and learns that murder and *amour* just don't mix, even in Paris.

In 1948, Henri-Georges Clouzot's *La Salaire de la Peur* (*Wages of Fear*) (page 228) merged the visual style of big-studio entertainment with a personal vision of pitiless misanthropy. The resultant critical firestorm gave way to box office success. *Wages* is that rare thing: an art film with all the kicks of mass entertainment; a subversive essay in which the thrills appear right on cue.

Nikita is the heir to *Wages*'s audacity.

Using dazzling colors and rock & roll camera movement, Besson combined the style of the Nineties—the contentless flash of music videos plus the cartoony ultraviolence of *Die Hard*—with the existential themes of classic noir. In Besson's vision, art and cheap thrills are so intertwined, there's no telling them apart.

Besson was pilloried even as he was praised. *Nikita* was all surface, critics claimed, with no substance beneath the flash.

Those critics are mistaken. Hidden within the MTV images are heartbreak, loss of home, loss of identity, the struggle to atone, and renunciation of the transformative power of love. . . . What could be more noir than that?

FOTOS INTERNATIONAL/ARCHIVE PHOTOS

Anne Parillaud and her best friend in *La Femme Nikita*

Anne Parillaud, Besson's wife, stars as a vicious street junkie sentenced to death for the murder of a policeman. Kidnapped by a clandestine government agency, she's offered a simple choice: Train as an assassin, or be executed. With the charismatic Tchéky Karyo teaching her about violence, and Jeanne Moreau(!) instructing her in feminine wiles, Parillaud grows up. That is, she learns to channel her aggressions for the good of the state.

Unleashed on the world, she falls for Jean-Hugues Anglade. Rather than lie about her past, she refuses to discuss it. They move in together. When she steals away to kill someone in cold blood, it's both heartbreaking and exhilarating. Besson, like Peckinpah in his prime, makes violence terrible, yet totally escapist.

Parillaud carries the picture. She's a beauty and finds the range to express Nikita's rough edges, reflexive brutality, and loving kindness. Tchéky Karyo's cat-like face expresses emotion reluctantly, and his cool masks a cold, cold heart. Anglade keeps it simple; he plays a heroically gentle man. Karyo's infatuation with Parillaud grants him the humanity his job destroys. Angland's love for Nikita grants him the courage his personality seems not to require. In other words, Parillaud's affection makes men of both of them.

Shooting in the hard colors of rock videos, Besson finds an equivalent to the shadowy B/W of the classic period. During violent or sinister sequences, where a classic director might slice the world into shadows, Besson shoots in brilliant, cold blues and greens. During the quieter, more sentimental moments, he softens the color tones, and browns predominate. No modern director frames with Besson's wit, and nobody, but nobody, matches him for camera movement. There is neither a dull moment nor an unimaginative shot. The plot might go to hell in the last fifteen minutes, but the mood never falters.

The oppressive, conformist society so feared in classic noir has been replaced by a government that controls its citizens by force. In a clever inversion, Besson shows day-to-day domesticity—considered in noir's hipster heyday to be the absolute destroyer of a man's poetic soul—as the only viable haven against the physical and spiritual violence of the outside world.

Besson does not neglect the classic themes: that the sins of the past must be paid for in blood; that those sins will forever prevent genuine intimacy; and that Nikita's character will be the source of her fate. In the end, that is Nikita's tragedy.

A modern masterpiece, and, like it or not, the face of noir to come.

Other recommended rentals directed by Luc Besson:

The Big Blue
Le Dernier Combat
The Fifth Element
Subway (Beware the dubbed version—rent the subtitled version *only*.)

20 CENTURY FOX/ARCHIVE PHOTOS

Laura (1944—USA)

Mood Guide: Elegant, sinister romance

Director: Otto Preminger; *Camera:* Joseph La Shelle; *Screenplay:* Jay Dratler, Samuel Hoffenstein, Betty Reinhardt

Cast: Gene Tierney, Dana Andrews, Clifton Webb, Vincent Price, Judith Anderson

In English; B/W

Plot: Somebody's killed Laura, a mysterious society beauty. Is it

> her gold-digging fiancé? His rich, older girlfriend? Or the upper-class smoothie who introduced Laura to the finer things in life? Only the tough cop knows the score, and he's got problems of his own. For one thing, he's so in love with Laura he can hardly think straight . . . and all the suspects know it.

With a brutal killing at its core, *Laura* functions as a fine whodunit. But lurking within its elegant construction is a noir melodrama, a masterpiece of shadowy cinematography and witty dialogue, and a perceptive, unsentimental study of men's need to mythologize women. Because the story relies on psychological tension and affairs of the heart rather than action, *Laura*, released in 1944, remains remarkably current.

Laura has been murdered. Or has she? Her fey guardian, played by Clifton Webb, accuses her gold-digging boyfriend, Vincent Price. Dana Andrews plays a hard-boiled detective who must unravel the nasty skeins of jealousy, lust, and greed that bind this community of indolent upper-class New Yorkers. Like every other man in the story, Andrews becomes obsessed with Laura. Director Preminger presents Andrews' fall as particularly piquant because Andrews has never even seen the object of his love. All he knows of Laura is her ever-present portrait and the possessive emotions she evokes in others.

The mystery then, is not "who killed Laura?" or even "who is Laura?" but rather whose version of Laura—which man's idealized construct of her—will dominate?

Even when we finally meet her, Laura remains unreal. Preminger presents Gene Tierney as the mirror in whom men see what they want. Laura has no personality of her own: Her placid beauty functions as the prism through which men reflect their sexual tension regarding one another. These three very different men are rendered with superb, understated acting.

Clifton Webb's character possesses great feeling and intellect, but has no sexual interest in Laura. Price plays a man of passion and charm who lacks depth, emotion, or virtue. Dana Andrews' tough-nosed cop is all man: He feels a bit, thinks a little, connects to his sexuality with ease, and wastes no time on subtlety. Given that this film was made during the war, there's little doubt which model of masculinity will emerge as worthy of Laura's hand.

The atmosphere of the film is of cynical withdrawal and pointless decadence. Society has grown too rotten, too hypocritical to be worth protecting. Only Andrews, his hard shell of integrity intact, can move in this world uncorrupted. Uncorrupted by money, that is; his love for Laura inflames him.

Pure anarchy fuels Andrews' desire to solve Laura's murder, which is inseparable from his desire for her. For him, Laura's death is an indictment of the society in which she lives. He yearns to tear that society down and to return to simple, working-class love. Again, Preminger's puzzle-box cynicism strikes. The only man capable of protecting society loathes it; society is dependent upon a man whom it regards with contempt.

Though Andrews' vision of Laura seems more wholesome to him, it's no less fantastic than that of his rivals. Laura neither confirms nor denies anyone's opinion. She floats above the fray, serene and untouchable. Is Preminger mocking man's infinite capacity for self-delusion? Or a woman's need to hold herself above the emotional carnage she inflicts by passivity? If only modern movies were as willing to embrace such fiendish, sophisticated ambiguity . . .

A great mystery, a font of feminist cinema theory, and, in a subculture of boy-movies, a film that men and woman can both really enjoy.

The Long Goodbye (1972—USA)

Mood Guide: Cynical revisionist private eye

Director: Robert Altman; *Camera:* Vilmos Zsigmond; *Screenplay:* Robert Altman, Leigh Brackett

Cast: Elliott Gould, Henry Gibson, Sterling Hayden, Jim Bouton, Nina Van Pallandt

In English; color

Plot: It's L.A. in the 1970s: sex, gloss, and money. But Marlowe's got other concerns. His best friend is framed for murder. A classy dame hires Marlowe to find her missing husband. The husband kills himself, and Marlowe smells a rat. Is the husband connected to the crime Marlowe's best friend is accused of? Is the two-timing wife a deadly liar?

A modernist, absurd take on the classic Raymond Chandler novel featuring Hollywood private detective Philip Marlowe. Elliott Gould brings an offhand, shambling grace to a character burned into America's memory (by Humphrey Bogart) as hard-boiled and in control. Gould's Marlowe never even attempts control: He's much too aware of the power of fate.

For Altman, Marlowe remains a man of the 1940s trapped in the 1970s. Marlowe wears old suits, drives an antique car, and holds himself to an outdated moral code. His morality includes loyalty, fair play, and a lack of greed. Any man adhering to such a code, Altman contends, will experience serious problems living and working in modern Los Angeles.

Alienated yet determined to survive, Marlowe's mantra is, "It's okay with me," by which he keeps himself separate from the grasping of those around him. Marlowe's anachronistic personality functions as his salvation and the root cause of his lack of success—the struggle between the two (personal morality versus career striving) being a recurring Altman theme.

More than pace or rhythm, Altman is a master of mood, and his shift from sequence to sequence is usually dependent on one mood ending and another taking hold. This narrative shift in mood is enhanced by Leigh Brackett's sarcastic but sincere screenplay. (Brackett contributed to the screenplay of another Raymond Chandler work, 1946's classic *The Big Sleep*.) Brackett sees Marlowe (and Hollywood) through the prism of thirty years of personal experience; her nasty humor and unexpected violence give the story its edge.

The constantly shifting, constantly searching camera mirrors Marlowe's quest and reveals a shadowy world hidden beneath L.A.'s sunshine. That world includes a drunken author, his scheming wife, and a vicious, neurotic gangster played by director Mark Rydell (*Cinderella Liberty*). Everyone except Marlowe is neurotic in that L.A. showbiz way: They're neurotic and proud of it.

Sterling Hayden, almost unrecognizable behind a huge hippie beard and gray tangled mane, is the doomed writer; *Ball Four* author Jim Bouton plays Marlowe's missing friend; 1970's flash in the pan—and erotic powerhouse—Nina Van Pallandt is the femme fatale; and Arnold Schwarzenegger enjoys his second screen appearance, as a hoodlum tough guy. Blink, and you might miss him.

A hundred wonderful, hidden jokes (and references to other noir films) run through the film. Among the most subversive is that the film's theme song plays on whatever music source is nearest to hand: Gould listens to a jazz version of the song on his car radio; when he walks from his car into a supermarket, a Hollywood Strings rendition plays on the store's Muzak. When Marlowe visits a remote Mexican village, the funeral band marches by blaring the theme.

A touching, funny, suspenseful parody of detective movies that is among the best detective movie ever made.

Other recommended rentals directed by Robert Altman:

Brewster McCloud
Buffalo Bill and the Indians, or Sitting Bull's History Lesson
McCabe and Mrs. Miller

Mood Guide: Horror film as noir

Director: Fritz Lang; *Camera:* Fritz Arno Wagner, Gustave Rathje; *Screenplay:* Thea von Harbou, Paul Falkenberg, Adolf Jansen, Kark Vash

Cast: Peter Lorre, Gustave Grundgens, Otto Wernicke, Theo Lingen

In German, with English subtitles; B/W

Plot: A serial killer murders little girls. The cops can't catch him, so the criminal underworld mobilizes a search. But if they find the killer, what will be his fate?

The key pre-noir film, one that features every salient motif of the subculture. Lang's masterpiece of structure includes German Expressionist lighting, moral helplessness in the face of evil, a study in the contrasts and similarities between cops and crooks, a villain who is both repulsive and sympathetic, an atmosphere of overwhelming suspense, and a completely ambiguous (not to say existential) conclusion.

ARCHIVE PHOTOS

Peter Lorre in *M*

A city is gripped by fear. Someone is murdering young girls. As one girl bounces her ball off a poster advertising a reward for the killer's capture, his shadow falls across her. He takes the girl's hand, buys her the creepiest balloon on earth, and murders her. Lang shows her ball bouncing brokenly out of the bushes to suggest her feeble struggle for life. The eerie balloon, complete with humanoid arms and legs, flutters against a powerline, symbolic of the young girl's ghost looking down upon the evil that killed her.

The cops search, but in vain. Lang makes their methodology, their squabbles, and their power struggles amusing without undercutting the seriousness of the murders. Showing more ironic wit than his later works might lead you to expect, Lang deconstructs the helplessness of the well-intended burghers. He also shows how quickly folks will adopt a lynch-mob attitude when their comfortable lives are threatened.

As the cops organize, so does the underworld. They determine to find the killer if only because the constant police raids interfere with their criminal activities. The crooks show greater organization, discipline, and enthusiasm than the bumbling cops. Lang suggests that each world needs the other, but that criminals are by their nature more inventive and heroic.

The blind balloon seller recognizes the killer by the ominous tune he whistles. A crook gives chase. To identify the killer, the crook chalks an *M* (for ‘‘murderer’’) onto his hand, runs up and slaps the killer's back, transferring the *M*) onto the killer's coat. Peter Lorre plays the murderer as a cringing, pathetic wretch. Just as any search in noir becomes a search for self, one of Lang's most powerful moments is when Lorre's next intended victim tells him his coat is all dirty. Lorre looks over his shoulder into a mirror and recoils in horror at what he sees: himself, clearly marked as he is.

M is a thriller, the story of a murderer brought to justice, but Lang is using the thriller form (as noir would) to deliver more profound ideas. Though, as with the finest noirs, Lang's metaphors are absolutely ‘‘transparent’’: They never interfere with the story.

Employing only his eloquent framing (check out Lorre on his knees, begging for mercy, as the frame seems to collapse around him), precise visual grammar, and a cadenced editing rhythm, Lang suggests that the entire story is a parable of everyone's internal psychological struggles. The demon moves through us all, and in all of us a powerful, suppressive community stands in judgment. A building in which Lorre hides represents (in a singular mixture of Freudian, Symbolist, and Surrealist imagery) the ‘‘house’’ of his consciousness. For Lang, Lorre's trial in the cellar symbolizes the resilient arguments our demons advance in our deepest recesses of the subconscious. The id acts, the army of the super-ego condemns.

Lorre screams that he cannot help what he does—and in that moment shifts from monster to object of sympathy. As Lorre offers his only defense, Lang cuts to the immobilized faces of the accusers, every one of whom is clearly remembering a shameful moment when they could not help themselves, either. The monster has been given a human face.

Whatever his crimes, Lorre's torment makes clear his anguish. One voice defends Lorre. An appointed "lawyer" raises the classic moral question by stating that no one can be held responsible for actions he cannot control. The result is a concise and complete framing of the debate over capital punishment.

There is not one superfluous shot, or inelegant moment. In the midst of the most rigorous visual and narrative construction, the dialogue remains amazingly light and neo-realist. One of the ten best films ever made, and a primer of every visual, thematic, and narrative issue raised in noir.

Other recommended rentals directed by Fritz Lang:

The Big Heat (page 46)
Human Desire (page 134)
Metropolis
Scarlet Street (page 222)
The Woman in the Window (page 270)

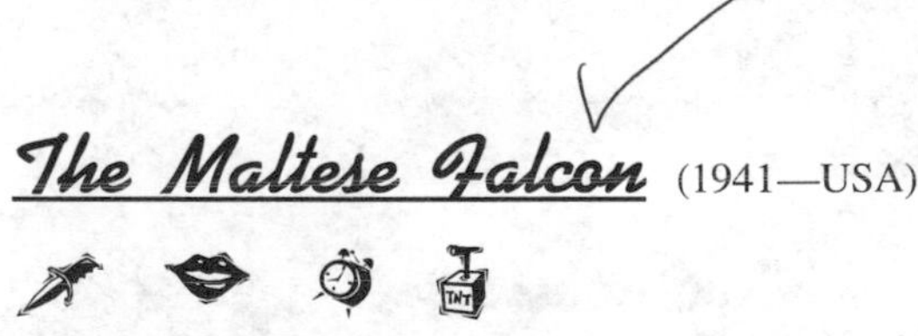

The Maltese Falcon (1941—USA)

Mood Guide: Banter amid the bleakness

Director: John Huston; *Camera:* Arthur Edeson; *Screenplay:* John Huston

Cast: Humphrey Bogart, Mary Astor, Sydney Greenstreet, Peter Lorre, Ward Bond, Elisha Cook, Jr., Barton MacLane

In English; B/W

Plot: Sam Spade gets hired to protect a dame. His partner gets shot. The cops want to hustle Spade downtown and work him over. What gives? Everybody, including the deadly dame, is after a little black bird. Spade falls in love, but does that mean he's lost his senses? Not likely, brother.

For once, the historians agree with the academics who agree with the filmmakers: *The Maltese Falcon* is the first film noir.

Why? Because in this, the third screen version of Dashiell Hammett's novel, director/screenwriter Huston's bemused misanthropy blends seamlessly with witty rapid-fire dialogue to set the requisite (hidden) agenda. That agenda reveals a world without friends or loyalty, where all goals are false and all effort leads to naught. Huston made the first hard-boiled thriller to look into its own heart.

ARCHIVE PHOTOS

Humphrey Bogart and *The Maltese Falcon*

Mary Astor comes to Bogart for protection. He assigns his partner to the job. The partner gets killed. The cops know Bogart was involved with his partner's wife and they think he did it. Bogart grills Mary Astor, and slowly, one seductive, misleading conversation at a time, Bogart learns of the existence of a mysterious, jeweled statue of a bird.

Peter Lorre, the soul of Continental neurosis, appears and searches Bogart's office. Elisha Cook, Jr., twitchy as a gerbil, plays a young gunsel who's not as tough as he thinks. Bogart takes away his guns and visits his boss, the deeply amused Sydney Greenstreet. Greenstreet tells Bogart the history of the bird and they begin to haggle.

After a few machine-gun dialogue exchanges, no one cares about the falcon or where it came from. The bird, and the plot itself, become of little consequence. This, again, makes the case for *Falcon* being the original text. For audience and filmmaker, the real drama lies inside Bogart's tortured soul. Bogart's character is the model for noir protagonists: He lives by his own contradictory moral code, regards the world with scorn and his own folly with particular contempt. But the life of the outrider takes its toll. Sam Spade enjoys humiliating Cook and Lorre. His violence has a sexual undertone. His anger betrays savagery.

Though the story nominally takes place in San Francisco, there are almost no exterior shots. The characters talk to one another in a series of cramped rooms, dislocated from everything except their emotions.

After a day and a night of badinage in a claustrophobic hotel suite, Bogart appears with the bird and comes to understand Mary Astor at last. That Astor's character lies, cheats, and murders, but remains capable of love, makes her fatally seductive: noir's first femme fatale.

The final shot in the final scene defines the noir subculture. Bogart denies his love and gives Mary Astor over to the police. The cops take her away; at that moment *The Maltese Falcon* is still just another thriller. But as the room empties, Bogart and Huston change everything. Bogart hefts the falcon and, straining, clasps the black bird to his chest. Bogart's smirk of triumph vanishes. He looks defeated, spent and bitter to the core.

Bogart walks out the door, shuffling under the weight of his load. The falcon he holds so tightly is the metaphor for his own black heart, for all the love he has denied, for all the death he has endured, for the dedication to his craft that keeps the world at bay, and for the inability to compromise that has left him, once more, alone.

Other recommended rentals directed by John Huston:

The Asphalt Jungle (page 36)
Fat City
The Red Badge of Courage
The Treasure of the Sierra Madre

The Man I Love (1946—USA)

Mood Guide: Drama of adult life

Director: Raoul Walsh; *Camera:* Sid Hickox; *Screenplay:* Catherine Turney, Jo Pagano

Cast: Ida Lupino, Robert Alda, Andrea King, Bruce Bennett, Martha Vickers, Dolores Moran

In English; B/W

Plot: A nightclub singer visits from New York to Long Beach to be with her two sisters and brother. She becomes embroiled in the problems of their lives and the lives of their neighbors, avoids the affections of a nightclub owner, and falls for a wayward piano player. When a murder wrecks her community, she must find a new way to love.

Ida Lupino plays the most fully realized, complex, and credible woman character of the postwar period—one of the most believable and three-dimensional woman characters in cinema. Perhaps because women wrote the screenplay, Lupino proves tough but vulnerable, sensible but emotional, and artistic but levelheaded. She embodies these contradictions without hypocrisy, and with her characteristic understated grace.

Lupino leaves her singing gig in a New York nightclub to visit her family in Long Beach. Before she does, director Walsh expresses his love for the late-night jazz milieu in an extended opening sequence that features Lupino singing as she sashays among the band members, effortlessly sipping her drink as she sings, gracefully blowing clouds of tobacco smoke out her nose as she croons the lyrics (no easy trick). Without a word of dialogue, Walsh establishes Lupino as a woman at home with herself, her lifestyle, and her fully aware sexuality. He presents her as a denizen of the demimonde, and when she surfaces, the workaday world seems too simple to contain her.

WARNER BROS./ARCHIVE PHOTOS

Lupino arrives at her sister's house in Long Beach and discovers a web of psychodrama: Her sister's veteran husband is hospitalized with a breakdown; her brother runs flunky errands for a nightclub-owning mobster playboy; her younger sister stays at home, nursing a crush on the virile, stupid, next-door neighbor. The next-door neighbor's slutty wife, bored with her twin babies and her preening hubby, is looking to mess around. Lupino provides some hard-earned common sense in this nest of folly and helps her family as much as she can.

Lupino takes a job singing at the mobster's nightclub. While fending off his advances, she meets a tortured jazz piano player played by Bruce Bennett. He gave up his promising career when his marriage to a society dame ended in heartbreak. Now, he's in the Merchant Marine and headed back to sea. Lupino and the piano player fall for one another. Bruce Bennett's part, like all the principals, is remarkably well-written and nuanced. Bennett can barely speak; the depth of his emotions choke him up. His music expresses all the tenderness he cannot. He's one tormented dude, and catnip to Lupino, who finds in his willingness to admit deep emotional pain the only adult behavior in her universe.

Naturally, their love—artist to artist, pragmatist to romantic, healing woman to wounded man—is doomed. Lupino loves too strongly to repress her feelings, and only by pretending to care less could she keep him. The pianist cannot reciprocate any deep emotional connection; he's overwhelmed by Lupino's care and would rather run away than fake a response. The mobster wants Lupino and doesn't care that she doesn't love him, just as Lupino doesn't care that the piano player doesn't love her. It's all too real.

The men, save Bennett, are presented (accurately and not unkindly) as greedy, feckless children who scamper from one urge, one half-baked idea, one momentary lust, to the next. The women can only react to the men and develop wisdom from a realistic, long-term view and their own powerlessness.

Walsh's visual expression of these ideas is astounding. The women speak to one another in simple frames, their figures level with one another. When men enter the picture, their shoulders crowd the edges of the screen, and they loom over the women in every shot. Walsh makes clear both the fear and sexual magnetism inherent in this power differential.

An air of tragic inevitability hangs over all the characters. Postwar malaise and disillusion inform every interaction. One husband has been driven insane by the war; another is so trapped by his boyish pride he cannot live like an adult; another seeks a daddy figure to guide him; and the mobster, though possessed of a potent life-force, retreats into exploitative cynicism. Only the piano player has retained his humanity, and at a price: He can no longer function in the world of emotions. He finds no salvation in Ida Lupino's love, but he's about the only man on the planet who wouldn't.

While maintaining the high production values—lovely costumes, expansive sets, complex lighting—and beautiful composition that are his trademarks, Walsh makes a purely American saga of neorealism. His characters go round and round, desperate to escape themselves yet enslaved by the unchanging rhythms of their natures. Only Lupino learns from her mistakes, and she—as the spirit of the modern, emerging, postwar soul—cannot stay in one place long enough to have a home.

Other recommended rentals directed by Raoul Walsh:
Captain Horatio Hornblower
High Sierra
They Drive by Night

Mildred Pierce (1946—USA)

Mood Guide: Tough love

Director: Michael Curtiz; *Camera:* Ernest Haller; *Screenplay:* Ranald MacDougall

Cast: Joan Crawford, Jack Carson, Zachary Scott, Eve Arden, Ann Blyth, Bruce Bennett

In English; B/W

Plot: Mildred, devoted to spoiling her daughters, leaves their father because he earns too little. She works as a waitress and then starts a chain of restaurants. Marrying a ne'er-do-well, she watches him bankrupt her hard-earned fortune. A final tragedy awaits, one that will reunite her family in the worst possible way.

Which is creepier? Watching Mildred Pierce's spoiled-brat daughters walk all over her or watching Joan Crawford play a kindly, self-sacrificing supermom? Joan's inner resources of toughness and vanity do finally emerge in the character she plays, but until that moment it's downright weird to see her play a good-natured doormat.

Mildred Pierce and her sappy husband Bert (the supersensitive, ultracraggy Bruce Bennett), have produced a pair of daughters. Veda's a stuck-up little prom queen, a social climber with a desperate sense of humiliation regarding her low-rent birth.

WARNER BROS./ARCHIVE PHOTOS

Zachary Scott and Joan Crawford in *Mildred Pierce*

Veda's status anxieties lead Mildred to open a restaurant, which grows into a chain of eateries. Mildred brings in a partner, a rich do-nothing with a wandering eye. His wastrel ways bankrupt Mildred's restaurants and bring about his own murder.

So much transgression . . . Mildred yearns for a life without men, one that includes only herself and her daughters. She strives for success and for that striving is punished by heartbreak. Forced to fight in a man's world, Mildred clings to her feminine side by remaining forgiving in the face of myriad aggressions and betrayals, most committed by her beloved Veda.

Mildred serves as a cautionary tale for the postwar movement that sought to drive women out of the workplace and back into the kitchen. Her resolute pursuit of success is presented as hardening her, as a waste of nurturing maternal energy. Mildred's constantly repeating trap is that she cannot escape her daughter (who represents Mildred's own repressed "feminine" sexuality), and so must continue to play a man's role.

Mildred's plight shows that even the most successful woman are flawed by the "weakness" of their femininity, their softheartedness. Underscoring the masculinity of her chosen life is that Mildred's destruction comes about because she trusts a femme fatale—her own daughter.

Veda provides the most negative possible view of feminine sexuality. She wants frivolous social success, she uses sex to achieve status; she abandons the object of her genuine affection to fulfill a sexual whim, and to ensure that her mother's return to the world of feminine sexuality will be corrupted and dishonorable.

Whenever her mother attempts to reconnect to her own abandoned sexuality, Veda is enraged. In the Freudian world of noir, Veda's an interestingly Jungian construction: the permanent girl-child living in the heart of, and destroying, the mother.

Though a woman's melodrama, *Mildred Pierce* is a study in noir flashback technique. The story is presented as a series of Mildred's disconnected memories. Violence opens and closes every chapter. Mildred, in the classic noir manner, recreates the chain of events, trying to make sense of life's unfolding.

Because James M. Cain wrote the book on which the film is based, fate remains cruel and anarchic. Because the characters' tragedies are so rooted in their natures, and because their natures are so clearly presented, the heartbreaking narrative seems crushingly inevitable. Crawford captures all the contradictions and frustrations of Mildred Pierce; she creates a character that lingers in the mind long after the film is over.

Other recommended rentals directed by Michael Curtiz:

The Adventures of Robin Hood
Casablanca

ARCHIVE PHOTOS

Murder, My Sweet (1944—USA)

Mood Guide: Enjoyable lightweight mystery

Director: Edward Dmytryk; *Camera:* Harry J. Wild; *Screenplay:* John Paxton

Cast: Dick Powell, Claire Trevor, Otto Kruger, Mike Mazurki, Anne Shirley

In English; B/W

Plot: Marlowe gets hired by a thug just out of stir. The thug wants Marlowe to track down his old girlfriend. When Marlowe asks about her, folks dummy up. So, Marlowe takes a new case, tracking down a murderous jewel thief. The two cases slowly intertwine, and everybody's chickens come home to roost.

Though seminal for its tough-talking private eye, Expressionist lighting, atmosphere of betrayal and decay, weird characters, and thematic links between of the corruption of the upper classes and the suffering of the lower, *Murder* hasn't aged well. As with *The Big Heat*, certain set pieces resonate strongly. But so many films since evoke similar themes with greater profundity, and now *Murder* now seems a bit lightweight.

Philip Marlowe, played by an adenoidal, swaggering Dick Powell, is approached by a gigantic hoodlum who's just out of jail. The hood, known for good reason as "Moose," is played with not-too-credible simplemindedness by Mike Mazurki. Moose wants Marlowe to track down his old girlfriend, Claire Trevor. Marlowe's usual sources prove recalcitrant where this dame is concerned, and Marlowe hits a dead end. He takes a job escorting a fey character who needs to pay a ransom for stolen jewelry. The fey-guy turns up dead, but his death leads Marlowe to Moose's girl. Marlowe brings Moose along, and the finale plays like a John Woo picture: everybody pointing guns at everybody else. By the time the end-credits roll, there're more bodies on the floor than in the last act of *Hamlet*.

As usual with Raymond Chandler, the plot connections are tenuous at best and few of the characters ring true. The dialogue goes over the top, and no matter how much Chandler loved his performance, Powell never seems more than an actor spouting cute lines. He delivers his snappy dialogue with a self-mocking petulance that draws needless attention to his performance rather than his character. Lacking the burning inner core of poetic self-distrust that grants profundity to Bogart or Robert Mitchum, Powell seems to be playacting.

But Powell alone cannot spoil the fun. Moose is a great character. He's always been the biggest, strongest guy in the room and he ain't interested in self-examination. Claire Trevor strikes just the right note of righteous indignation should any man be so stupid as to expect something of her. Her character plays as unfortunately two-dimensional; she remains nothing more than a spiteful manipulator, an unredeemed seducer.

Director Dmytryk brought from Germany a full-blown Expressionist sensibility to the visual construction. Harry J. Wild's cinematography provides a safe, ordered foundation for wilder flights of shadowy, more interpretive, films to come.

Other recommended rentals directed by Edward Dmytryk
Crossfire (page 85)

The Naked City (1948—USA)

Mood Guide: Dated police procedural

Director: Jules Dassin; *Camera:* Williams Daniels; *Screenplay:* Albert Maltz, Malvin Wald

Cast: Barry Fitzgerald, Howard Duff, Dorothy Hart

In English; B/W

Plot: New York. At night. Noon. Whenever. A beautiful young woman is murdered. The cops show up. They do their job. By the numbers. With a certain bitter resignation. The audience falls asleep.

Though director Dassin made one of the all-time greats (*Night and the City*, page 188), here he seems sadly overshadowed by the clammy hands of producer Mark Hellinger. Hellinger's style epitomizes the police-procedural school, wherein the filmmakers zealously follow each step taken by real cops. A virtue is made of verisimilitude, and any drama that might upset the procedures is missing.

Hellinger attempts a faux-documentary approach and makes a big deal out of shooting on location. The upside of using only real locales is a lovely portrait of New York City. The downside is that many character exchanges are shot on the street without benefit of synchronized sound; their voices are dubbed. Often, those speaking have their backs to the camera so the dubbers needn't worry about linking up with mouth motions. Another downside is the excruciating mock-realistic dialogue that so yearns to be hard-boiled. The acting is wooden and stiff, and the key plot elements coming roaring down Broadway with both doors open.

Most unbearable of all is Hellinger's constant, puerile voice-over. His smug, mock-ironic tone interferes with the story, breaks what little mood the acting can sustain, and serves mostly to remind us who was the boss of the whole misguided affair.

Avoid.

Other recommended rentals directed by Jules Dassin:
Night and the City (page 188)

The Naked Kiss (1964—USA)

Mood Guide: Anarchist moralizing in middle America

Director: Samuel Fuller; *Camera:* Stanley Cortez; *Screenplay:* Samuel Fuller

Cast: Constance Towers, Anthony Eisley, Michael Dante, Virginia Grey, Patsy Kelly

In English; B/W

Plot: A prostitute moves to a small town, seduces the local cop, and decides to quit the business. Taking work in a children's hospital, she goes straight and falls in love with the richest guy around. They plan to marry, but he has a secret even more horrible than hers.

Fuller's desperate to annoy everybody and he succeeds beyond his wildest dreams. The film's famous subversive aspects are instantly on display: The opening scene features a shaven-headed prostitute beating and then robbing her pimp. She seduces a small-town cop with the most brazen sex talk of any film of this era. The most brazen, that is, until the two of them have a postcoital chat about whether she can set up business in his little burg. First she tells him he's a lousy lay, then she cries because he hurt her feelings.

She decides to go straight and becomes the Florence Nightingale of a local children's hospital. There, she soothes crippled kids, keeps her fellow nurses (Russ Meyeresque top-heavy babes, the lot) from falling into the clutches of the vicious Candy, head madam of the local whorehouse (Candy is cast as an older, more jaded version of Kelly, our heroine), and falls for the richest guy in town, who also happens to be a poetry-spouting, jet-setting sophisticate. He finds in Kelly a rare combination of beauty, intelligence, and fancy sex tricks.

ARCHIVE PHOTOS

Constance Towers, unrepentant and unashamed, in *The Naked Kiss*

They decide to marry, she confesses her dirty past, and he accepts her all the same. Just when everything looks hunky-dory, her husband-to-be is revealed as a filthy pervert who only wants to marry her because, as a former whore, she'll put up with his repulsive lusts. Disgusted, and incensed because he calls her abnormal, she kills him. The cop arrests her for murder, but when her story of the guy's perversion proves true, she's set free. As she heads for the bus that brought her to town, all her friends appear to honor her for killing the pervert.

Now, ain't that America? First they revile Kelly for being a whore, then they throw her a parade for being a murderer. As prescient as Fuller was about how our current society could hold three different attitudes at once regarding sex, glamour, and violent death, the film remains both admirable for its ideas and almost impossible to watch.

Fuller's famous contempt for the hypocrisy of society is on display, as is his eye for starlets, his ability to shock, and his inexpressibly galling self-righteousness. But he remains at a distance from this anarchist fable and, except for the first fifteen minutes and one or two genuinely unhinged sequences, hardly applies himself as a filmmaker. Time slows to a crawl; only Constance Towers in the lead role bothers to act; the film looks clumsier than television of the same era; the characters are grotesque caricatures; Fuller substitutes inadvertently hilarious bathos for real emotion; and even his signature camera movement is absent.

On reflection, it's an amazing document, a scathing broadside at the sexual hypocrisy of movies as well as society. Fuller presents an America rotten to the core, obsessed with concealing its dirty lusts and determined to pit women against one another so they can remain subject to the sexual whims and financial power plays of men. Any woman who expresses her full nature, Fuller suggests, will be annihilated by the power structure or reduced to prostitution. Fuller wants us to love both sin and sinner, but he's so damn smug and lazy, he never bothers to make a real movie out of his radical ideas.

Other recommended rentals directed by Samuel Fuller:

Fixed Bayonets
Merrill's Marauders
Pickup on South Street (page 204)
Shock Corridor
The Steel Helmet
Underworld U.S.A. (page 264)

ARCHIVE PHOTOS

Richard Widmark in *Night and the City*

Night and the City (original version)

(1950—USA)

Mood Guide: Gripping, claustrophobic suspense

Director: Jules Dassin; *Camera:* Max Greene; *Screenplay:* Jo Eisinger

Cast: Richard Widmark, Gene Tierney, Googie Withers, Francis L. Sullivan, Herbert Lom

In English; B/W

Plot: A small-time American hood in London dreams of making it big. He wants to promote pro wrestling, but the London mob holds a monopoly. Using the father of the mob's biggest promoter as his protection, he betrays everyone he knows. When the father turns up dead, the hood might run, but he can't hide.

Some noir films are measured and moralistic (*Force of Evil*), some relentless and dispassionate (*The Asphalt Jungle*), but none burn with the pure searing energy and the out-and-out delirium of Jules Dassin's vision of a man driven by unquenchable self-hatred. Dassin's commitment to nihilism and cinematic flair infuse this grim tale with extraordinary passion.

The plot offers no crime caper, no seductive femme fatale, only a doomed and oddly compelling loser. The considerable suspense derives from watching Fabian spin his own web of destruction. That web encircles a seedy London of sleazy nightclubs, prostitutes, and thugs, all connected by a complex matrix of obligation and fear. Dassin draws this world with Dickensian detail.

Everyone strives as desperately as Fabian, but everybody else knows their place. Fabian's sin is that he seeks to rise above. Those who have accepted their lot despise Fabian for his ambition, pathetic though it may be. Those above are determined that Fabian shall not displace them.

Harry Fabian, as played by Richard Widmark, is a slimy rat—a thief, a sniveling toady, and a coward. He abuses his girlfriend and cheats anyone naive enough to trust him. Groveling, scheming, and grasping with manic energy, Fabian suffers from a gigantic ego and low self-esteem. In one of the most telling lines in the subculture of noir, a neighbor describes Fabian as "an artist without an art." Fabian lacks the one virtue that redeems even the most irredeemable noir bad guys: introspection. Of all the antiheroes in noir, none are so unheroic, and that's saying something.

Dassin's camera traps Fabian in a world of shadows, looming buildings, and tight, prisonlike camera angles. Strange window frames, doorways, and even street-lamp poles serve as the visual equivalent of prison bars. These vertical lines remind us that no matter where Fabian goes, he remains jailed by the pitiless city, permanently sentenced to the world he has made. There is no escape from the remorseless status quo, from the way things are and have always been.

Dassin uses shadow to great effect. It's rare that Widmark's face is entirely revealed. Fabian thus remains obscured, hidden in darkness.

Dassin suggests then, that Fabian hides his true soul from the world. He reveals himself to no one, not even himself. The only character not constantly in shadow is Fabian's goody two-shoes girlfriend, played with unlikely saintliness by Gene Tierney. She's lit as if a sun of goodness shines upon her every waking moment. And gazing upon Tierney's face, you can believe that it might.

Playing a sinister married couple, Googie Withers and Francis L. Sullivan, as Fabian's former lover and current boss, respectively, strike the perfect air of evil fatalism, and regret. Both have given up any search for meaning or happiness. What remains is rapacity and a pathological love-hate union. Sullivan evokes Sydney Greenstreet's world-weary cynicism. He's both the most heartless character and the only one who demonstrates any complex emotion. He's a bulky guy, and Dassin contrasts Widmark's constant motion with Sullivan's immobile, sedate menace.

Withers embodies the feminine opposite of Tierney's kindness. Withers ruthlessly pursues money, which she mistakes for freedom. Dassin shoots her in rigid, dominating angles; he never grants this gangland tough-ass a trace of feminine softness.

This is noir at its best, as acting, writing, and camerawork combine to create a pitiless and inescapable universe. Despite it's unrelieved darkness, the story remains hypnotic, gripping and even, at moments, fun.

Night Moves (1975—USA)

Mood Guide: 1970s psychodrama and ultraviolence

Director: Arthur Penn; *Camera:* Bruce Surtees; *Screenplay:* Alan Sharp

Cast: Gene Hackman, Jennifer Warren, Melanie Griffith, Harris Yulin, James Woods

In English; color

Plot: A former football player agrees to track down a missing teenager. His search leads both to the end of his own marriage and a complex web of smuggling, incest, and murder. The football player wants to trust, but his instincts tell him to shoot first and ask questions later. If he does, he just might survive.

With his roles in *The French Connection, The Conversation,* (page 80) and *Night Moves*, Gene Hackman incarnates the mid-Seventies noir sensibility as much as Robert De Niro (*Taxi Driver,* page 114). As in *The Conversation*, Hackman plays a nosy outsider, a former football player turned private eye, who spies on others to earn a living but also to search for clues to his own mysterious motivations.

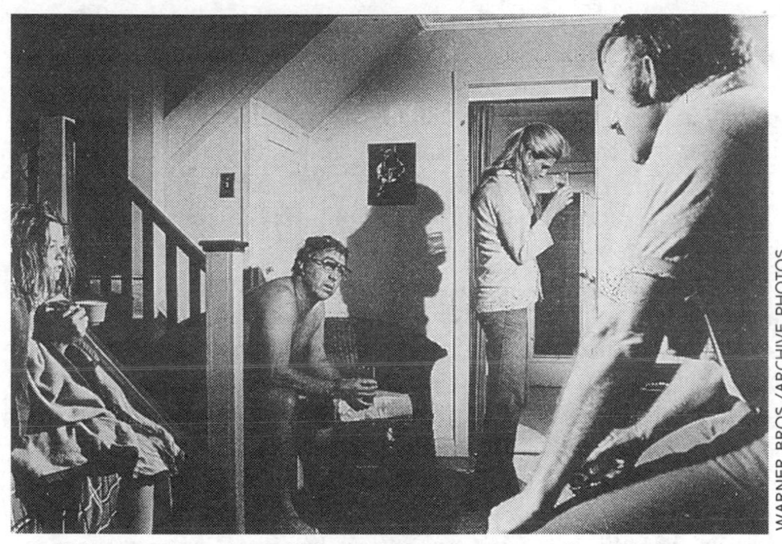

WARNER BROS./ARCHIVE PHOTOS

Melanie Griffith, Harris Yulin, Jennifer Warren, and Gene Hackman in *Night Moves*

Yet where *The Conversation* and *Taxi Driver* take liberties with the noir form to deliver a more profound message, *Night Moves* chooses an old-fashioned route: The deeper questions of trust, love, betrayal, and identity are subsumed within a rock-'em, sock-'em murder mystery with plenty of sex, violence, and gratuitous nudity.

For all its self-aware modernity as regards the psychoanalytic questions, *Night Moves* is structured like classic noir.

Tormented by an untimely injury that ended his football career, Hackman suffers from an uncontrollable temper. Sick of his outbursts, his wife leaves him. To make matters worse, she savages him with a New Age lecture on his unexplored psychic recesses. Because Hackman knows she's right, he despises her all the more. Hackman's frustration at his inability to connect fuels his constant rage. His anger drives away those who might help end his isolation. It's a frustrating and very modern trap from which Hackman finds little escape.

Hackman takes on a missing persons case that turns tricky and then fatal. As he searches for a runaway daughter who fled a mom worth running away from, Hackman also searches for his own father. When he finds his dad, Hackman takes control the only way he knows how: by avoiding personal contact, hiding out, and spying. He pulls the same trick on his ex-wife, but gets caught. She accurately identifies the sexual charge Hackman derives from his voyeurism.

In pursuit of his missing person—the barely pubescent but definitely postcoital Melanie Griffith—Hackman stumbles into a remote outpost of crime run by an old pal hiding in Florida. Thus director Arthur Penn contrasts modern Los Angeles with all its new-thinking, hapless claptrap, and the ages-old swamp, where life's more natural and brutal patterns unfold with far less internal censorship. Free from the civilized expectations of the big city, Hackman loosens the reins on the bitterness and seething violence within. Neither serve him well.

As Hackman tries to unravel the story's central mystery (which doesn't make much sense), he also tries to figure out himself. One measure of self is his ex-wife, another is Jennifer Warren as the inexplicable accomplice of Hackman's old pal. She seduces Hackman in a very Seventies way: First she discusses her painful childhood memories, then she takes her clothes off as he watches. For a guy who both craves intimacy and needs to spy, it's the best possible technique. Thus, while the script might lack narrative clarity, it delivers sharp, idiosyncratic characters who perfectly reflect their time. Caught between the dwindling freedom of the Sixties and the dubious adult responsibilities of the Seventies, everyone prefers to pretend that they're someone else. When the truth finally hits, it packs a wallop.

A strong cast of character actors includes James Woods, in one of his first roles, and Harris Yulin. Beware the nihilist shocker of an ending.

Other recommended rentals directed by Arthur Penn:

Bonnie and Clyde
The Chase
The Missouri Breaks

Notorious (1946—USA)

Mood Guide: Sadistic love and espionage

Director: Alfred Hitchcock; *Camera:* Ted Tetzlaff; *Screenplay:* Ben Hecht

Cast: Cary Grant, Ingrid Bergman, Claude Rains, Louis Calhern, Leopoldine Konstantin

In English; B/W

Plot: A hard-hearted playboy recruits a party girl to spy on a group of Nazis. She falls for the playboy, but he refuses to reciprocate. To punish him for his rejection, she snares one of the Nazis, who marries her despite the protests of his protective mother. When the Nazi discovers that the party girl is an American agent, he and his mother plot her slow, painful death.

The plot relies on a pack of postwar Nazi conspirators, but the drama that compels Hitchcock takes place beneath the surface. There, Grant and Bergman torment one another as only the passionate know how, and Claude Rains suffers from the stifling caresses of his monstrous mother's love.

Bergman plays a Florida party girl, the daughter of a German immigrant, a Nazi spy. Grant works for American intelligence and recruits Bergman to infiltrate a group of former Nazis living in Rio. Bergman falls for Grant, and he for her, but he cannot admits his feelings. Hiding behind a mask of duty, Grant brings Bergman to Rio and sets her up with her former flame, played by Claude Rains. When Bergman learns that Rains is one of the Nazis, Grant encourages her to marry him.

Though rich, sophisticated, and as capable of murder as his fellow Nazis, Rains comes off as the most sympathetic character in the film. Little goes right for the poor guy.

ARCHIVE PHOTOS

Rains marries Bergman out of love, but she despises him and yearns for Grant. Rains's mother demonstrates her affection by helping Rains kill the woman he loves. And if Rains ever revealed his heart to his comrades, they'd slaughter him like a chicken. Hitchcock likes to torment his characters, and Rains gets the full treatment. His miserable life is presented as punishment for his own moral cowardice. His eventual death is photographed like an ascendance to heaven, a release from all Rains's earthly woes.

Madame Konstantin, in the role of Rains's jealous, condemning mother, is the matriarch from hell. She puts Rains down at every opportunity and loves him most when he fucks up the worst. Drawing herself imperiously from beneath her silken sheets, rustling ominously in her cascading lace nightgown, she pronounces to Rains in a voice of doom: "We are protected only by the enormity of your stupidity." More Hitchcock perversity: In this topsy-turvy world, Rains's mom is the femme fatale.

Meanwhile, Grant torments Bergman, concealing his jealousy and forcing her into ever more desperate situations. She responds by self-destructively following his every order. He's appalled that she won't stop the whole thing and run off with him. She feels exactly the same way.

Compared to the B movies and noirs of the day, with their noisy promiscuity and explicit violence, Hitchcock's reliance on innuendo seems downright dainty. But his repression has its virtues. Bergman's courting of Grant is unbearably erotic. She was never more beautiful; her eyes seem directly connected to her soul. Bergman's passionate nature is accessible to her in a way that Grant's is not. His condemnation of her as a drunken slut who cannot change seems the ultimate hypocrisy. She lives precisely as he would, if he had her courage.

Hitchcock's detailed portrait of the underneath—a world of emotional manipulation and denial, of jealousy, of homicidal rage, and Oedipal lust, and of multiple horrors committed under the banners of love and country—earn this picture its place in noir. Certainly, Hitchcock's elegant surface, perfect frames, star-friendly lighting, and insistence on an apparently happy ending are at odds with a strict interpretation of the canon. But his haunting air of danger, and the inordinate pleasure he draws from the cruelty of lovers, make this the perfect prelude to his masterpiece, his noir paean to hopelessness, *Vertigo* (page 267).

Other recommended rentals directed by Alfred Hitchcock:

Vertigo (page 267)
Suspicion
Rear Window
The Wrong Man (page 273)

ARCHIVE PHOTOS

Ida Lupino *On Dangerous Ground*

On Dangerous Ground (1951—USA)

Mood Guide: Romantic, unsentimental thriller

Director: Nicholas Ray; *Camera:* George Diskant; *Screenplay:* A. I. Bezzerides

Cast: Robert Ryan, Ida Lupino, Ward Bond, Ed Begley

In English; B/W

Plot: The toughest cop in town is so tough, his pals think he's a psycho. Sent upstate to track a killer on the run, the cop meets a lady who can show him another kind of life. If she does, is he too far gone to recognize redemption when it's staring him in the face?

A gripping romantic thriller with not a moment of sentimentality; the only Nicholas Ray (*In a Lonely Place*) picture with an unambiguously happy ending.

Working from a screenplay based on his own idea, and supported by producer John Houseman, Ray cast Robert Ryan as a cop driven crazy by loneliness. Ryan savages the criminals he arrests. As he beats one young offender, his face a mask of frustration and rage, Ryan cries: "Why do you punks make me do this?" When the chief warns him about his brutality, Ryan defends himself—sounding like the model for *Dirty Harry*—by arguing that violence is necessary in such a violent world. The chief, and Ryan's friends, fear that the violence is not in the world, but in Ryan himself.

By way of a working vacation, Ryan is ordered upstate to investigate a murder. Ryan's city is all dark streets, deep shadows, and tight compositions. As he heads into the country, everything changes. The frames open wide to encompass mountain vistas, and the somber tones lighten up as snow, rather than shadows, dominates. The city stifles Ryan, but the great outdoors proves welcoming. Ray gives us just a moment to appreciate this potential sanctuary before reminding us that tragedy is everywhere.

Ryan arrives as the local townspeople chase a suspected child killer. He meets Ward Bond, the grief-stricken father of a murdered girl. Bond, insane with sorrow and mad for revenge, says he intends to murder the murderer. Ryan recognizes himself in Ward's homicidal rage. Ryan seldom speaks, but his performance is proof of Ray's greatness as a director of actors. Ryan's every conflict, every contradictory moment of rage and reflection, flashes across his face.

Ray captures obsession like no other director, and Bernard Herrmann's powerful music fuels Ward Bond's obsessive chase. Ward and Ryan run through snow-covered fields, race along icy roads in a stolen car, and finally corner the fugitive in a remote farmhouse.

Here, Ryan meets Ida Lupino, and the film changes tone again. In Lupino's farmhouse the light is soft and comforting. Lupino's domestic tranquillity elicits the first signs of tenderness in Ryan. Ray, the master storyteller, places Ryan and Lupino together in frames composed to suggest their instinctual, immediate intimacy. Ryan and Lupino are well-matched. Both communicate volumes without speaking. The camera loves Lupino, and no actress today has her combination of capability, adult self-containment, and sweetness. Here is a woman who can grant Ryan the forgiveness he cannot grant himself. But does he recognize the opportunity she represents?

Ray has done the apparently impossible. He mixes the classic themes—a cruel man lost in a cruel universe, the pointlessness of any effort, the difficulty of escaping one's past patterns and habits—with a strangely modern "woman's" melodrama. Ray arrives at a simple, heartfelt conclusion: A man needs a strong woman to show him his innate kindness; a woman needs a strong man to protect her from the world. It's an old—and possibly anachronistic—story, but Ray makes it sing.

Other recommended rentals directed by Nicholas Ray:
Bigger Than Life
In a Lonely Place (page 137)
The Murder of Fred Hampton

Ossessione (1942—Italy)

Mood Guide: *Postman,* with a twist

Director: Luchino Visconti; *Camera:* Domenico Scala, Abdo Tonti; *Screenplay:* Luchino Visconti, Giuseppe De Santis
Cast: Massimo Girotti, Clara Calamai, Juan deLanda, Dhia Cristiani
In Italian, with English subtitles; B/W
Plot: A wandering tramp falls for the neglected wife of a filling station owner. Together, they kill her husband, but the tramp wanders off once more. Reunited, they try to love, but karma comes a'calling.

An Italian take on James M. Cain's *The Postman Always Rings Twice*, featuring what appears to be the birth of neorealism—non-studio locations, natural-light exteriors, nonactors in bit roles, a detailed portrait of peasant life, a shocking matter-of-factness about sex, grubby *mise-en-scène*, obvious "real life" in the background of many shots, a decidedly nonglamorous natural setting for the action—and a truly perverse twist on Cain's already contrary tale.

A charismatic tramp wanders into a filling station. He supposedly falls for the hot-blooded but neglected wife of the filling station owner, a fat slob. But something's askew. The tramp looks like a matinee idol, but the wife is merely an attractive woman, hardly a bombshell. The tramp gets much more flattering lighting and adoring close-ups. When the tramp kisses the wife, she's filled with passion, but he's barely interested. He takes off his shirt and poses languidly for the camera. She keeps her clothes on.

The tramp comes alive only when another tramp shows up. Their eyes suggest a passionate connection, they speak longingly of the open road and, sure enough, the tramp splits with his new pal only moments after promising to love the wife "forever." The two tramps share a bed and embark on a life of selling umbrellas on the street. That's where the wife finds her lost lover and entices him back to the gas station. The tramp and the wife kill the husband in a staged auto wreck. The police investigation is not half as thorough as in the American *Postman,* but Visconti wastes little time on anything so mundane as cops.

The second tramp shows up at the gas station and begs his pal to join him once more. The two men share a lingering walk down by the river, which turns into a quarrel. Tramp one smacks Tramp two. Tramp two, his face as horrified as only a betrayed lover's can be, takes off back down the road. This is the most moving separation of the film, and Visconti makes it clear that Tramp one's heart is now broken.

He flees the wife and picks up a young girl in town. Displaying Visconti's Continental matter-of-factness regarding sex between men and women (as opposed to his coy suggestions about sex between men and men), the girl immediately removes her clothes. Tramp one stops her with a shake of his head. "You are not like other men," she says, wonderingly. Well, *duh.*

In his novel, Cain suggests that ironic fate and unavoidable karma collude to bring the tramp to justice. But Visconti takes it an astounding step further. Visconti suggests that this cruel justice springs from the tramp turning his back on his true nature (he's gay) and his true love (Tramp Two). That thesis certainly must have blown a few minds fifty-five years ago . . . what courage Visconti had.

And what a sparse vision, using natural locations and shooting simply, but with poetry. There's a particularly lovely sequence of the husband and a priest riding their bikes onto a ferry, which drifts into the river as they continue their conversation. It's neorealism in its purest form.

Even so, Visconti makes a mighty slow movie, and *Ossessione* barely creaks along, stopping now and then for inexcusable folksy moments like the fat-slob husband singing opera in a bar. There's little suspense, and as a noir it's most interesting for its unusual theme.

Other recommended rentals directed by Luchino Visconti:
Death in Venice
The Leopard

Out of the Past (1947—USA)

Mood Guide: Noir incarnate

Director: Jacques Tourneur; *Camera:* Nick Musuraca; *Screenplay:* Daniel Mainwaring

Cast: Robert Mitchum, Kirk Douglas, Jane Greer

In English; B/W

Plot: A retired hood reluctantly returns to the world of mobsters to track down the missing girlfriend of a mob boss whose request he cannot refuse. When he finds the girlfriend, he does the worst possible thing: He falls in love with her. Together, they go home to face the music.

Screenwriter Daniel Mainwaring wrote *Invasion of the Body Snatchers*. Cinematographer Nick Musuraca shot the surreal *Cat*

People (1942). Director Jacques Tourneur's approach—in fact, his life—was noir incarnate. These B-movie all-stars combine to create a classic; a bleak, enthralling tale of a man struggling to escape his fate even as he knows he is utterly and deservedly condemned.

Robert Mitchum plays a hoodlum dragged out of self-imposed exile by mobster Kirk Douglas to track down Douglas's runaway girlfriend, the fatally seductive Jane Greer. Even as Mitchum recognizes the mortal danger of falling for her, he does. Does he condemn himself out of profane love, a yearning for redemption from his dirty past, weariness of life, or sheer perversity? As you might have guessed, all of the above. Douglas has never seemed so evil, nor so reveled in his own physique. He swells with menace when confronting Mitchum, and his final threats to Jane Greer are downright terrifying.

ARCHIVE PHOTOS

Virginia Huston and Robert Mitchum in *Out of the Past*

Director Tourneur's sense of hopelessness and existential dread were hard-earned during a career that featured seminal but underappreciated work like *I Walked with a Zombie*. These themes find expression in a desolate compendium of classic noir elements: violence, sexual obsession, alienation, betrayal, and (justified) paranoia, all presented in eerie, shadow-laden lighting and dreamlike camera work.

Everyone betrays; some for love, some for money, some out of boredom, and one, a French teenage deaf-mute garage attendant living in the middle of rural Nevada(!?!), for no discernible reason except to add to the pervasive air of tragedy. For spooky directorial flourishes amid a hopelessly confusing (and ultimately unimportant) plot, this film has no equal. Nor for B/W cinematography, acting, or soul.

Mitchum's alienation is key; he's alienated from himself, from sacred love, and, by his betrayals, even from his own kind: gangsters. In typical noir fashion, Mitchum never "blames" Kirk Douglas for his troubles. He recognizes the villain as nothing more than an actualizer of evil forces long extant in the world of men, and in his own psyche. Mitchum's only faith is his absolute lack of faith, his conviction that things will only worsen no matter which course he follows. No other actor could present such knowing resignation when confronted with the absurd universe of his own folly. Mitchum shines in this role, sappy as a schoolboy in love one moment, psychotically violent the next, with never an apparent contradiction.

Jane Greer, likewise, is the classic femme fatale: the embodiment of sexual terror, a seducer/destroyer, who is smarter than any man but needy, too—she not only outwits you, she steals your heart as well. Her will to power—in the noir tradition—automatically means snatching it from a man. No woman in noir is sexually active without being destructive, and Greer's character is no exception. She's both, and damn compelling either way.

One of the all-timers: fierce, poetic, suspenseful, complex, intelligent, heartbreaking, and lovely to gaze upon.

Other recommended rentals directed by Jacques Tourneur:
Cat People
I Walked with a Zombie

The Phenix City Story (1955—USA)

Mood Guide: Crude, wacky docudrama

Director: Phil Karlson; *Camera:* Harry Neumann; *Screenplay:* Crane Wilbur, Daniel Mainwaring

Cast: John McIntire, Richard Kiley, Kathryn Grant

In English; B/W

Plot: A small town lies helpless in the grip of the mob. Dope, prostitution, and gambling make the innocent live in fear. A gallant crusader tries to fight the powers that be, but they fill him full of holes. His son steps up to the challenge. Will good prevail, or will the son go the way of the father?

Here's proof that even bad movies can be seminal.

Director Paul Schrader (screenwriter of *Taxi Driver* and director of *The Comfort of Strangers*) describes the final phase of classical noir as having a ''hysterical'' style. ''Hysterical'' is the only word for this lurid, cheapo docudrama that comes at the end of the classical cycle. B-movie director Phil Karlson presents the true story of a struggle between a crime organization and the citizens who oppose it, set in the actual southern town where the real-life events occurred.

A young man returns home to discover that his town is ruled by prostitution and gambling. As mob violence escalates, the young man urges his father to join his campaign of reform. Initially reluctant, his father agrees to run for Attorney General. But when his father's quest is interrupted, the young man encourages the U.S. military to take over the town, and they do! This truly strange film features an equally strange ending: a call for a military coup as the proper solution to corrupted democracy.

Karlson's baroque technique and florid melodrama have proven to be a magnet for cinema scholars and noir historians. His pulp writing, relentless close-ups, crude camera work, and commingling of local townspeople with actors create a consistent, if unintentional, style. Perhaps Karlson's overstatement suggests the depth of his desire for a return to conformism and normalcy—even at the price of a military takeover. Whatever, the picture works better as an object of academic study than as entertainment. Everything that makes it sound so interesting also makes it almost unbearable to sit through.

The dramatic emphasis of every scene seems out of whack; the presentation is badly dated and lacks rhythm. The "real" actors chew the scenery shamelessly. Their constant Method shouting stands in hilarious contrast to the stiff, wooden-faced locals, who appear to be paralyzed with self-consciousness. The narration is overbearing and moralistic. The intensity never flags, so viewer exhaustion sets in early.

And yet . . . . Karlson breaks away from his amateur theatrics to present violence with shocking intimacy. A young black girl is thrown from a speeding car like garbage, a pistol shot blasts into a man's face, thugs stomp a voter at a tolling place—all presented with an offhandedness that makes these violent moments the most real.

If you are a true noir buff, or one who can enjoy a bad picture made with verve, this may prove a worthy rent. Otherwise, check out the later films that refined *Phenix City*'s pornographic energy.

Other recommended rentals directed by Phil Karlson:
Kansas City Confidential (page 144)
The Silencers

Pickup on South Street (USA—1953)

Mood Guide: Urban hysteria and the Red Scare

Director: Samuel Fuller; *Camera:* Joe Macdonald; *Screenplay:* Samuel Fuller

Cast: Richard Widmark, Jean Peters, Thelma Ritter, Richard Kiley

In English; B/W

Plot: A pickpocket takes possession of something he shouldn't have. The cops want it. Commie agents want it. The gal he filched it from wants it, too. He wants her, but is he willing to pay her price?

There's this prostitute, see, and there's this pickpocket, and since this is 1953, there's also this Commie spy and a tough cop who doesn't care whose heart he has to break . . . you get the idea. Richard Widmark picks the purse of a streetwalker without knowing she's unwittingly carrying microfilm planted on her by a dirty Commie rat.

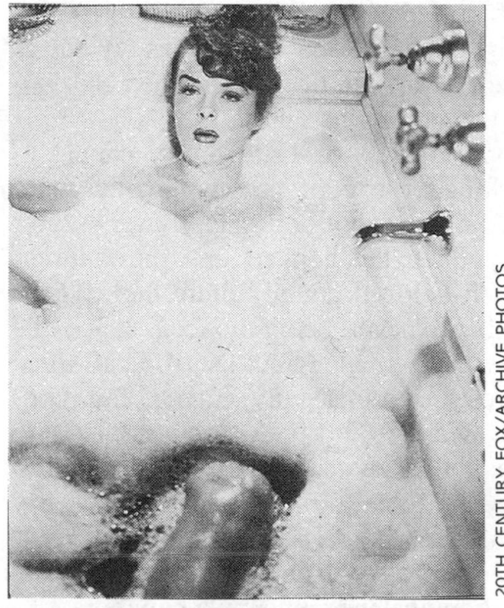

20TH CENTURY FOX/ARCHIVE PHOTOS

Jean Peters in *Pickup on South Street*

Fuller, a rabid antitotalitarian, made a film with a hero who repeatedly opines that politics are stupid, and only suckers would give their lives for their country. Was Fuller challenging his own beliefs, or just trying to irritate the censors? Not that he really cared about the Red Scare. When the cops try to manipulate Widmark through his (dormant) patriotism, Widmark sneers: "Don't wave the flag at me."

But Widmark comes around, for love of the hooker or his country, it's hard to say. He leaves his seamy little hut by the waterfront and does battle with the Reds, all the time feeling like a number-one sap. Thelma Ritter plays Widmark's conscience, a classic tough-gal, heart-of-gold waitress. Like Widmark, she fills her pulp role with surprising depth. In a career of tough waitresses, this is Ritter's most moving performance.

Of all of Fuller's cartoonish characters, these resonate with a singularly credible life-force. Jean Peter's hooker is particularly touching, with her vulnerable face and hard-ass manner. She's the physical embodiment of the oft-described Mickey Spillane girl, the one with the mouth so soft and ripe that Widmark doesn't know whether to kiss it or punch it. With Peters in his arms, Widmark looks convincingly confused, as his life of independence and violence is threatened by the tenderness she evokes.

Fuller, per his obsessions, focuses on little people caught in the cogs of the big machine. The cops are marginally more palatable than the Commie stooges, but both happily serve their absent masters. The pickpocket, the hooker, and the waitress have found in Fuller's much-beloved gutter culture the existential freedom that comes from never being noticed. Once the dominant society (that previously reviled and discarded all three protagonists) evinces interest, even that puny, fragile, and hard-earned liberty is snatched away.

Fuller trumpets his distaste for duty, patriotism, and even common decency if any force one to conform. The director clearly prefers an outright criminal to a hypocritical "good citizen." There's just enough anti-Commie fervor in his story to keep the censors from detecting his genuine and subversive beliefs.

Fuller was the pulp-meister, the American Melville—or was Melville the French Fuller? He wrote aggressively naive noir films and shot them with an economy (he had no money) and a pure technique (he was a genius) that made him a favorite of Europeans thirty years before America cineastes came to properly revere him. Coppola, Milius, and Spielberg all came to Fuller for advice, and in his retirement he became a script guru to a new generation of directors.

Short, crude, and simplistic (this description applies to both the film and to Sam Fuller himself), *Pickup* endures on the strength of Thelma Ritter's performance, Fuller's contradictory passions, and his startling camera movement.

Other recommended rentals directed by Samuel Fuller:
Fixed Bayonets
Merrill's Marauders
The Naked Kiss (page 185)
Shock Corridor
The Steel Helmet
Underworld U.S.A. (page 264)

ARCHIVE PHOTOS

Lee Marvin in *Point Blank*

Point Blank (1967—USA)

Mood Guide: Mean-spirited corporate gangsters

Director: John Boorman; *Camera:* Phillip H. Lathrop; *Screenplay:* Alexander Jacobs, David Newhouse, Rafe Newhouse

Cast: Lee Marvin, Angie Dickinson, John Vernon, Keenan Wynn, Carroll O'Connor

In English; color

Plot: A tough gunman pulls a robbery with his best friend. His best friend double-crosses him and runs off with the gunman's wife. The gunman wants revenge. He also wants his money. Only his mortal wounds and every single member of organized crime in Los Angeles stand in his way . . .

Lee Marvin plays an old-fashioned gangster who doesn't much care for the modern world. John Boorman is a forward-looking director desperate to create a whole new genre. That the Boorman-Marvin genre contains only one film is not their fault. Maybe nobody else had their combination of hubris, vision, cynicism, and guts.

Boorman harnesses Marvin's boorish, all-American, semi-psychotic energy to a visual design based on the super-alienated, wide-screen European cinema of such emerging auteurs as Michelangelo Antonioni and Alain Resnais. Filling these arty, distanced frames with raging energy, *Point Blank* showcases shockingly explicit violence and even more explicit sex. What makes both disturbing even to our jaded modern eye is Boorman's determination that the violence be sexy and the sex violent. This brutality fuels Boorman's presentation of a world without sentiment; no characters share a moment of genuine warmth or connection.

Marvin pulls off a heist with an old pal. The old pal double-crosses him and steals his girl. Marvin doesn't care about the girl; he wants his money back. With the subtlety of a rhinoceros, and packing the biggest pistol ever seen on the screen (at that time), Marvin plows through the faceless corporate underworld of a bright, shiny, indifferent Los Angeles.

His mobster victims agree that Marvin was wronged, but they don't understand his rage. "It's just business," they tell him, baffled, as Marvin fills them full of holes. All ruefully shake their heads at the archaic methods of this man of action, this fool who doesn't understand that the business of modern criminality is business. Carroll O'Connor does a hilarious turn as the head of the Organization, the corporate Mafia that has Marvin so upset. O'Connor scolds Marvin, reminding him that "nobody uses cash nowadays."

Marvin's character owes much to the self-contained ferocity

of Ralph Meeker's Mike Hammer in *Kiss Me Deadly* (page 151). Like Hammer, Marvin requires little in the way of sex, sleep, or human companionship. When not chasing his money, Marvin sits motionless, his big arms hanging slack. Without a task to perform, Marvin's body serves no purpose and provides him no pleasure.

Marvin's a blunt object, a bull searching for a china shop. Among the pieces he smashes in his hunt is Angie Dickinson, who plays a tough-minded, good-hearted moll. Marvin uses her unashamedly. She falls for him. He's not interested. A crooked cop offers to help him. He's not interested. The Organization offers to settle. He's not interested. All that interests him is his quest, and his quest has no purpose, meaning, or resolution. It's self-generated, self-perpetuating, and pointless: the perfect metaphor for modern ambition.

Boorman references noir conventions by turning them on their head. Where classical noir is B/W, *Point Blank* is shot in luridly modern colors. Where noir uses first-person narration to clarify the (anti) hero's twisted motivations, Boorman leaves Marvin's strategies opaque. Where classical noir uses framing to underscore story points, Boorman's superwide compositions are deliberately meaningless. Everyone stands far away from everyone else, or shouts when they're standing side by side, or kisses madly while gazing at one another with wide-open suspicious eyes.

Boorman's unadorned style and Marvin's Cro-Magnon sexiness influenced filmmakers from Godard to Tarantino to Woo. In the great noir tradition—and without ever evoking the classic visual style of noir—Boorman entertains with violence, sex, and greed while commenting on the distrust, commercialism, and heartlessness of the modern world.

Be sure to rent the Letter-Boxed version.

Other recommended rentals directed by John Boorman:

Catch Us If You Can
Deliverance

Police (1985—France)

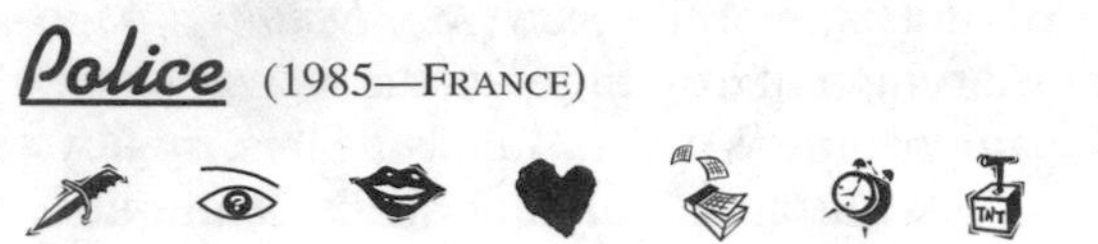

Mood Guide: Blunt, unsentimental tour of Paris's seamy side

Director: Maurice Pialat; *Camera:* Luciano Tovoli; *Screenplay:* Maurice Pialat, Catherine Breillat, Sylvie Danton, Jacques Fieschi

Cast: Gerard Depardieu, Sophie Marceau, Sandrine Bonnaire, Richard Anconina, Franck Karoui

In French, with English subtitles; color

Plot: A tough but corrupt cop is out to bust the Algerian gangsters who deal heroin. A young girl steals money and drugs from the gangsters and turns to the cop for protection. Maybe she loves him, maybe not. But if he falls for her, he'll make an enemy of everyone he knows.

Think of it as a French version of *The French Connection*, with trickier social issues and a more ambivalent heroism. Pialat's remarkably intimate, complex *policier* is fueled by forbidden love across the boundaries of crime and race.

Concerned equally with the mechanics of police work and the rotting souls of those who perform it, *Police* brings a near-documentary approach to the war between Parisian drug cops and their Arab heroin-dealing adversaries. In this misanthropic universe, the races loathe one another, men have the power, women use sex to take it away, and those who ignore the rules end up heartbroken, dead, or both.

Depardieu plays a hard-assed, jovially corrupt detective. He beats prisoners, turns allies into snitches, steals drugs for his informants, and makes no apologies for his sexism or his helter-skelter amorous urges. Sophie Marceau, in a seductive, self-contained performance, plays the duplicitous common-law wife of an incarcerated Arab dope seller. At first she appears an exploited innocent, but—and the viewer understands this far sooner than the lovesick Depardieu—she's more hardened and Machiavellian than she seems.

And she's running a far more dangerous game than the happy-go-lucky Depardieu. Marceau plays the cops against the Arabs and her husband's murderous family against itself. Everyone falls for her, except the homicidally unsentimental Algerians. They stand in stark contrast to the sappy Europeans. Marceau describes the Arab world as a place "where it is impossible to tell what anyone thinks." She prefers their violence and stoicism to the self-righteous hypocrisy of the Europeans, who lie with disdain but become furious when someone lies to them.

In contrast to most femmes fatale, Marceau understands her duplicitous nature, but is helpless before it. "I've always lied," she says, sounding very much like a man. Very much, in fact, like Depardieu. In Marceau, he sees his own corrupted soul, and aches to protect her. Wrongly convinced of his own ruthlessness, he hasn't a clue how ruthless she can be.

Yet, when Marceau's world of deceit crumbles, she turns to Depardieu. To rescue her will mean ruining himself, though it also offers redemption. As with most noir heroes, Depardieu's redemption and downfall are indistinguishable. The bitter, lingering taste of his failure is Depardieu's one satisfaction—however perverse—from the whole miserable affair.

Depardieu and Marceau (who hated the director and later accused him of sadomasochistic mind-games in order to elicit a great performance) are superb, and the minor players are a revelation. Richard Anconina plays a charming street hoodlum of a lawyer who foolishly betrays both sides. Future French superstar Sandrine Bonnaire, with her sweet smile, makes believable the noir chestnut of a whore with a heart of gold. The Arab family members, led by Franck Karoui, mumble in a harrowing, impenetrable style. Pialat intends that they be impervious to European understanding, and they are. They're fucking scary.

The violence is realistically matter-of-fact. The nit-picking bureaucratic bullshit seems as real as a day at the office. The sex is arousing, if nihilistic, and the visuals are as beautiful as they are simple. Pialat explains nothing, including his own cynicism.

He presents the violence, racism, abuse of power, and corruption as normal life. His matter-of-fact approach earned him the enmity of both the police and the French Arab community. Both claimed they had been misrepresented. It's hard to tell about that from this side of the Atlantic, but every moment has the ring of truth.

ARCHIVE PHOTOS

The Postman Always Rings Twice (1946—USA)

Mood Guide: Suspenseful fable of karma

Director: Tay Garnett; *Camera:* Sidney Wagner; *Screenplay:* Harry Ruskin, Niven Busch

Cast: John Garfield, Lana Turner, Cecil Kellaway, Hume Cronyn, Leon Ames

In English; B/W

Plot: A drifter falls for a dame and agrees to work at her husband's café. She falls for him, too. They kill the husband and fail to make it look like an accident. Together, they go on trial. Will love prove stronger than suspicion?

One problem with the (cinematic, sociological, feminist, deconstructivist, Lacanian, etc.) critical analysis unleashed on noir is that the compelling theoretical aspects of a film may be cited as if separate from the picture itself. That is, an awful film can resonate through the critical literature for its symbolic rather than cinematic virtues. And this is an awful picture: silly, badly paced, self-parodying, dated, suspenseless, and, ultimately, unconvincing.

For the theorist, however, *Postman* offers a mother lode of compulsive love, murderous feminine duplicity, failed redemption, and quirky fate. For the film renter, it's a laugh-inducing snoozer, with just enough great scenes to keep you from hitting Rewind.

It resembles a typically bungled modern big-studio effort, with worthy intentions frustrated by commercial concerns. If you strain, you can make out the brilliant source material (the novel by James M. Cain). But you can also see the studio's determination to make a star of Lana Turner at the expense of the story. Her spotlessly white (and unintentionally amusing) costumes do provide a nice (theoretical) counterpart to her "dark" soul, but they hardly blend with the neo-realist *mise-en-scène*. Feminist critics might argue that this is deliberate, that certain women characters are separated—by lighting and costume—from the story in order to emphasize their status as "the other." In *Gilda*, for example, it seems plausible, but here, that dog won't hunt.

John Garfield's great, as usual, but there is no chemistry between Turner and him. Compare any of their pallid, close-mouthed, Hollywood kisses to a single melting glance between John Dall and Peggy Cummins in *Gun Crazy*, or—for sheer perversity—the sidelong, soul-searching looks between Glenn Ford and George Macready in *Gilda*.

Fortunately, the story comes to a halt to showcase the best scenes: the courtroom sparring between Hume Cronyn as a cocky, cynical lawyer and Leon Ames as an equally faithless district attorney. Their interplay has the snap, great dialogue, and suspense the rest of the picture lacks. There are other worthy moments: Turner and Garfield alone in a surreal nighttime ocean, a stunning car crash, the terror on Garfield's face when he knows the end is near, the grisly explosion of a cat pawing an exposed electrical wire, the nastiness in Cronyn's voice as he excoriates Turner. These scenes share Cain's hopeless outlook and his appreciation for the futile.

And you know what? The modern remake with Jack Nicholson and Jessica Lange is even worse.

Prince of the City (1981—USA)

Mood Guide: Compelling police drama

Director: Sidney Lumet; *Camera:* Andrzej Bartkowiak; *Screenplay:* Sidney Lumet, Jay Presson Allen

Cast: Treat Williams, Jerry Orbach, Bob Balaban, Lindsay Crouse

In English; color

Plot: A corrupt cop with a bad conscience, hoping for redemption, rats out his fellow cops. No good comes from it. The rat is made an outcast from cops and even from the criminals he chases. Justice is not served. Based on a true story.

A dark, dramatic, and at times agonizing study of the Byzantine corruption of New York City cops, district attorneys, petty thieves, and mobsters. The story is told through the eyes of one tormented soul who decided to confess everything and brought the wrath of the whole interlocking structure down upon his head.

Directed by New York City cop-crook-movie avatar Sidney Lumet (*Serpico, Dog Day Afternoon*) and based on a true story, *Prince* follows Treat Williams as a cop in an elite squad of crime fighters who make more arrests and secure more convictions than any other squad in the city. They also steal money and drugs from those they bust. Williams, a working-class cop from the outer boroughs, is driven by the potent dualities of giant ego/self-loathing plus heroic urge/class inferiority. He lets himself be seduced by two white-bread Manhattan DAs. They flatter his sense of his own importance and exaggerate the importance of their crusade against police corruption. Williams takes them at their word and informs on his partners.

His heroism hardly receives the laurels he anticipates. He is made outcast, the Mafia tries to kill him, his partners go to jail, and others attempt suicide. Williams watches, appalled, as the corruption cases created by his testimony labor through the bureaucrat swamp. His DA/protectors get plush new assignments and move up the ladder. New DAs break long-standing deals and treat him not as a hero, but a snitch. The confusion depresses him to the point of suicidal folly.

Lumet toyed with this territory in *Serpico* and *Q & A*, but in those melodramas he never addressed the pervasive ambiguity of the life of cops. Contradictions rule the day: Mafiosi offer to save Williams's life, and cops try to kill him. The high-minded white upper class, represented by lawyers, DAs, and judges, break their word and fight for career advancement. Ethnic working-class cops and crooks offer Williams loyalty long after he has proven himself to be a rat. It's a bleak study of class brotherhood, shot with simplicity and acted sincerely.

The underappreciated Treat Williams has the complex charisma of a movie star from the old studio era; he's a strong guy with an underlying river of pain. His performance is among the finest in any American film of the last twenty years and should have won him an Oscar, or, at the very least, a lifelong dispensation against ever having to costar with Joe Piscopo.

Williams delivers all the intricacy of this character, with his wild swings between physical heroism and moral cowardice, the love he feels for the men he betrayed, and his lust for the praise of those richer than he. In a subtle and nuanced performance, Williams disappears into this tortured cop.

Lumet lets the actors carry the day and subordinates the camera work to their performances. Because the film has so many different characters and scenes, a decision was made to concentrate on the acting and to shoot on location as simply as possible. The reliance on location provides the gritty, street feel so necessary to understand the pressures on Williams's character.

Long, difficult, and wrenching, the film features fine cop action, shoot-outs, and courtroom drama. There's also great Noo

Yawk cop/crook slang and amazing work from a deep supporting cast that includes Jerry Orbach (tough cop), Bob Balaban (sleazy bureaucrat), and Lindsay Crouse (cop's loyal wife). Also, some of the most inventive cursing you will ever hear.

Other recommended rentals directed by Sidney Lumet:

Q & A
The Verdict

ARCHIVE PHOTOS

Raw Deal (1948—USA)

Mood Guide: Masterpiece of cinematography

Director: Anthony Mann; *Camera:* John Alton; *Screenplay:* Leopold Atlas, John C. Higgins

Cast: Dennis O'Keefe, Claire Trevor, Marsha Hunt, John Ireland, Raymond Burr

In English; B/W

Plot: A tough dame breaks her man out of jail. She doesn't know he's falling for someone else, but she finds out when he brings the second dame along on the lam. Together they dodge roadblocks, hoods sent to kill them, and even a murderer. Plotting their escape to Panama and revenge for a vicious double-cross, the dame and her man still have to reckon with the other woman.

Forget Ingmar Bergman. Forget John Woo. And while you're at it, forget Durante Alighieri, too. For images of salvation achieved, salvation denied, love's betrayal, man's savagery, the perversity of the romantic urge, the loneliness of existence and the surreal, sexual intimacy of hand-to-hand combat, Anthony Mann and cinematographer John Alton—especially cinematographer John Alton—beat 'em all, hands down.

Dennis O'Keefe (and his big, knobby face) break out of prison into the waiting arms of Claire Trevor. She provides a rare voice-over; rare in that voice-overs (the Greek chorus of noir) are hardly ever spoken by women, and this one is doubly surprising because Claire appears to be a secondary character. Though the narrative engine is Dennis O'Keefe (and his big, knobby face), it's clear by movie's end that the story's heart belongs to Claire. And that all the violence and suspense are secondary to her obsessive love.

And obsessed she is. To Claire, Dennis is the center of the universe. Unfortunately for her, Dennis feels exactly the same way. And although Claire doesn't know it at first, O'Keefe is falling for their semiwilling hostage, Marsha Hunt.

With their three-way lusts, jealousies, and resentments shaping every verbal exchange, the three hit the road, bound for O'Keefe's promised payoff from superscary Raymond Burr. Director Mann shoots the massive Burr from the floor looking up, so Burr's broody face appears to be the size of Mount Rushmore. Burr earns his villain stripes early when he flings a flaming dessert onto a woman who bumps into him. Then he stares at her, meanly.

Burr sends two hoods after O'Keefe. One tries to kill him in a brutal fight sequence that ends with mild-mannered Marsha gunning down the hood, but only after O'Keefe tries to blind the guy by impaling him on a deer antler. A second hood (who looks so much like the first one that you may be confused) kidnaps Marsha. Self-centered O'Keefe is thus forced to admit his love for Marsha, turn his back on his faithful Tonto (Claire), and head to the rescue. His final battle with Burr is unmatched in noir for its ferocity.

Since this is a Mann picture, it's a waste of energy to be bothered by the inane dialogue or silly plot turns. No one, save John Ireland as the hood Fantail, can "act." Nor does anyone bother trying. Instead, the actors deliver their lines in monotone, their face and bodies unmoving. When one of the players speaks *and* shifts any part of their bodies at the same time, it's a shock.

Alton's work here is untouchable. It's the richest cinematography in noir outside of Orson Welles's pictures. Indeed, *Raw Deal* looks a lot like *Citizen Kane*: deep focus frames, pools of impenetrable black and startling white, one face looming in the foreground and another barely visible in the background shadows, crystal-clear chiaroscuro close-ups shot through blowing fog (How did he do that?). The fight sequences and the final shots are Alton's crowning glory. Each shot in the fights brings a new, ornate, almost impenetrable composition, with lurching figures shifting around from blackness to lightning-sharp blasts of white light. That it takes a moment to understand each new frame only adds to the suspense and heightens the brutality.

Mann's most pessimistic view of fate, his most psychologically complex characters, and his most graphic violence. It's Mann's best noir, the one that justifies his critical reputation as a master of the form.

Other recommended rentals directed by Anthony Mann:

Border Incident
The Furies
T-Men (page 239)

Alain Delon contemplates existence in *Le Samourai*

Le Samourai (The Samurai) (1967—France)

Mood Guide: Dreamlike noir-Zen

Director: Jean-Pierre Melville; *Camera:* Henri Decaë; *Screenplay:* Jean-Pierre Melville, Georges Pellegrin

Cast: Alain Delon, Cathy Rosier, François Périer, Nathalie Delon

In French, with English subtitles; color

Plot: A silent, mysterious hit-man is ordered to kill the one witness to his earlier hit. Perhaps he will, perhaps he won't.

Clearly as influenced by the spare, virtually silent, genre-busting Westerns of Sergio Leone as by the Japanese hero of its name,

Melville's pared-down, spiritual masterwork is a paean to method, to moral courage, to style as a weapon against corruption, and to the crime movie itself, and as to numerous cool-guy movie icons, of whom star Alain Delon is unquestionably the coolest.

Delon plays a hit-man. In the opening shot of the film he lies alone in an bare, anonymous room, silent on his bed, smoking. Only, you can't see him. Our first glimmer of the man is the puff of smoke announcing his presence. Delon appears, then, like a genie. He's all mythology, with no greater realist weight than a puff of smoke.

Like Leone's Westerns, *Le Samourai* invents a genre while transcending it; like Leone, Melville makes art that delivers every cheap thrill genre was created to provide. He shoots with economy and grace, drawing attention only to the Zen simplicity of his frames. After proving himself a master of B/W, Melville here bends color to his ends, shooting Delon in a steely-gray palette, his room in washed pastels and the rest of the universe in harsh, stark colors. There's little music and seemingly deafening ambient sound. The ambient sound is loud because each room works its power on those who occupy it, and because Melville wants to remind us how attuned Delon's character is to every perceptible nuance of the world. The colors are strident for the same reason. They represent the oppressive acuity of the Samourai's discernment.

With his blank-faced, malevolent grace, Delon pulls a hit and uncharacteristically leaves one witness alive. His employers try to kill him for this apparent treachery, but he's too tough to die. The idiot cops come after him with their eavesdropping devices, but Delon's canary(!) alerts him to their presence, and the bug is foiled. Finally, the crooks return to pay Delon his original fee. Thus satisfied, Delon heads out to do the job, as all honorable Samurais must.

Though Melville succumbs to sentimentality in other films, here his style is cold-blooded and purposeful, a cinema stripped of all unnecessaries. The least American and most French of Mellville's pictures (its style and substance are so intertwined as to be inseparable), *Le Samourai* is, unsurprisingly, also the most Japanese.

Delon almost never speaks and takes no apparent pleasure from life Since, unlike many monosyllabic noir heroes, he derives no transcendence from the day to day via his violent acts, why does he continue to live in the face of the meaninglessness of life? Because, as a Samourai, Delon is devoted to method, to the perfect doing (by his standards) of every task.

Watch him steal a car: Delon calmly jimmies the door. He sits behind the wheel and produces a ring of keys the size of a large pizza. One by one he tries the keys, putting each in its turn on the seat beside him. When he inserts the proper key and the car starts, he drives away. No wasted motion, no elation, no apparent response at all: Delon is the existential master of his life. He accepts that he cannot control fate, but he insists on controlling himself.

Delon/Melville's devotion to method is not the devotion of Bresson's *Pickpocket.* Bresson found in the doing perfectly a path to spirituality. For Melville, method is the refuge of a man without real-world accomplishments or middle-class trophies. The Samourai (like *Bob le Flambeur* [page 63] in an earlier age) is the ultimate hipster. His sole accomplishment is the clarity with which he lives each moment. His skill and technique have nothing to do with Bressonian transcendence. There is nothing in the Melville universe for the Samourai to transcend and nowhere for him to transcend to. Things are as they are, and then you die.

And so, after spending all this time demonstrating the effectiveness of Delon's manner of coping with meaninglessness, Melville shows it to be without meaning. The beautiful, enigmatic witness should betray Delon, but she won't. He should kill her, but he refuses. In a good world, they would become lovers, but they can't. Delon finds the only solution, and that's damnation.

When the Samourai sacrifices himself, it's because he failed his Bushido, his own code. For him the sacrifice is small, because the Samourai credits himself as already dead, hence his corpse-like movements, his disinterest in sex, his refusal to speak . . . nothing in life grants him ecstasy. And the one person who might, he must kill.

Other recommended rentals directed by Jean-Pierre Melville:

Le Doulos (page 112)

Bob le Flambeur (page 63)

Le Deuxième Souffle (page 99)

ARCHIVE PHOTOS

Scarlet Street (1945—USA)

Mood Guide: A little man self-destructs

Director: Fritz Lang; *Camera:* Milton Krasner; *Screenplay:* Dudley Nichols

Cast: Edward G. Robinson, Dan Duryea, Joan Bennett, Margaret Lindsay

In English; B/W

Plot: A henpecked old fellow falls for a dangerous woman. She steals his money, drives him to crime, takes credit for his artwork, and ridicules his very manhood. Then things turn ugly.

Fritz Lang's narrative is a silk locomotive. Events fuel one another with invisible, crushing momentum, and the process (of life) is so smooth and apparently irresistible that no one ever notices a) they're being run over or b) that they set the whole train (of events) in motion by their own cupidity/poor moral judgment/shitty luck/ineffectual nature/inappropriate obsessions/horniness/greed/simple human needs.

Pity's tough to come by in noir, and no one doles it out with greater parsimony than Lang. His characters suffer crueler fates than those of any other director. (Though Hitchcock is certainly a close second.) In fact, Lang is meaner to his characters than any artist I can think of, except Evelyn Waugh or Vladimir Nabokov. And like Waugh, Lang inflicts the worst fates on those who deserve them the least. In *Scarlet Street*, Edward G. Robinson's only flaw is that he possesses no discernible courage of any kind. For this, Lang condemns him to the Seventh Circle of Hell.

The story opens with poor *schlemiel* Robinson receiving a commemorative watch for twenty-five miserable years as a cashier at some two-bit company. Robinson's deeply touched by his coworkers' care, and admires the watch with guilty pleasure. Meanwhile, Robinson's boss sneaks out of the dinner to meet his gorgeous young mistress. Thus does Lang establish the hierarchy of things: Robinson is a lowly, contented dog, barely aware that above him on the food chain others are living less dutiful but more voluptuous lives.

Robinson paints for pleasure, but his horrible, overbearing wife refuses to allow his paints anywhere but the bathroom. Robinson scurries around trying to please this monster until he meets the most selfish and self-indulgent of femmes fatales, "Lazy Legs," played by Joan Bennett. Bennett fakes love for Edward G. at the behest of her psycho pimp-boyfriend, played with sadistic charm by Dan Duryea. Smitten, Robinson embezzles money from his firm and sets up the lady in a little penthouse.

In return, Bennett spurns his advances, has Duryea over to spend the night and, when confronted by a big-deal art critic (the fanciful engines of Lang's plots always seem so perfectly credible—how does he get away with it?), claims to have painted Robinson's works. The critic buys the paintings and the femme fatale is suddenly a respected artist. Robinson, thrilled to see his work admired, doesn't care that he will never get his proper due.

All he cares about is that a twist of fate enables him to leave his grotesque wife. Racing to Bennett to share the happy news, Robinson catches her with Duryea. Robinson, for once, takes control of events, with disastrous consequences.

Lang collapses the world until it's sufficiently contained to reflect his implacable moral vision. He shoots in deliberately artificial environments. Robinson's seamy apartment is a claustrophobic hell, his office a cage in a zoo, and his beloved penthouse a trashy little aerie. Like his preposterous dreams of happiness with a willing floozy (what would Robinson do with her if he really had her?), Robinson's ambitions in the art world are revealed by Lang to be as false as his other fantasies of escape. Robinson never really tries to alter his nature or his world, and neither does anybody else. Having made their ghastly fates by lying down on the tracks, they let the locomotive roll right over them.

Everyone, Lang argues convincingly, is flawed by dint of their humanity, and therefore not only doomed, but deserving of every punishment we inflict on ourselves.

Other recommended rentals directed by Fritz Lang:

The Big Heat (page 46)
Human Desire (page 134)
M (page 170)
The Woman in the Window (page 270)

The Set-Up (1948—USA)

Mood Guide: Heavy-handed boxing movie

Director: Robert Wise; *Camera:* Milton Krasner; *Screenplay:* Art Cohn

Cast: Robert Ryan, Audrey Totter, Percy Helton, Alan Baxter

In English; B/W

Plot: An aging, punchy, low-rent boxer dreams of one more big bout. His manager throws the fight without telling the boxer, who goes into the ring thinking he should give his all.

With its obvious irony, overt message-mongering, and heavy-handed cutting, *The Set-Up* feels more like a full-length *Twilight Zone* than a movie. Unfortunately dependent on the plight of the working man (as rendered by the unconsciously condescending Hollywood elite), *The Set-Up* cannot escape its era. Worse, by attempting a grotesquely fake neo-realism, it never rises above it's own devices. The sole saving grace is Robert Ryan's performance of a man who doesn't know when he's beaten.

Robert Ryan plays an aging, second-rate fighter of great, if dented, dignity. His long-suffering wife, Audrey Totter, has had enough. She refuses to attend his fight. Ryan's manager, unbeknownst to him, throws the fight to the local mob big-wig, Little Boy. The manager, played by George Tobias, is convinced that Ryan is such a stiff he'll lose on his own. Tobias does not share fifty dollars' worth of blood money with his own fighter.

Meanwhile, Ryan suffers plenty of premonitions. An older, even more punchy version of himself sells fight cards in front of the arena. In the locker room awaiting their bouts is a parade of ham-and-eggers, each either a more hopeful or more pathetic version of Ryan. Each speaks of his dreams of winning, of the big-time, and of the sweet retirement awaiting. Most return to the locker room beaten like drums. Ooh—the cruel disparity between the simple yearnings of the working man and the impassive grindings of fate!

Ryan's wife walks the nasty little town, stacking up epiphanies of her own. She sees reminders of their own wasted years, and normal folks who appear to live mundane but fulfilling lives. In this noir, normality is presented as a haven. The life of the outsider/artist (Ryan's life as a boxer) is shown as lacking in reward, either material or existential.

Finally, after a parade of Fifties antistereotypes (quiet Brooklynites, muscular Jews, the Noble Negro, etc.), Ryan fights. Though it seems far longer, the picture has at this point taken up only about forty minutes of the viewer's life. How will the filmmakers fill the remaining forty minutes? With Ryan boxing.

We see a number of actual three-minute rounds of Ryan and his young, blond opponent pretending to fight each other. It's pretty tedious, especially when intercut with the stereotypes in the arena who respond to the violence in a variety of supposedly revealing, but extremely hackneyed ways.

The Set-Up's heavy-handed tragic ending is no more affecting than its heavy-handed editing or its portrait of a world without loyalty except among the downtrodden. Whatever its noble intentions, the film is undone by its reliance on cheap manipulation.

It's hard to find worthwhile boxing noir: The message-mongering is so heavy, it strips the films of narrative credibility. Perhaps boxers symbolize the low-class, old-school masculine characteristics that Hollywood writers/executives want to overcome. Whereas they identify with the battered, noble private eye (who, after all, suffers economically for his accurate but unpopular vision, as do all writers), the past-his-prime boxer is either a) the bully who beat the shit out of them in high school; or b) symbolic of the ignorant working-class immigrant who attacks American society with his hands and not his brains. In other words, try as they might to ennoble Robert Ryan, the screenwriters look at him and see (an Irish version of) their dads. Or worse, they see the noble working-class guy whom they admire but wouldn't trade places with in a million years.

Only Martin Scorsese (and screenwriter Paul Schrader) had the artistic courage to look at a champion boxer and perceive the sexy, poetic psychopath lurking within. *Raging Bull* may not be noir, but it's the best boxing movie ever made.

Other recommended rentals directed by Robert Wise:

Run Silent, Run Deep
The Sound of Music
West Side Story

ARCHIVE PHOTOS

Charles Vanel and Yves Montand in *Le Salaire de la Peur*

Sorcerer/Le Salaire de la Peur (The Wages of Fear)

Sorcerer (1977—USA)

Mood Guide: Suspense with the lid off

Director: William Friedkin; *Camera:* John M. Stephens, Dick Bush; *Screenplay:* Walon Green

Cast: Roy Scheider, Bruno Crémer, Francisco Rabal, Amidou

In English; color

Le Salaire de la Peur (The Wages of Fear) (1952—FRANCE)

Mood Guide: Ditto, in French

Director: Henri-Georges Clouzot; *Camera:* Armand Thirard; *Screenplay:* Henri-Georges Clouzot

Cast: Yves Montand, Vera Clouzot, Charles Vanel

In French, with English subtitles; B/W

Plot: Four men on the lam with nothing to lose drive two trucks filled with nitroglycerin over a nightmare mountain road in the most isolated country on earth. If they blow up—so what? Their lives weren't worth much, anyway. If they make it—enough money for total redemption.

A suspense and adventure classic, first told by French director Henri-Georges Clouzot as *Le Salaire de la Peur (The Wages of Fear). Sorcerer* is the American remake.

The essential existential stuff: Do things right, be brave, and triumph. Provided, of course, that fate and coincidence don't make a mockery of all your efforts. And provided that you don't get what your corrupt soul really deserves no matter how brave you pretend to be.

Fresh off his triumph of *The Exorcist*, William Friedkin laid his money and credibility on the line to make the very first bloated Hollywood thriller—*Sorcerer* cost twenty-two million dollars. In 1976! Unlike most arrogant, self-indulgent Hollywood guys, however, Friedkin put every dime onto the screen. It fairly glistens, lit with piercing, glowing blues under an action-movie sheen of diamond-hard white light.

Roy Scheider stars as a lowlife Boston hoodlum on the run. His fellow fugitives—a French swindler, an Arab terrorist, and a Latin American hit man—live in an uneasy community of expatriates in the most appalling vision of a South American backwater ever created for film. In fact, the worst aspects appear all too real. Somewhere in this miserable country, terrorists have blown up an oil well. Scheider's mission—and he has no choice but to accept it—is to drive with three companions across mountains, rivers, swamps, and deserts. Their trucks are unreliable, slow, and packed with explosives so cranky, they might be set off by a vigorous sneeze.

Friedkin, who shot in eight different countries, creates a detailed back-story for each fugitive, so the film begins—with no explanation—by jumping from one character's prologue to the next. No apparent connection exists until Scheider wakes up in hell and he meets those who screwed up as badly as he, those who ran until they could run no further.

Now they want redemption, meaning a return to the world, and they will do anything to get it. And that's the whole of the plot: First you meet the guys—which takes the first half of the film—then they drive the trucks, which takes the second half. Pure adrenaline fuels the economy of expression; not one wasted moment from start to finish.

The Wages of Fear, the original version, is longer, meaner in spirit, slightly cruder in cinema, features more harrowing stunts, and suffers from 1940s sexism and costumes. It's also French, which means that the lash of fate is both crueler and funnier. If the roads Yves Montand and his three compatriots drive over are not quite so terrifying as those in *Sorcerer*, the suspense is greater. Nothing is faked; those ancient trucks appear to be hovering on the brink every second . . .

With his single lens, unmoving camera, and apparent determination to kill his cast, Clouzot merges the (basically Hollywood) pre-war action extravaganza (*The Four Feathers*) with the (basically European) post-war personal statement picture. In keeping with prevailing European trends—meaning no one had any money—Clouzot shoots mostly outdoors in a simple visual style. His function-over-form approach stands up fifty years later; the spare, elegant frames grant the stunts and suspense center stage. The most harrowing physical and emotional carnage is shot in long, unbroken takes, and the agony on his actors' faces cannot be entirely make-believe. Without such a restrained style, the unceasing tension might be lurid or even stupid. With it, Clouzot achieves a classic.

Try not to let the extremely dated opening wreck *The Wages of Fear*'s credibility. Due to the aforementioned 1940s sexism, women may find it difficult, but the thrills of the remaining two hours reward endurance handsomely. Though both films share a story line, they are so different, and so compelling on their own terms, that both should be seen, though on separate nights.

Looking for suspense? Rent either of these and claw all the upholstery off the arms of your chair.

Other recommended rentals directed by William Friedkin:
The French Connection
To Live and Die in L. A. (page 257)

Other recommended rentals directed by Henri-Georges Clouzot:
Les Diaboliques (page 102)

The State of Things (1982—USA)

Mood Guide: Meditative film within a film

Director: Wim Wenders; *Camera:* Henri Aliekan; *Screenplay:* Wim Wenders

Cast: Patrick Bauchau, Samuel Fuller, Allen Goorwitz, Viva, Roger Corman

In English, with some German with English subtitles; B/W

Plot: A troubled director on location in Europe watches his cast and crew sink into ennui as they await money from America. He goes to Hollywood to track down his producer, who's being pursued by the Mob.

Fleeing the corporate hell that directing and editing his Hollywood debut (*Hammett*) had become, Wenders wrote and directed this bitter, ravishing tale of the unending war between creativity and commercialism that is the Hollywood experience. Only Wenders would make an independent art house noir as relaxation from the stress of making a big studio commercial noir. And only Wenders could make a self-conscious arty semi-ode to noir that works perfectly as the most modern and post-modern entry in the subculture.

The State of Things marked the beginning of Wenders' collaboration with the lyrical cinematographer, Henri Aliekan, who photographed the films of Jean Cocteau. His B/W cinematography is less Expressionist than in Wenders's better-known *Wings of Desire*. The compositions are more photographic; they recall the still-photography of Robert Frank. The visual style harkens to the low-contrast, all-gray tones of John Ford's *My Darling Clementine*. Unlike Ford, Wenders uses the gray scale to suggest a universe of slight moral differences. No one in this washed-out world has a better grip on reality, a more effective set of values, or a clearer path to salvation. There's little physical violence in this saga. The characters are perfectly capable of destroying themselves. They don't need anyone's help to do the job.

Gathering a cast of eccentrics (Warhol actress Viva, auteur Samuel Fuller, Paul Getty, Allen Goorwitz), Wenders shot half his story in Lisbon and then returned to L.A. for the finale. Seminal independent/trash film producer-director Roger Corman plays a flint-hearted studio executive, and Allen Goorwitz (née Garfield) should have won an Oscar for his portrayal of a failed producer fleeing loan sharks.

Hiding from pursuing hit men, the "director" and the "producer" cruise L.A. all night in a borrowed Winnebago. As they ride, Wenders's doppelgänger sits in silence while Goorwitz's character talks endlessly about the film business. Though an eerie, unnamable tension suffuses the entire picture, this all-night ride, this chase scene without a chase, is as claustrophobic as any in noir. Wenders's alter ego finds himself not in the happy state of remove he prefers—making movies—but in the horrible dislocated condition of a man pursuing money in America. Wenders makes it clear that this is a dangerous position to be in.

Wenders has seldom been as insightful, as compact, or as assured. *The State of Things*, though demanding in the usual Wenders way—slow and not well-explained—has a fierce uplifting quality. There's genius in Wenders' patient building of the story and in his deep appreciation for the beauty of the world as it appears in B/W.

Other recommended rentals directed by Wim Wenders:
Alice in the Cities
The American Friend (page 31)
Lightning over Water
Paris, Texas
Wings of Desire

The Stranger (1946—USA)

Mood Guide: Small-town hypocrisy and hysteria

Director: Orson Welles; *Camera:* Russell Metty; *Screenplay:* Anthony Veiller, John Huston, Orson Welles

Cast: Edward G. Robinson, Orson Welles, Loretta Young, Billy House

In English; B/W

Plot: A postwar Nazi hunter tracks a concentration camp mastermind to a bucolic New England town. There, the Nazi has hunkered down; he's a schoolteacher about to marry the prettiest girl in town. The Nazi hunter must unmask his quarry, solve a murder, and keep the Nazi from killing his lovely new bride.

Unfairly dismissed as Welles' most mainstream picture, *The Stranger* is his third film, made to convince the studios that Welles could deliver a conventional commercial script. Though more straightforward than Welles' masterpieces, it still offers plenty of hysteria, paranoia, and hidden identities as well as a truly warped gothic ending. The climax is played over ten straight minutes of night-for-night high-contrast, so make sure you get a good rental print. A poor one will turn everything into a big shadowy mess.

Edward G. Robinson plays a cold-blooded Nazi hunter. He lets a little Nazi escape in hopes of catching a bigger one, a genocidal commander played with matinee idol charm by Welles. Welles' character, who escaped Germany at war's end, has woven himself a hiding place deep in the fabric of American life. He's a schoolteacher in a postcard-perfect New England town, about to marry the daughter of a Supreme Court Justice. The daughter is played as overcivilized and highly strung by an actress riven with those qualities, Loretta Young.

Welles dramatizes the unreal nature of the town when a shot of a postcard melts into the town itself. Though first presented as the apogee of propriety, the town proves a hotbed of corrosive hypocrisy and unspoken malevolence. The kindly shopkeeper incarnates repressive small-town conformism; he's a miserly fussbudget and a cheat. Young's upright younger brother happily turns informer. The neighbors who welcomed the Nazi later cheer his grisly demise. Thus, Welles' character serves as a metaphor for the postwar corrupting darkness that everyone refuses to see. His character also represents the Devil as presented in many New England tales: the smooth seductive stranger who must be cast from the community to restore it to goodness.

Most traumatized by that casting out is Loretta Young, who plays Welles' wife. The slowly unveiled truth about her beloved drives her mad. First refusing to believe that her new husband could be such a monster (the failure of love to sanctify evil), Young then tells Welles that she doesn't care, she will stand by him no matter what (the crippling dependence of love). She's the classic noir innocent bystander transformed by fate into a victim.

Finally, abused and abandoned by all the men in her life (her husband wants to kill her; her father is willing to let her get killed; her brother spies on her; the external authority figure, Robinson, puts her into harm's way), Young rises up and provides her own empowering solution.

The hysterical collapse of Young's perfect little life is Welles's commentary on the fragility of any sanctuary. But it's also coscreenwriter John Huston's typically unsympathetic rendition of the feminine psyche; his women characters exist only at the poles of slavish devotion and overwrought revenge. The more human middle ground eludes him.

Similarly, the more metaphorical aspects of Young's plight may well elude viewers who find her instant melodramatics less than credible. Another weakening factor is the speed with which Welles abandons his smooth, hard-won personal and unleashes the vile murderer within. Despite these problems, the mood of imminent anarchy holds. The rapid, overlapping dialogue, Robinson's somber characterization, and Welles's inventive visual and narrative solutions to every plot problem (he was Orson Welles, after all) make *The Stranger* compelling beyond its flaws.

Dislocating but also compelling are the continuous warring contradictions between Welles's earnest attempt to make a commercial movie and his ornate impulses to utterly sabotage his own efforts.

Other recommended rentals directed by Orson Welles:

Citizen Kane
The Magnificent Ambersons
Touch of Evil (page 258)

Sunset Boulevard (1950—USA)

Mood Guide: Hollywood and its discontents

Director: Billy Wilder; *Camera:* John F. Seitz; *Screenplay:* Billy Wilder, Charles Brackett, D. M. Marshman, Jr.

Cast: Gloria Swanson, William Holden, Erich von Stroheim, Nancy Olson, Jack Webb, Cecil B. DeMille

In English; B/W

Plot: Fleeing his creditors, a down-and-out screenwriter stumbles into the Hollywood mansion of a long-forgotten silent movie star. He agrees to edit her screenplay, but becomes romantically involved and financially dependent. When he seeks to return to real life, he discovers just how powerful her fantasy has become.

In the opening shot, William Holden's voice-over establishes his character as: 1) the cynical commentator on the action to come; 2) the victim of that action; 3) the femme fatale; and 4) dead. Holden floats motionless in a swimming pool, telling us his tale in flashbacks from beyond the grave. Billy Wilder thus immediately sets a rather high standard for heartlessness, black humor, and adventurous story-telling technique.

ARCHIVE PHOTOS

William Holden and Erich von Stroheim in *Sunset Boulevard*

Holden plays a failed, glib screenwriter. Escaping his creditors, he hides in the garage of what he mistakes for an abandoned mansion. Turns out the house is occupied by a faded movie star, Gloria Swanson, and her faithful, deadpan servant, played by silent-era director Erich von Stroheim. (Where today could you find stars of this magnitude willing to mock themselves so shamelessly?) Holden has no money; Swanson has a deranged, endless screenplay in need of editing. Holden moves into the garage, but slowly succumbs to Swanson's advances (and her generosity). With von Stroheim as a constant, silent observer, Holden moves into the house and Swanson's arms.

Their love scenes are indescribably creepy. Swanson clings to Holden with her long, sharp nails as Holden fights to keep the disgust from his face. As the femme fatale, Holden's good looks allow him to seduce himself into a situation his financial ruin prevents him from escaping. He's not wholly untouched; he develops a certain distant affection for Swanson, though her lavish life occasionally repels him. His illusion, like many femmes fatales before him, is that he regards his current situation as aberrant to his true nature rather than as the inevitable product of it.

Swanson's life bores Holden to tears. In a mind-blowing joke sequence, Wilder presents Swanson's weekly night of bridge with other faded stars. Her guests include Buster Keaton and Douglas Fairbanks, Jr. Holden escapes Swanson's clutches and attends a party hosted by Jack Webb. There, he meets Nancy Olson, and they fall in love. Holden sneaks away from Swanson to meet Nancy and collaborate on a screenplay. Holden regards Nancy and their work together as his salvation.

Wilder presents Holden as remarkably feminized in his powerlessness: Holden holds illicit assignations with a lover he admires for her independence and creative spirit. These scenes also provide Wilder's biting commentary on the Hollywood writer's fate: Doesn't every writer sneak resentfully away from their commercial hackwork to pursue the one project they just *know* to be art?

Swanson, meanwhile, is convinced that Cecil B. DeMille wants to film her screenplay with her in the starring role. As Swanson becomes increasingly unhinged, she learns of Holden's affair. Inviting Nancy to her mansion, Swanson reveals Holden as the gigolo he is.

Holden finds himself no more than amused by Nancy's shocked reaction. He's strangely relieved that the one person who believes in him finally understands just how thoroughly corrupt and worthless he really is. Holden experiences noir's revelatory moment: Nancy's horrified face is the mirror that reveals himself to himself without delusion. Again, Wilder inverts the gender conventions of noir; it's usually the trusting guy who learns that his lady love is the tramp. And usually it's the lady love who revels in transcendent truth of her discovery/ruin.

Holden understands that his sloth, self-delusion, and indifference to his own talents have led to his destruction. Like everyone else in noir, Holden cannot escape the consequences of his nature.

Jettisoning one delusion for another, Holden decides that his soul is not wholly bankrupt, that he can change if only he had the pure, cleansing love that Nancy Olson might provide. He chases after her, but Swanson, outraged and heartbroken, shoots him down. (I'm not giving anything away here, the movie starts with him dead in the pool, remember?)

Whether Wilder redeems his Old Testament view of man's nature, his contempt for all vanity and ambition, his too-clear understanding of the Darwinian swamp that *is* the movie business, and his laughing at noir to make great noir depends entirely on whether you find the willful, sophisticated bleakness of Wilder's vision as funny as he does.

Other recommended rentals directed by Billy Wilder:

Ace in the Hole (*aka The Big Carnival*)
Double Indemnity (page 107)
Sabrina
Witness for the Prosecution

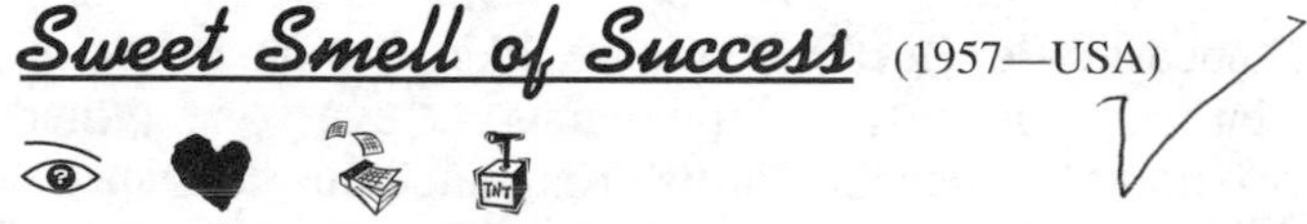

Sweet Smell of Success (1957—USA)

Mood Guide: Mean-spirited urban morality tale

Director: Alexander Mackendrick; *Camera:* James Wong Howe; *Screenplay:* Clifford Odets

Cast: Burt Lancaster, Tony Curtis, Susan Harrison, Martin Milner

In English; B/W

Plot: The most powerful gossip columnist in America runs Manhattan nightlife with an iron fist, using a flunky who will do anything he says. Together they chase glitz and ruin lives. The columnist wants the flunky to do one more evil favor. If he can't, all his hustling will be for naught.

Playwright Clifford Odets didn't indict society with this screenplay, he burned it to the ground. The story concerns a purely American ambition and renders the components of such—ass-kissing, corruption, betrayal, lost love, doomed good deeds—in avid detail. Yet, for all of Odets's meanness of spirit, the film is no morality tract. Its characters are eagerly evil, jovial in their viciousness; their enthusiasm for the depravity of their lives is never subsumed to anything so corny as a "message."

Burt Lancaster plays a ruthless, omnipotent gossip columnist in New York City. Lancaster's shamelessly ambitious assistant, played by Tony Curtis in the performance of his lifetime, will do anything to curry favor with Lancaster.

Lancaster holds court in a New York nightclub while Curtis scrambles around the nighttime city, wrecking reputations, lying, and wheedling, all on Burt's behalf. Lancaster assigns Curtis the odious task of derailing the current romance of Lancaster's psychologically frail younger sister. Lancaster is obsessed with keeping his sister's love to himself; he'd rather destroy her than let her become an adult. Lancaster's repressed incestuous urges seem even creepier because his character's lust is so unconscious, so masked in fatherly well-meaning. In the carrying out of Burt's assignment, Curtis finds himself smitten by the urge to do a good deed. If he succumbs, Burt will make him pay.

The story moves quickly. The self-revealing, sexually laden dialogue (Lancaster to Curtis: "You're like a cookie full of arsenic.") emerges in furtive little bursts as everyone either whispers or shouts. Lancaster shifts from unctuous to vicious in an eye-blink. Odets parses New York's never-mentioned but ironclad class system; he notes the tiny snubs that can shatter twenty years of social climbing.

The cinematography by American legend James Wong Howe combines typically classic composition with a gritty, on-location edge. For Howe, the dark city offers no shortage of visual metaphors. The shadow lines that fall across Lancaster's face are sharp enough to shave with, and never have the pools of light thrown by streetlamps promised such salvation, or the inky darkness around them such despair.

This either/or world is tinged by tragedy, as Lancaster and Curtis play out an intense Oedipal competition, both striving for the adoration of Lancaster's sister. Odets presents these themes with a blithe straightforwardness, as if daring the censors to admit that they recognized the archetypal struggles underlying it. Adding to the amorality is that Odets makes it clear that corruption allows his characters to achieve their goals of money, sex, and public recognition. For Odets, achieving these goals demands the sale of one's soul.

It's practically a Scorsese picture, with its merciless, classically derived themes, after-hours netherworld, and neorealist dialogue. As in *Casino* and *Mean Streets*, the characters move through a shabby, barbarous, self-contained universe. As in Scorcese's best work, the characters are so compelling that their flaws do not diminish our interest. They sustain it.

It's a nervy piece of work: complex, adult, and spiteful.

T-Men (1948—USA)

Mood Guide: Overwrought documentary-style *policier*

Director: Anthony Mann; *Camera:* John Alton; *Screenplay:* John C. Higgins

Cast: Dennis O'Keefe, Mary Meade, Wallace Ford, Alfred Ryder, June Lockhart

In English; B/W

Plot: Two Treasury agents infiltrate a vicious ring of counterfeiters. After months of building their cover story, one has a chance encounter with his wife in the presence of the gang. That agent makes the ultimate sacrifice, but the other sticks to his charade at the cost of his marriage, his sanity, and, maybe, his life.

The Anthony Mann conundrum: If his movies are so damn important, why are they so hard to sit through?

Two Treasury agents are assigned to infiltrate a gang of counterfeiters. They speak in monosyllabic grunts until they change out of their drab cop clothes and into fancy criminal silk suits and wide ties. Then they speak in ludicrous comic book jargon.

With their change of clothes, they've changed identities. Except they're exactly the same dullards they were before.

With cartoonish ease, the cops join the gang. One particularly psychotic crook suspects them. When one of the cops gets nervous just before a heist, the psycho says to him: "What's the matter? Got the whim-whams?" That's about as realistic as the dialogue gets.

ARCHIVE PHOTOS

In their zeal, the cops turn their backs on normality and become criminals. The married cop, while in the company of the counterfeiting gang, runs into his sweet-faced wife, played by June Lockhart. He pretends not to know her. Her friend keeps insisting that he's Lockhart's husband. When the cop finally gets away, his cover is irrevocably blown. Mann closes the sequence with a close-up of June Lockhart teary-eyed with pride, overcome that her husband is dedicated enough to ignore her.

The perversity of the gulf between the apparent message ("What a man!") and the underlying message ("Look at the mess this guy made of his life in the name of duty!") lies at the heart of Mann's appeal to film scholars. Such a contradiction should be fascinating. And it might, if this weren't an Anthony Mann picture. The guy's a real enigma.

Are Mann's simpleminded plots, high-school acting, and plodding pace only vehicles for his bizarre but sincere subtextural messages? Those messages include men's virtually sexual attachment to duty; the criminal mentality dormant in every cop; reductive characterizations that suggest the absence of depth in any modern man; and an abandonment of middle-class values by the most valiant defenders of those values—cops.

Scholars point out how Mann's subtext completely subverts the "plot," and they argue (correctly) that in noir, style carries the meaning. But they never mention how tedious Mann's noirs can be. In *T-Men* the subtext does not justify the leaden pacing and stupid mock-tough dialogue. John Alton's cinematography, however, makes up for every boring, silly, or pretentious moment.

Alton here defines the subculture with his weird angles, alienated placement of figures in relation to one another, cutting shadows, and constant inventiveness. He shoots double reflections, jams three faces tight into the camera or sets two black silhouettes against rising white jets of steam. Ignoring the idiotic story, Alton creates the tone. And that tone is all or nothing, life or death, black or white, good or evil, salvation or damnation.

For noir scholars, for the curious, and for those who enjoy the emotional power of pure image.

Other recommended rentals directed by Anthony Mann:

Border Incident
The Furies
Raw Deal (page 216)

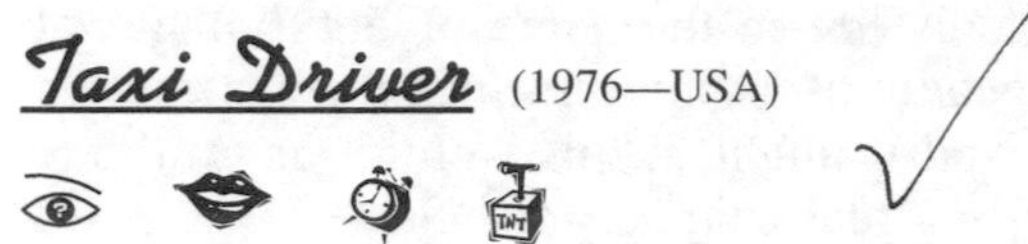

Taxi Driver (1976—USA)

Mood Guide: American psychosis

Director: Martin Scorsese; *Camera:* Michael Chapman; *Screenplay:* Paul Schrader

Cast: Robert De Niro, Albert Brooks, Jodie Foster, Harvey Keitel, Cybill Shepherd, Peter Boyle

In English; color

Plot: A disaffected veteran who cannot sleep takes up taxi driving through the nighttime city. But the city repels him and magnifies his alienation. He fixates on a lovely blonde who's way out of his class. Her rejection fuels his growing need for violence. He determines to save a young whore from her pimp, no matter what the cost.

This is the most subjective screenplay in noir, told from the protagonist's increasingly disturbed point of view. Scorsese made obsolete the old forms of noir narrative and thrust the audience into the mind of his protagonist with an intimacy never seen before. In fact, Scorsese created the dividing line between the abandoned classical period and (the more self-conscious) neo-noir with a single shot: a sinister, twisting zoom down into Robert De Niro's bubbling glass of Alka-Seltzer.

The bizarre zoom represents De Niro's point of view both literally (he stares into the glass) and psychologically: As the water churns, De Niro enters a fugue state. Ignoring the polite conversation around him, he fixates on the blue bubbles. It's our first hint that De Niro may not be simply disaffected, but insane. It's a moment full of foreboding, terrifying on an instinctual level, and among the most original pieces of foreshadowing ever created. The shot makes clear just how vested in De Niro's outlook the film's will be.

It's also Schrader's/Scorsese's way of telling us that for the subject of this tale, the world functions as a collection of symbols, signs, and inexplicable phenomena. By forcing us to decipher De Niro's neurotic codes, the screenplay makes us pay unusually close attention. But it also enables us to empathize with every new disappointment that befalls De Niro, who would otherwise generate little empathy.

On the rare occasion that Scorsese moves outside De Niro, it's to show us how De Niro views himself in the world. His cab cuts through the cold city fog, or is submerged in a blast of water. The rushing spray is momentarily soothing, then entrapping. De Niro hits the wipers, and the moment is past. Cocooned against a world he experiences at a crippling distance, De Niro uses his cab as his only conduit to human contact and as his protection against it.

In the manner of frustrated, dislocated Americans everywhere, he turns—with psychotic, religious fervor—to pornography, guns, solitary TV watching, and physical fitness. As Scorsese's commentary on the early noir hero's tendencies to fall for regal blondes, De Niro works up an attachment to the ultimate unattainable blonde fantasy: a slightly ditzy, tough-minded campaign worker played with uncharacteristic subtlety by Cybill Sheperd. Scorsese makes good use of Sheperd's irritating, innate, prom-queen arrogance. She's a worthy object of desire and contempt.

Unable to conceal his self-loathing or control his self-destructive impulses, De Niro takes this sheltered, self-important child of the suburbs to a sleazy porno house on their first date. She bolts, leaving De Niro ashamed and alone once more. Recognizing that he cannot socialize up the class ladder, he moves down, fixating on a new blonde, a thirteen-year-old street whore played with heroic clarity by Jodie Foster. De Niro cannot save himself, but he determines to rescue Jodie and he certainly possesses the arsenal for the job.

In one of the most raw, famously graphic, and disturbingly violent sequences in cinema history (which is also, astoundingly, among the least exploitative), De Niro kills Foster's pimp, a floor manager in the hooker hotel, and tries to kill himself. His rampage, shot as real, anti-glamorous, and horrible, plays in yellowy, muted colors and deranged jump-cuts that suggest De Niro's ragged perception of the forces he has unleashed. The strange colors actually come from problems with the ratings board. Scorsese did not want to downplay the graphic violence, so he agreed to make the red blood less vivid. The hallucinatory tones add fuel to the nightmarish sequence and place us vividly into De Niro's deranged mind-set.

And in the end, what catharsis has De Niro achieved? He sought those two big-time American goals: transcendence through violence, and transformation of self, yet the aftermath suggests that both eluded him, somehow.

Thus, where *Kiss Me Deadly* (page 151) closes with an apocalypse of finality, Schrader and Scorsese espouse a more solipsistic, less political, and profoundly renewable end of the world.

So many key noir themes are expressed here: the destructive power of obsession, the alienation inherent in modern urban life, the impossibility of enduring human connection, and the torments of one lost soul suffering on the edges of society. Bernard Herrmann's unsettling score sets the tone, and, in keeping with the noir tradition, the script offers many great character parts. Among the best are Albert Brooks; Steven Prince as a streetwise gun dealer; and Scorsese himself as a cuckolded husband who shares his violent fantasies with De Niro.

Other recommended rentals directed by Martin Scorsese:

GoodFellas
Mean Streets
New York, New York
Raging Bull

Other recommended rentals written and/or directed by Paul Schrader:

Blue Collar
The Comfort of Strangers
Hardcore
Light of Day
Light Sleeper
Patty Hearst
The Yakuza (screenwriter only)

BARSON COLLECTION/ARCHIVE PHOTOS

They Live By Night (1948—USA)

Mood Guide: Overwrought love on the run

Director: Nicholas Ray; *Camera:* George E. Diskant; *Screenplay:* Charles Schnee

Cast: Farley Granger, Cathy O'Donnell, Howard da Silva, Helen Craig

In English; B/W

Plot: A naive kid breaks out of prison with two tough cons. He meets his soul mate and tries to live right, but the cons drag him back into the world of crime.

Nicholas Ray opens his debut picture with one of the first helicopter shots in cinema. Ray's hovering camera frantically chases a car carrying three escaped cons: smooth-cheeked innocent Bowie (Farley Granger), and tough, hardened crime vets T-Dub and Chickamaw. Bowie falls for Keechie (Cathy O'Donnell), the daughter of a man who helps the cons escape.

Ray introduces his hero and heroine with a written sentence on the screen: "This boy and this girl were never properly introduced to the world we live in." If that line seems melodramatic and over the top, just wait.

Bowie has violence in him and tries to suppress it. Keechie's so naive and loving, it hurts. Together, they make a noble primitive couple as Ray contrasts their uncorrupted, childlike natures with the money-grubbing society all around them. Too unsophisticated to do anything but love each other like illiterate little Bambis, Bowie and Keechie are due for some harsh lessons.

Chickamaw has little patience with their sweetness. Howard Da Silva, who plays silky, uptown villains in other noir films, presents Chickamaw as a subhuman beast. Ray's framing makes his terrifying, outsized physicality all the more oppressive. Chickamaw dominates all interior compositions—horizontal visual lines radiate out from Chickamaw, all paths lead to him. In a signature sequence, Chickamaw crushes Keechie's beloved Christmas ornaments as a warning to the couple: Criminals they are, and criminals they will stay. There is no place in Chickamaw's life for anything as sincere as Christmas.

In this dysfunctional family, Keechie and Bowie are the innocent kids, and Chickamaw, the abusive father. The love he sees between Keechie and Bowie only reminds Chickamaw of his own misspent life. Meanwhile, Bowie fails to comprehend the level of Chickamaw's hatred. Bowie tries to protect and support Keechie as a man should, but he lacks the moral strength or attention span to do things right. Although Keechie sees the proper path, she hasn't the authority to make Bowie walk it.

Ray, an intellectual and artist, loved to portray himself as a man driven by uncontrollable passions. His florid romanticism and refusal to let a subtle moment pass without firing a twenty-one-gun salute add to the wearying air of frenzy and hysteria. His worthy impulses are often inseparable from his carny shamelessness;

trying to tell one from the other is tiring. The picture further suffers from a preachy air, as if Ray felt himself the only person capable of reminding his audience that the lower classes have their share of saints and profundity, too. While the directorial vision is passionate, brilliant, and technically revolutionary, the directorial voice is strident, self-congratulatory, and off-putting.

The backbone of the noir subculture are films that deliberately submerge their critical themes within a pop-entertainment plot, thus supplying art *and* kicks. Ray reverses the equation, playing his themes as the main point of the film and the whammies as mere incidentals. Sadly, this is another classic and scholar's favorite that has become increasingly difficult to watch. It's the only Ray film that seems dated.

Other recommended rentals directed by Nicholas Ray:
Bigger Than Life
Johnny Guitar
In a Lonely Place (page 137)

They Won't Believe Me (1947—USA)

Mood Guide: Gripping, understated suspense

Director: Irving Pichel; *Camera:* Harry J. Wild; *Screenplay:* Jonathan Latimer

Cast: Robert Young, Susan Hayward, Jane Greer, Rita Johnson, Tom Powers

In English; B/W

Plot: A gold-digging playboy wants his wife's money and his girlfriend's affection. When fate deals him an easy way out, he jumps at the chance. Will the law catch on, or can he be saved by divulging the horrible truth?

This is a true hidden gem: a well-written, accessible suspense thriller, with the unusual casting of Robert Young as a money-grubbing, weak-willed Romeo. It's the nastiest role he ever played.

Young's rich wife discovers his unconsummated but intense affair with Jane Greer. Young promises Greer he'll leave his wife, but Young's wife bribes him with a new life Out West. So, Young dumps Greer without a backward glance. After a few faithful months, Young falls again, this time for a very young, lovely, and seductive Susan Hayward. She's ripe as a peach, with glowing skin and none of the hardness that marks her later roles. Susan appears to be the femme fatale, but it turns out she really loves Young, miserable louse that he is.

RKO PICTURES/ARCHIVE PHOTOS

Robert Young and Rita Johnson in *They Won't Believe Me*

A tragic accident provides Young with a way out of all his romantic dilemmas that also satisfies his greed. He takes a chance, but becomes haunted by his sordid past. The film presents the story in classic flashback, but with a suspense-making twist. Young tells his own story from the stand while on trial for murder. Young confesses his contemptible nature, and several rather cold-blooded acts, but pleads his innocence of murder.

Young makes a clean breast of his own rotten nature. It's clear he never before fully understood how selfish and destructive his feckless habits had become. As he describes his greed and inability to love, he creates the noir universe of solipsism, missed connections, cruel fate, and inevitable hard dues. In an amusing switch, Young also proves himself to be the femme fatale. His restless seducing, his lust for money, his basic untrustworthy nature, his ability to break hearts without remorse and, most critically, his inability to live without a woman's attention cause all his problems.

And, in the end, it's his self-indulgence that once more leads to his doom.

Young's self-evisceration adds the necessary emotional underpinning to the story, which tears along with never a flat section or unconvincing scene. The only unfortunate moments derive from an overly literary, descriptive voice-over and from the visual distraction of Young's stylish ties and their perfect knots, which seem to occupy center frame in every one of his close-ups.

Though photographed with competence and plot-serving simplicity, no metaphorical profundities emerge from the visuals or the story. Even so, *They Won't Believe Me* remains inventive, gripping, and unfairly underrated.

Thief (1981—USA)

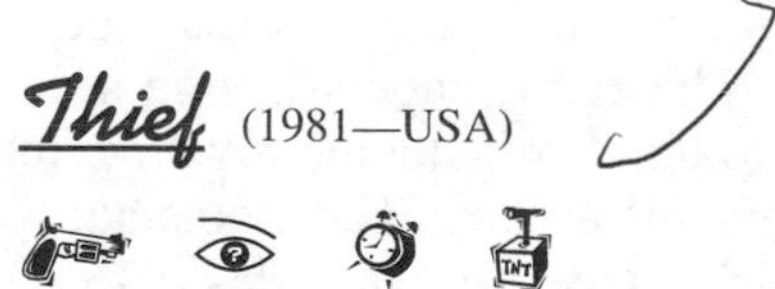

Mood Guide: Riveting monosyllabic modern noir

Director: Michael Mann; *Camera:* David Thorin; *Screenplay:* Michael Mann

Cast: James Caan, Tuesday Weld, James Belushi, Robert Prosky, Willie Nelson

In English; color

Plot: A solitary jewel thief is offered partnership by the mob. He joins them to build his new life, with a new wife and an adopted child. But the mob doesn't care for freelancers, and the thief must relearn how to survive on his own.

Only once did Michael Mann (*The Last of the Mohicans*, *Heat*) put a lid on the compulsive mythmaking that makes his later work so overblown. Only once did he understate, and when he did, a classic emerged.

James Caan, a jewel thief—and a living, breathing, cool-guy metaphor for the outlaw/artist in society—makes the classic artist-guy mistake of trading his freelance ways for the illusion of security. Way more security than he prefers, compliments of his new partners, the Mob. Caan discovers that once having compromised in order to join, he must be absolutely uncompromising—that is, he must kill people—to escape. The (criminal) corporate world is a nasty place for the artist willing to defend his art.

The artist-metaphorical stuff does not dilute the pure Americanness of Mann's vision, and nobody's more American than he—remember *Crime Story*? While wrestling with his artist's dilemma, Caan strives to create a home life with Tuesday Weld (American corrupted innocence incarnate), to get his mentor, Willie Nelson (American integrity incarnate), out of jail and to pull off the most compelling, most gear-intensive safecracking (American ingenuity incarnate) in movie history.

Caan's *Thief* is as American as can be: He distrusts language, derives his identity from his work, and has a chip on his shoulder the size of Mount Rushmore. The crime capers feature sexy high-tech tools/techniques, and Mann loves them, reveling in their *Popular Mechanics*/do-it-yourself aspects. He shoots adoring close-ups of every tool, which, naturally, includes a bevy of sexy side arms. He follows a lock-breaking device into the lock itself in that rarest of moments: a shot never before attempted. It's a measure of Mann's visual inventiveness, and of his determination that every frame be compelling.

Mann tamps down the story's emotions. Everyone seems under intense pressure from within. Characters speak in oblique references, using an almost impenetrable street slang. The mood starts out claustrophobic, and the options get chipped away one by one. Something has to give. That something turns out to be

Caan's notions of the Good Life. His fantasies of merging freedom and security go to hell, and Caan follows them.

Caan both underplays and, for the only time in his career, acts. Willie Nelson's role is brief, but iconic. Tuesday Weld, impossibly beautiful and remote, stifles the bitchy undercurrent that mars her later work, and even James Belushi justifies his presence. Mann got everyone to do their best work and, in so doing, did his own.

Stylish (streetlights reflected in gleaming car hoods), moody (late-night, rain-slick streets), trendy in the best possible way (a hypnotic, pulsating score from Tangerine Dream), nice explosions, guns galore, ex-cops as character actors, and plenty of bitchin' Armani—albeit circa 1980—on everybody, even the sleazy cops.

Other recommended rentals directed by Michael Mann:
Heat
The Last of the Mohicans
Manhunter

The Third Man (1948—England)

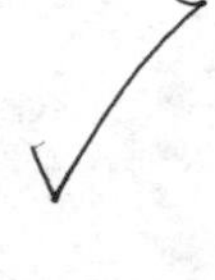

Mood Guide: Witty thriller of moral decadence

Director: Carol Reed; *Camera:* Robert Krasker; *Screenplay:* Graham Greene

Cast: Orson Welles, Joseph Cotten, Trevor Howard, Alida Valli

In English; B/W

Plot: An American writer comes to post-war Vienna to meet his friend. But his friend's been murdered . . . or has he? Intrigue and broken hearts abound.

Joseph Cotten flies into post-war Vienna, drawn by a telegram from his old pal Harry Lime, played as the avatar of cynical bemusement by Orson Welles. When he arrives, he's told that Orson's been killed in a hit-and-run. So, Cotten is stuck in Vienna without money or prospects. An urbane military policeman—Trevor Howard, as the last outpost of civilized, upper-class disdain—offers to fly Cotten home, but Cotten gets a glimpse of Orson Welles's girlfriend, Alida Valli. Smitten, Cotton decides to stay, the better to investigate his old pal's death. The girl, grief-stricken over Orson, barely notices him. But, like all Americans abroad, Cotten's a romantic fool who must get in over his head to be disabused of his romantic notions.

ARCHIVE PHOTOS

Orsen Welles in *The Third Man*

By way of bumbling persistence, he untangles a web of smugglers and murderers who operate with a genial but charming Old World savagery. They tolerate his meddling, and eventually he discovers what everybody knew about his old pal, except him. Orson appears, and recruits Cotten for the new world order. Cotten isn't interested and, after some soul-searching, sells Orson out to the military police. While he disapproves of Welles' smuggling, Cotten turns Judas to protect Orson's girl from arrest. When she discovers Cotten's motives, she warns Orson, thereby dooming herself.

Though it offers little overt spiritual or psychological content (save some crushing insights into the stupidity of love), *The Third Man* delivers a very Greeneian message on the necessity of developing a functional, flexible morality to deal with the destruction of prewar values. The result is a perfect story, perfectly told. The visual style precisely suits the narrative; each actor occupies precisely the space on screen that his character occupies in the story, and the wacky Anton Karas zither music comments on the action with the cunning of the insane.

It's a morality tale, an amusing anecdote, a brokenhearted essay on the limits of friendship and the impossibility of love, and a rather nasty postwar European assault on all those well-meaning Henry James American do-gooders wandering around the wreckage of a civilization far too sophisticated for them to understand and too dangerous for them to survive. Featuring two famous set-pieces—Welles's harsh conversation with Cotten on a Ferris wheel, and Welles's doomed race through the Vienna sewer system—*The Third Man* also ends with the single most eloquent, heartbreaking, closing sequence in cinema.

The legends abound: Did Greene and Welles crack semi-hack director Carol Reed like a walnut between them, or did they inspire him to his greatest glory? Was it Reed or Greene who resisted producer David Selznick's demand that Noel Coward play the Orson Welles role? And was it really Reed who discovered the incredible zither player, Anton Karas, in a Vienna sausage bar and then insisted on using Karas's sprightly tune as the ironic counterpoint for all the misery this tale uncovers?

As for the question of who really directed what: Reed's slanty camera angles, ironic music, bravura lighting, and operatic exterior locations do seem mighty Wellesian, and Welles's performance is phenomenal—relaxed, scurrilous, self-knowing, and absolutely dominant. Like his character, Welles controls the action even when offscreen.

And, as Greene said, *The Third Man* is ultimately what movies are all about: entertainment. There's entertainment for those literate in film, art, literature, and politics, and for the moronic action/thrills movie-junkie. *The Third Man* remains necessary proof that entertainment created with a scrupulous eye to character, an adamant lack of sentimentality (and that includes none of sentimentality's flip side—easy cynicism), devotion to narrative detail, and the absence of pretension can become something even greater: art.

Only the dream alliance of Orson Welles and Graham Greene could create a tale this profound, universal, personal, funny, and mean-spirited, and still tell it in such a relaxed, civilized, and amusing manner.

Other recommended rentals directed by Carol Reed:
Odd Man Out

This Gun for Hire (1942—USA)

Mood Guide: Moody, slightly comic chase

Director: Frank Tuttle; *Camera:* John Seitz; *Screenplay:* Albert Maltz, W. R. Burnett

Cast: Alan Ladd, Veronica Lake, Laird Cregar, Robert Preston

In English; B/W

Plot: A hit-man is engaged by a Nazi agent to whack a pair of recalcitrant spies. Seeking to get rid of him after the job is done, the agent pays the hit-man with stolen, marked money. The cops chase the hit-man, who chases his dishonest client. In the midst of the chase, the hit-man becomes entangled with a young girl who may be his angel or his grim reaper.

Ladd plays Raven, a psycho, a professional hit man who murders to satisfy the bitterness he feels because his mother abused him (Freudian motivation alert!). He whacks out a guy on behalf of Laird Cregar, who plays early-noir archetype—the oversized, soft-spoken villain with the palette of an urban sophisticate and the implied sexual preferences of a degenerate. Cregar's manners and methods make him less than a manly man (think Peter Lorre, only big and fat). He chooses refinement over action, and so loses the moral high ground to Raven.

Raven may be a killer, but he takes responsibility for his actions and creates his own sins. Cregar hires folks to do his dirty work and then welshes on the deal.

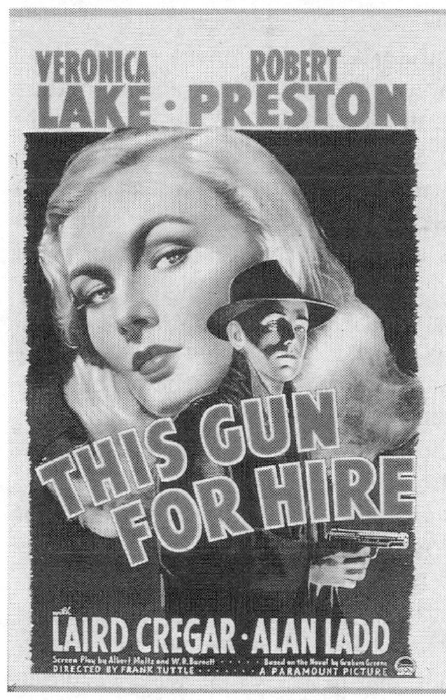

ARCHIVE PHOTOS

Cregar double-crosses Ladd by paying him with stolen, easily traceable money. Ladd spends the first bill and is transformed into a fugitive. Raven prizes his anonymity, and so being identified—his photo fills the front page of every paper—is as emotionally painful as being on the run. His sympathetic aspects are clear to Veronica Lake, who befriends Raven as he rides the train to L.A. in pursuit of Cregar. Unaware that Lake is the girlfriend of the cop tracking him, Ladd confides in her and accepts her help.

Unfortunately for Ladd, he doesn't know that Lake is a government agent who's also after Cregar. Raven is thus twice-betrayed by those he mistakenly trusted. Lake creates another early noir type—the woman who is both redeemer (when she allows her emotions to rule) and femme fatale (when she behaves as duty demands). Later femmes fatales would reverse her motivations.

While the cynicism of Graham Greene's novel (*A Gun for Sale*) has been muted to the point of invisibility, Ladd embodies it all on his own. His performance is a star-making wonder. He plays a man too wounded to show emotion, and so shows far more than he realizes. His still face seems to gather light, to demand our attention. Because Ladd is more a movie star than a convincing actor, it's to his advantage that his character is so undemonstrative.

His vicious killer with a wounded heart is very noir. And it produces a very noir side effect: Lake's straight-arrow cop boyfriend, the ostensive hero, seems boring and unpoetic when contrasted to the cold-blooded, sensitive killer. The romanticization of evil and the glamorous allure of villainy key to noir gets an early and seductive presentation.

John Seitz's camera work is also seminal. He blasts great shafts of shadow and light down upon his star's faces, but his magnum opus is a baffling search through a fog-shrouded factory. As the cops scurry to and fro, Ladd slips away among the fantastical, dreamlike, industrial shapes. It's another key early-noir moment, as the inanimate world is vested with Freudian magical power, and the villain escapes through the moral ambiguity of the obscuring fog.

While the story might seem downright silly, and the propaganda badly dated, Seitz's moody cinematography and Alan Ladd's performance combine to qualify *This Gun* as important, if simpleminded, noir.

To Live and Die in L.A. (1985—USA)

Mood Guide: Sexy cops and cool counterfeiters

Director: William Friedkin; *Camera:* Robby Müller; *Screenplay:* William Friedkin, Gerald Petrivich

Cast: William Petersen, Willem Dafoe, Debra Feuer, John Pankow, John Turturro, Darlanne Fluegel

In English; color

Plot: A dangerously macho cop tracks a murderous counterfeiter. The cop seeks revenge for his slain partner, while the counterfeiter's only protecting his turf and looking for thrills. As the cop grows obsessed with revenge, he crosses the line into lawlessness.

Friedkin's *The French Connection* may be a great picture, but it remains a straight-up *policier.* It lacks noir's necessary subtext of dread and existential confusion. Gene Hackman's Popeye Doyle suffers few doubts about his compulsion to catch the French Connection. And without those doubts, he's just another tough cop.

Conversely, *To Live and Die in L.A.* shows how much Friedkin learned about life, cops, and heroes in the fifteen years that separate the two pictures. *To Live . . .* masquerades as a cop thriller, and it delivers the car chases, sex scenes, and shootouts required. But Friedkin's nonstop action illuminates a complex ethical universe, where the cops are criminals and the crooks admirable for their rigorous morality.

An aggressive, uptight, and unself-aware cop (Petersen) goes mad for revenge when his partner is murdered by the first downtown/Bohemian counterfeiter in movie history (Dafoe). Petersen sets out to trap Dafoe, even if it means he has to rob the FBI, threaten his stripper girlfriend with jail, lie to his superiors, and ruin the career of his new partner.

Petersen's all rough edges and random urges, but Dafoe maintains an artist's ironic distance. He's cool; for him, counterfeiting is both a creative act (which places him in the cinematic tradition of poetic criminals) and a search for kicks. Because Dafoe suffers ennui, he uses violence to wake himself up. This adds to his perverse sexiness. Dafoe follows the classic antihero's moral code: He does things his way or dies trying. If this were a Melville picture, he'd be the hero.

Petersen, on the other hand, has no morality. He's result-oriented and cares only about winning. Petersen symbolizes the repressive world of business and can-do guys, with all their sexual brutality, bad clothes, and lethally short attention spans. Thus, Friedkin makes it clear that the outlaw life (when lived with a certain ironic poetry) makes one cool, and that macho conformity drives one insane.

The character parts are acted to perfection. Dean Stockwell seems vastly self-amused playing a corrupt dope attorney, John Turturro shines as a violent hood, and Darlanne Fluegel plays Petersen's stripper girlfriend with just the right level of whiny self-righteousness and greed. Debra Feuer says very little, but her stillness gives her character a subversive profundity. She's also a babe.

Add to this the most breathtaking, complex, and grandiose car chase in movie history; sinister, really hot sex (Friedkin prefers lanky, affectless blondes); neon colors from Wim Wenders's cinematographer, Robby Müller; and a shocking ending, and you've got one of the most inexplicably neglected wonders of the last twenty years.

Other recommended rentals directed by William Friedkin:
The Exorcist
The French Connection
Sorcerer (page 227)

Touch of Evil (1958—USA)

Mood Guide: Orgiastic camerawork and corruption

Director: Orson Welles; *Camera:* Russell Metty; *Screenplay:* Orson Welles

Cast: Orson Welles, Charlton Heston, Janet Leigh, Akim Tamiroff, Marlene Dietrich

In English; B/W

Plot: A reforming Mexican district attorney lands in a border town to investigate a murder and a corrupt sheriff. The sheriff fights back by framing the D.A.'s wife and killing his own gangster ally. The D.A. must save his wife, surmount the entrenched local power structure, and get the sheriff, once and for all.

After the stately mind-warping and brick-by-brick character construction of *The Lady from Shanghai* (page 158), Welles turns to anarchic street-noir. He was slated only to act, but got to direct when Charlton Heston leaned on Warner Brothers to make it so.

ARCHIVE PHOTOS

Orson Welles, Janet Leigh, and Akim Tamiroff in *Touch of Evil*

Heston plays a Mexican-American attorney with a blond bombshell wife, Janet Leigh. He dares to bring her to a hellish border town where he investigates a car bombing and the local corrupt sheriff, played by Welles. The car bombing—presented as the opening credits roll—is revealed by the most difficult, poetic, and mind-blowing tracking shot ever attempted. Welles infuses the noir moving camera with new levels of hysteria and danger, and suggests an end to cinema itself; the shot closes with Welles' name on the screen, and the car blowing sky high.

Heston suspects Welles of faking evidence to get a confession from a poor Mexican accused of the crime. Welles retaliates by ordering a gang of pachucos to abduct Heston's wife. The pachucos, whom Welles grants a menacing sexual ennui, fill Leigh full of marijuana and dump her in a seedy downtown motel. Welles shows up, commits a murder, and leaves Leigh to be framed for it. Heston puts the squeeze on Welles's old partner, and the partner betrays his lifelong protector.

Welles's stubbly, worn-out sheriff hasn't a chance. Heston is the new order: clean-cut, articulate, and completely assimilated. He's a bureaucrat, and can always find a paper solution to a real-world problem. Welles's sheriff spent a lifetime fixing one filthy mess after another. It's no surprise his hands are so unclean.

Welles embraces the sleaziest aspects of noir in all its self-contradicting, grimy glory, and seals the end of the classical period. No film is so passionately ambivalent about good and evil, purpose and pointlessness, duty and corruption, or the constraints of law and the sexiness of anarchy. No measly crime saga could justify such camera movement or bravura cutting precisely timed to that movement. Welles yanks the camera this way and that, shifting from cheesy gothic effects (the shadows cast on a dead man's face by a sputtering neon sign) to moments of sublime beauty (Welles's shadow cast large upon a bridge as he walks through the night).

Every shot is strange and frightening. On first viewing, many are difficult to figure out. Welles's framing is almost Cubist; everyone is presented from myriad angles. Thus Welles makes it clear that that no one possesses a single true self. Everyone, save Leigh, is multilayered and, by definition, corrupted, capable of anything. The sound design, with its shifting volumes, discordant music, and echoing silences, adds to the air of dislocation and sensory anarchy. The world is spinning apart, and the gravity of the entrenched corrupt order will not hold.

In theme and technique, *Touch of Evil* is Welles's most modern picture, and the most shocking for Welles's embrace of his own loss of physical beauty. That is, Welles got fat, which he equates in this picture with a loss of moral compass, so draw your own conclusions about self-hatred.

Suspenseful, filled with wild-ass fifties-type action and, like *Citizen Kane*, with one technical surprise after another. Also, it's the best work Heston ever did. While history has revealed marijuana to be not quite so potent as the film suggests, Marlene Dietrich's turn as an inscrutable gypsy fortune-teller makes up for any flaws.

Only, there aren't any.

Other recommended rentals directed by Orson Welles:

Citizen Kane
The Lady from Shanghai (page 158)
The Magnificent Ambersons
The Stranger (page 232)

Undercurrent (1946—USA)

Mood Guide: Weirdly compelling Freudian romance

Director: Vincente Minnelli; *Camera:* Karl Freund; *Screenplay:* Edward Chodorov

Cast: Katharine Hepburn, Robert Mitchum, Robert Taylor, Edmund Gwenn

In English; B/W

Plot: A spoiled young girl falls for a rich businessman who's strangely obsessed with his supposedly dead brother. But the businessman proves rather shady himself, and Hepburn has visions of a mysterious stranger. When her new husband reveals his true nature, will the brother emerge to save Hepburn from herself?

Katharine Hepburn might seem the least appropriate actress to star in a noir, but here she puts aside her usual tricks to deliver a restrained, affecting performance.

She plays a naive young woman who falls for an industrialist, the ominously slick Robert Taylor. Taylor, an urbane, accomplished daddy-figure, seems obsessed with his long-missing brother, Robert Mitchum. Taylor tells Hepburn that Mitchum committed a murder, that he abandoned the family business, that he hasn't been seen in years. Because Taylor speaks of his brother so often, Hepburn finds herself increasingly curious about him. Taylor takes her curiosity as a betrayal.

ARCHIVE PHOTOS

Katharine Hepburn and Robert Mitchum in *Undercurrent*

He grows insecure and reveals some less than admirable qualities, including a fearsome temper. Hepburn meets a mysterious caretaker on the family estate who warns her about Taylor. Hepburn wants to love Taylor, but he's a childish despot, desperate for constant approval and mean as a snake if it's not instantly forthcoming. As fear replaces love, Hepburn develops a fantasy attachment to the brother she has never met.

In a jarring break of narrative flow, Minnelli presents a meeting between Taylor and Mitchum. Mitchum is revealed as quite different from Taylor's fearful characterization. Mitchum asks only that Taylor speak honestly about his past to Hepburn. If he refuses, Mitchum says, Mitchum will do so himself. Taylor wants to come clean, but old habits die hard. Can he own up to the harsh truth about himself, or will he kill to conceal it?

It's a super-Freudian melodrama, in which the competing men serve as complements to warring aspects of Hepburn's personality. If she misdirects her love, her life may be in jeopardy. This is Minnelli's literal metaphor for (what he perceives to be) every woman's dilemma: A woman is defined by the man she chooses. The threat to Hepburn's life equivalates the threat to the spiritual life of any woman who picks an unworthy man.

''Bad'' noir women take power by sexual assertion. Otherwise powerless in a man's world, seduction is their only weapon. Such women are ''bad'' because their seizing of sexual power subverts the usual order. Here, Minnelli takes the high road: Hepburn is never remotely sexual. She has brains, breeding, and status. She's a ''lady,'' who controls—and expects to control—by her approval or the withholding of it. When civilization cracks, and Hepburn finds herself in a situation where moral force cannot carry the day, she's helpless.

The film is more gripping than it has any right to be, with its gothic mansions, flickering firelight, mysterious brothers, and simple-minded notions about gender politics. The production details and luscious camera work only add to the feminine atmosphere—contrast the lush sets, complementary lighting, and fancy costumes to the stark world of such ''male'' films as *Kiss Me Deadly*. But there's an arresting dreamlike quality to Hepburn's imaginings of Mitchum, and Minnelli suggests a moral corruption within Hepburn, the possibility that she, too, has a darker side

While men make the world, a woman's contribution is to love. As men fail in the world, women fail with their hearts, with equally disastrous consequences. Whether you agree with Minnelli's notions, this is the truth of the world for Hepburn's character, and she makes a fascinating study.

Other recommended rentals directed by Vincente Minnelli:

An American in Paris
The Bad and the Beautiful
Meet Me in St. Louis

COLUMBIA PICTURES, ARCHIVE PHOTOS

Underworld, U.S.A. (1960—USA)

Mood Guide: Overwrought gangster melodrama

Director: Samuel Fuller; *Camera:* Hal Mohr; *Screenplay:* Samuel Fuller

Cast: Cliff Robertson, Beatrice Kay, Dolores Dorn, Richard Rust, Larry Gates

In English; B/W

Plot: A tough young hood watches his father get beaten to death in an alley. He dedicates his life to finding and killing those who killed his dad. He goes to jail and ends up working for the biggest crime syndicate in the land. Can his quest keep him pure, or will he turn out no better than his dad?

Cliff Robertson, a street punk with a protective surrogate mom—played with heartbreaking affection by Beatrice Kay—watches as a gang of hoodlums stomps his (hoodlum) dad to death in an alley on New Year's Eve. Since the picture opens with Robertson rolling a drunk, and his surrogate mom is a stripper, if not worse, this is clearly life at the bottom of the American barrel.

Robertson vows revenge on his dad's killers. He goes to reform school and then to prison, where he finds one of the murderers dying in the prison hospital. Robertson smothers him with a pillow. Out of jail and acting on impulse, as he always does, Robertson saves a girl from a savage beating. She turns out to be a good-hearted semi-hooker who doesn't want to deal dope for a crime syndicate. By returning the dope she wouldn't sell to the mob, Robertson becomes one of their favorites. Robertson has good reason for infiltrating the syndicate: The top bosses are the men who killed his dad. Robertson intends to draw close enough to the leaders to murder them and, as much as he's able, he falls in love with the girl.

Robertson's time in the trenches has taught him nothing but self-reliance. He cannot experience love and treats his surrogate mom and his girl the same: When they provide him with information or service, he's grateful. When they do not, he's enraged. Likewise, he offers the syndicate no more loyalty than they offer him. He informs on the crime bosses to the FBI, and colludes with the feds in various schemes to turn the bosses against one another. In this world, Robertson remains pure because he makes no bones about his own corruption.

Only Sam Fuller would present such shades of moral order: Robertson is the hero, even though he murders a helpless old man in his bed, deals heroin, and informs for the FBI. Robertson's holy quest for revenge anoints him in Fuller's eyes. Robertson's harsh life has robbed him of any degree of humanity, and for Fuller, this is punishment sufficient. Besides, in the Fullerian universe, there's no innocence, only varying degrees of guilt. Fuller's real villains, as always, are the fat cats who run things.

On one side, those fat cats are federal agents. On the other, executives of a national crime syndicate. Both operate from office towers and both send poor slobs like Robertson into the streets to do their dirty work. Fuller presents Robertson as a typical, frantic American trying to carve out a little piece of paradise, caught between the towering pillars of suppressive good and invasive evil. Robertson might attain his immediate goals, but the cost will be high, and the basic order of America will never be overthrown.

Fuller moves the camera with his usual low-budget inspiration and infuses his cornball dialogue with seething, potboiler passion. Fuller's style is energetic and crude, even off-putting. Described accurately by director Jim Jarmusch as an "anti-totalitarian anarchist," Fuller shamelessly douses his story in cheap irony and even cheaper sentimentality.

Fuller's raw emotional fireworks cannot, however, deflate his brilliant screenwriting moments . . . as when the head crime boss relaxes by his indoor swimming pool, basking under his tanning lamp with cucumbers over his eyes.

"There will always be people like us," he tells his underlings, snuggling contentedly in his poolside chaise lounge. "Always have, always will."

Other recommended rentals directed by Samuel Fuller:

Fixed Bayonets
Merrill's Marauders
The Naked Kiss (page 185)
Pickup on South Street (page 204)
Shock Corridor
The Steel Helmet

ARCHIVE PHOTOS

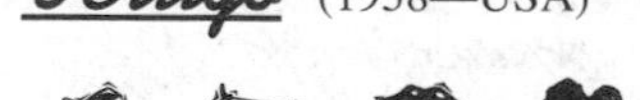

Vertigo (1958—USA)

Mood Guide: Obsession

Director: Alfred Hitchcock; *Camera:* Robert Burks; *Screenplay:* Alec Coppel, Samuel Taylor

Cast: James Stewart, Kim Novak, Barbara Bel Geddes, Henry Jones

In English; color

Plot: A cop is pensioned off the force because his fear of heights caused the death of another officer. Hired by a friend to shadow the friend's wife, Stewart falls in love with her, but is unable to prevent her suicide. Meeting her apparent double, Stewart falls once more, and the old pattern repeats itself.

Vertigo serves as the summing up of Hitchcock's most cherished themes, which, not coincidentally, are the themes that fueled much of noir. Coming well after the demise of the classical cycle, and bereft of most of noir's visual signatures, Hitchcock's masterpiece is the ultimate noir.

ARCHIVE PHOTOS

Kim Novak, Jimmy Stewart, and Kim Novak in *Vertigo*

It embraces lost love, obsession, cruel fate, the role of coincidence, destiny as a product of character, self-loathing, redemption achieved, redemption snatched away, the isolation of existence, and the fundamental perversity of love = human nature. Hitchcock affects a dispassionate, dreamlike style that makes *Vertigo* his most passionately felt work.

James Stewart plays a cop with vertigo. He can't handle heights. Taken literally, this means he cannot come to the rescue of a fellow cop dangling from a rooftop. The cop falls to his death, and Stewart leaves the force. On the metaphorical level, Stewart is a man best suited to keeping both feet on the ground. If he lets his romantic side take flight, he's a menace to himself and others.

Slowly recovering from a nervous breakdown with the help of his pal, Barbara Bel Geddes, Stewart accepts an assignment from an old friend to tail the friend's wife. The friend believes that his wife, played with a spacey, wholly 1950s glamour by Kim Novak, is cracking up.

Bel Geddes is another classic Hitchcock construction: the desexualized woman who yearns for a man who never sees her as feminine. With her horn-rim glasses, asexual perkiness, and shelflike breasts, Bel Geddes loves Stewart, but not wisely. She could be the healer he needs, but his mind is elsewhere.

Bel Geddes tries to suffer in silence as Stewart becomes increasingly obsessed with Novak. But when Bel Geddes makes the mistake of mocking his interest in Novak, Stewart drops her from his life without a backward glance. In one of Hitchcock's most harrowing portraits of self-hatred, Bel Geddes pulls her own hair and curses herself, crying, "Stupid, stupid, stupid." In the film's last glimpse of Bel Geddes, she walks stooped down an empty corridor that symbolizes the long and lonely life awaiting her.

Stewart follows Novak around the city, an unreal space devoid of traffic, shot in crystalline, overly simple Technicolor frames and haunted by Bernard Herrmann's typically eerie score. When Novak attempts suicide, Stewart rescues her and they fall in love. She takes him to a church tower, but he cannot climb with her. She throws herself from the tower, and Stewart is once more plunged into despair.

But he meets a woman who appears to be the double of his lost love, also played by Novak. Pursuing her madly, Stewart wins her affection and forces her to dye her hair, to dress and to move like the dead woman. In a heart-wrenching sequence that displays all of Hitch's compassion for the obsessive vagaries of love (that is, none), Stewart urges Novak to put on a certain dress. In this perverse, reverse striptease, Stewart says to her: "It can't matter to you, it can't . . . ," illustrating Hitch's view that men have no capacity for recognizing a woman's emotions when in pursuit of their own gratification. And Novak replies: "If I do this, will you love me?" Stewart nods, and Novak surrenders to his fetish, wherein Hitch demonstrates his notions of the pure masochism of feminine love. Or, perhaps, his belief that a woman in love will accept any humiliation to keep her man.

Using a muted palette of colors, and little of his self-conscious cinematographic virtuosity, Hitch creates an atmosphere of distrust and hopelessness that unfolds with the inevitability and weight of Greek tragedy. Stewart's nature makes his fate. Mistaking the overcoming of his weakness for a newfound strength (as movie heroes always do), Stewart leads himself straight to perdition.

Other recommended rentals directed by Alfred Hitchcock:
The Birds
Notorious (page 193)
Rear Window
The Wrong Man (page 273)

The Woman in the Window (1944—USA)

Mood Guide: Literate tale of entanglement

Director: Fritz Lang; *Camera:* Milton Krasner; *Screenplay:* Nunnally Johnson

Cast: Edward G. Robinson, Raymond Massey, Joan Bennett, Dan Duryea

In English; B/W

Plot: A married, mild-mannered professor meets the woman of his dreams. Their meeting, though innocent, turns violent, and the professor finds himself mired in murder and blackmail.

Edward G. Robinson, a university professor with an obliging aspect, is obsessed by a portrait of a woman. On the evening that he sends off his wife and kids on a summer vacation, he receives a warning. Raymond Massey, the district attorney and Robinson's best friend, tells him that tragedy can grow from the tiniest, most innocent action. A man with a sane, normal life should keep it that way, Massey intones. Robinson defends himself as a stalwart member of the terrified middle class. But his passion for the woman in the portrait reveals his yearning for a forbidden adventure.

RKO PICTURES/ARCHIVE PHOTOS

Edward G. Robinson transfixed by (a portrait of) Joan Bennett in *The Woman in the Window*

That night, while staring at the portrait, he meets the living, breathing woman who modeled for it. Smitten, he accepts an invitation for a drink at her place. There, her lover bursts in and assaults Robinson, who kills the man with a pair of scissors. With the woman's help, he disposes of the body. The dead man turns out to be famous, and the cops want the killer. Robinson also deals with a conniving bodyguard who comes skulking around for blackmail. Robinson decides, with the woman's help, to murder the blackmailer.

Joan Bennett, the woman in the window, is no femme fatale.

She proves basically good and helps Robinson at every turn. She seems almost a frightened schoolboy's fantasy: She's beautiful and provocative, but never pursues Robinson, and seems helpless in the face of her own nature. Dan Duryea, as the blackmailing bodyguard, sees through her gentle facade and treats her as the sexual creature she is.

Raymond Massey makes a great D.A. With his godlike voice and relaxed manner, he tells Robinson of every newly discovered clue—and they all lead straight to Robinson. On a trip to the crime scene with Massey, Robinson makes several self-incriminating blunders. It's as if Robinson wants to get caught, or at least wants credit for being the bad-ass everyone knows he could never be.

Fritz Lang prefers a straightforward visual approach, no-nonsense acting, and metronomic editing that give the story an irresistible momentum. Lang's concerns are the thin line between guilt and innocence, how even the best will overthrow morality to do the worst, and the power of (bourgeois) man's conscience to enslave him. The deceptive simplicity of Lang's technique adds unobtrusively to the power of the story.

In Lang's view, it is not the act of murder that damns Robinson, but that by concealing it, Robinson contradicts his own moral code. This is foreshadowed in the opening scene, when Robinson lectures his class on degrees of culpability in murder. What Lang finds most reprehensible is that Robinson commits terrible acts only to protect his good name. Hypocrisy is Robinson's real crime.

Yet, in a surprise ending that is at first irritating and then amusing, the film's secret heart turns out to be painting a portrait of its own. That portrait is of a fearful little man desperate for relief from his stultifying life, who discovers with infinite gratitude that there is none. Lang pierces the self-made myths of the middle-class with a cynical wit that is a match for Billy Wilder's, and second to none.

Other recommended rentals directed by Fritz Lang:

The Big Heat (page 46)
Scarlet Street (page 222)
You Only Live Once

ARCHIVE PHOTOS

Vera Miles, Henry Fonda, and Anthony Quayle in *The Wrong Man*

The Wrong Man (1956—USA)

Mood Guide: Police procedural in reverse

Director: Alfred Hitchcock; *Camera:* Robert Burks; *Screenplay:* Maxwell Anderson, Angus MacPhail

Cast: Henry Fonda, Vera Miles, Anthony Quayle, Nehemiah Persoff, Werner Klemperer

In English; B/W

Plot: An innocent musician is mistaken for a holdup man and arrested for his crimes. All witnesses who support the musician's alibi prove to be dead or untraceable. His wife cracks under the strain. His trial provides no justice. Where can he turn?

Henry Fonda, a mild-mannered musician at a New York nightclub, is mistaken for a holdup man. Whisked away from his family before he understands what's happening, Fonda is misidentified in a line-up and thrown into jail. A reticent son of immigrants—with a childlike faith in the righteousness of the cops and a terror of impropriety—Fonda's too respectful to make a fuss. Bearing his sudden burdens with a naive, heartbreaking patience, Fonda believes there's justice inherent in the American system, and that the truth will set him free.

Less optimistic is Fonda's poor wife, played as a tarnished, insecure saint by Vera Miles. Faced with an onslaught of bills, the raising of two sons, and the absence of her reliable husband, she cracks. Miles goes slowly mental in her own quiet way, until even the somewhat opaque Fonda recognizes the seriousness of her plight. Hitch again shows Fonda's destructive trust in authority as a series of somber psychologists announce that Vera must be put away. And so she is.

Fonda's nightmare worsens as the only witnesses who might corroborate his alibi have either died or moved away. He finds a willing attorney, played with jarring Shakespearean volume and presence by Anthony Quayle, but Quayle can do little with the meager evidence available.

Based on a true story, the film presents two of Hitchcock's lifelong phobias: imprisonment and false accusation. Hitch finds no relief in American "justice" and little solace in the useless good intentions of cops, but he doesn't blame the system as such. Hitch considers Fonda a victim of the randomness of fate, and proof that a moral, well-lived life offers scant protection against the dark side.

It's a very Hitchcockian (and noir) message and certainly the most understated and least fantastical picture Hitch ever made. Hitch needn't exaggerate a thing to provide terror; he shoots the clanking jailhouse doors and hand-cuffed, dispirited cons with neo-realist dispassion. Using shadows, entrapping vertical lines, and a constantly narrowing fame, Hitch subsumes his trademark visual style into a recognizable noir motif (something he does not do, for instance, in *Vertigo* [page 267]). But the most powerful moments are still undistilled Hitchcock, as when his lens tracks right through the narrow viewing slit in Fonda's jailhouse door to suggest the claustrophobic horror that Fonda suffers in his cell.

As the noir cycle wound down, it seemed that audiences no longer wanted to be reminded of the destructive chaos underlying day-to-day life. The police procedural, acting as a counter to noir, sacrificed plot and thrills to concentrate on the calm, deliberate, and, above all, rational methods that cops employed to defeat criminals (and therefore the anarchy that threatened the new mass bourgeoisie). Police procedurals carried a reassuring message: Cops are a bulwark of sanity against an insane world.

Hitch brilliantly inverts the conventions of the police procedural. Here, every time the cops make a calm, rational move, they're not only dead wrong, they're wantonly destructive. The little guy, whether harassed by the system or by simple bad luck, has nowhere to turn.

Other recommended rentals directed by Alfred Hitchcock:

The Birds
Notorious (page 193)
Rear Window
Vertigo (page 267)

Noir Not Available

Sadly, many great noir films remain unavailable in home video formats. The following is a list of worthy films that should be rented as soon as they appear. Please pester your video store and keep on eye out for:

Ace in the Hole (*aka The Big Carnival*) (1951—USA) Director: Billy Wilder
Angel Face (USA—1953) Director: Otto Preminger
The Blue Gardenia (USA—1953) Director: Fritz Lang
Border Incident (USA—1949) Director: Anthony Mann
Brute Force (USA—1947) Director: Jules Dassin
The Crimson Kimono (USA—1959) Director: Samuel Fuller
Fallen Angel (USA—1946) Director: Otto Preminger
The File on Thelma Jordan (USA—1950) Director: Robert Siodmak
Radio On (1980—United Kingdom) Director: Christopher Petit
The Reckless Moment (USA—1949) Director: Max Ophuls
Ride the Pink Horse (USA—1947) Director: Robert Montgomery
Thieves' Highway (USA—1949) Director: Jules Dassin
The Unsuspected (USA—1947) Director: Michael Curtiz
Where the Sidewalk Ends (USA—1950) Otto Preminger

Renting or Purchasing Videotapes and Laser Discs by Mail and the Internet

If you don't live in a big city with a specialty video-rental shop, the more obscure, interesting noir films may be difficult to find. The foreign noir may prove impossible. Fortunately, renting by mail is getting easier, and rental catalogs grow more comprehensive every day. Only a rent-by-mail house can keep up with films that are newly available on tape, and their staff are usually as helpful as they are knowledgeable.

Mail-order rental houses print catalogs, for which they charge, or they offer memberships. Most update their catalogs with smaller, magazinelike mailings, and all can be reached via 800 numbers. Though the rental charge will be higher than at your local video store—as much as ten dollars per film—renters can keep a movie for three days. Usually, the rental price includes return postage, and tapes are sent in a reusable mailer-box. All require a credit card deposit. While each catalog listed below strives to be comprehensive, if you subscribe to all three you should be able to find any noir currently available on video.

As always, the Internet is an excellent source of sources. Because Web addresses change so frequently, I'm reluctant to list any here. You can find several videotape and laser disc sales houses by calling up any search engine—such as Yahoo or Webcrawler—and typing in "laser disc."

RENTAL CATALOGS
Video Library 1-800-669-7157
Home Film Festival 1-800-258-3456
Facets Video 1-800-532-2387

VIDEO AND LASER DISC PURCHASE
Ken Crane's Laser Disc 1-800-624-3078
Scarecrow Video 1-800-700-8554
Lazer Perceptions 1-415-753-2016

Recommended Reading

Bandy, Mary Lea. *Rediscovering French Film.* New York: Museum of Modern Art, 1983.

Bluestone, George. *Novels into Films: The Metamorphosis of Fiction into Cinema.* Berkeley, CA: University of California Press, 1957.

Bobker, Lee. *Elements of Film.* New York: Harcourt, Brace & World, 1969.

Boorman, John, and Walter Donohue. *Projections 4.* London: Faber and Faber, 1995.

———*Projections 4½.* London: Faber and Faber, 1995.

———*Projections 5.* London: Faber and Faber, 1996.

———*Projections 6.* London: Faber and Faber, 1996.

———*Projections 7.* London: Faber and Faber, 1997.

Brown, Royal. *Focus on Godard.* Englewood Cliffs, NJ: Prentice-Hall International, 1972.

Buss, Robin. *French Film Noir.* London: Marion Boyars Publishers, 1994.

Campbell, Joseph. *The Hero with a Thousand Faces.* Princeton, NJ: Princeton University Press, 1949.

Christopher, Nicholas. *Somewhere in the Night: Film Noir and the American City.* New York: The Free Press, 1997.

Clarens, Carols. *Crime Movies: An Illustrated History of the Gangster Genre from D. W. Griffith to Pulp Fiction.* New York: Da Capo Press, 1997

Copjec, Joan. *Shades of Noir.* London, England: Verso, 1993.

Cowie, Peter. *The Cinema of Orson Welles.* New York: Da Capo Press, 1993.

Crenshaw, Marshall. *Hollywood Rock*. New York: Harper Perennial, 1994.

Davis, Mike. *City of Quartz*. New York: Vintage Books, 1990.

Deivert, Bert, and Dan Harries. *Film and Video on the Internet*. Studio City, CA: Michael Weiss Productions, 1996.

Dixon, Wheeler Winston. *The Films of Jean-Luc Godard*. Albany, NY: State University of New York Press, 1997.

Doane, Mary Ann. *Femmes Fatales: Feminism, Film Theory, Psychoanalysis*. New York: Routledge, 1991.

Dymtryk, Edward. *On Film Editing*. Boston: Focal Press, 1984.

Fariello, Griffin. *Red Scare: Memories of the American Inquisition*. New York: Avon Books, 1996.

Garnham, Nicholas. *Samuel Fuller*. New York: The Viking Press, 1971.

Haskell, Molly. *From Reverence to Rape: The Treatment of Women in the Movies*. Chicago: University of Chicago Press, 1987.

Hebdige, Dick. *Subculture, The Meaning of Style*. London: Methuen & Co., 1979.

Hillier, Jim. *Cahiers du Cinéma, The 1950's: Neo-Realism, Hollywood, New Wave*. Cambridge, MA: Harvard University Press, 1985.

———*Cahiers du Cinéma, The 1960s: New Wave, New Cinema, Reevaluating Hollywood*. Cambridge, MA: Harvard University Press, 1985.

Hirsch, Foster. *Film Noir, The Dark Side of the Screen*. New York: Da Capo Books, 1981.

Kael, Pauline. *Kiss, Kiss, Bang, Bang*. New York: Bantam Books, 1968.

———*For Keeps: 30 Years at the Movies*. New York: Dutton, 1984.

Kaplan, E. Ann. *Psychoanalysis and Cinema*. New York: Routledge, 1990.

———*Women in Film Noir*. London: The British Film Institute, 1978.

Katz, Ephraim. *The Film Encyclopedia*. New York: HarperCollins, 1994.

Katz, Stephen. *Film Directing Shot by Shot*. Studio City, CA: Michael Wise Productions, 1991.

Kitses, Jim. *Gun Crazy*. London: The British Film Institute, 1996.

Kolker, Robert, and Peter Beichen. *The Films of Wim Wenders: Cinema of Vision and Despair*. New York: Cambridge Press, 1993.

Krutnik, Frank. *In a Lonely Place: Film Noir, Genre, Masculinity*. London: Routledge, 1991.

McArthur, Colin. *The Big Heat*. London: The British Film Institute, 1992.

———*Underworld USA*. London: The Viking Press/The British Film Institute, 1972.

Mamet, David. *On Directing Film*. New York: Penguin Books, 1991.

Meyer, David N. *The 100 Best Films to Rent You've Never Heard Of: Hidden Treasures, Neglected Classics and Hits from Bygone Eras*. New York: St. Martin's/Griffin Press, 1996.

Milne, Tom. *Godard on Godard*. New York: Viking Press, 1992.

Melville, Jean-Pierre. *Melville on Melville*. Edited by Rue Noriega. New York: Viking Press, 1971.

Nelson, Thomas. *Kubrick: Inside an Artist's Maze*. Bloomington, ID: University of Indiana Press, 1982.

Palmer, R. Barton. *Hollywood's Dark Cinema: The American Film Noir*. New York: Twayne Publishers, 1994.

Peary, Danny. *Guide for the Film Fanatic*. New York: Fireside Books, 1986.

———*Cult Movies 3*. New York: Fireside Books, 1988.

———*Cult Movie Stars*. New York: Fireside Books, 1991.

Polan, Dana. *In a Lonely Place*. London: The British Film Institute, 1993.

Rafferty, Terrence. *The Thing Happens: Ten Years of Writing About the Movies*. New York: Grove Press, 1995.

Roud, Richard. *Cinema, A Critical Dictionary: The Major Film-Makers*. New York: Viking Press, 1980.

Schatz, Thomas. *The Genius of the System: Hollywood Filmmaking in the Studio Era*. New York: Henry Holt and Company, 1988.

Schickel, Richard. *Double Indemnity*. London: The British Film Institute, 1992.

Schrader, Paul. *Schrader on Schrader*. Edited by Kevin Jackson. London: Faber and Faber, 1990.

———*Transcendental Style in Film: Ozu, Bresson, Dreyer*. New York: Da Capo Press, 1972.

Selby, Spencer. *Dark City: The Film Noir*. Jefferson, NC: MacFarland, 1984.

Silver, Alain, and Elizabeth Ward. *Film Noir: An Encyclopedic Reference to the American Style,* 3rd ed. Woodstock, NY: Overlook Press, 1995.

———*Film Noir Reader*. New York: Limelight Editions: 1996.

Sklar, Robert. *Movies Made America*. New York: Vintage, 1976.

———*Film: An International History of the Medium*. New York: Harry N. Abrams, 1993.

Stephens, Michael L. *Film Noir, A Comprehensive Illustrated Reference to Movies, Terms and Persons*. Jefferson, NC: McFarland & Company, Inc., 1995.

Telotte, J. P. *Voices in the Dark: The Narrative Patterns of Film Noir*. Urbana, IL: University of Illinois Press, 1989.

Time Out Editors. *The Time Out Film Guide, 5th ed.* London: Penguin Press, 1996.

Vale, V., and Andrea Juno. *Incredibly Strange Films*. San Francisco: RE/Search Publications, 1986.

Vaughan, Dai. *Odd Man Out*. London: The British Film Institute, 1995.

Wenders, Wim. *Emotion Pictures*. London: Faber and Faber, 1994.

———*The Logic of Images, Essays and Conversations*. London: Faber and Faber, 1991.

ARCHIVE PHOTOS

Anthony Caruso and Sterling Hayden in *The Asphalt Jungle*

Index of Actors/Actresses

Index of Cinematographers

Index of Directors

Index of Movie Titles in Chronological Order

Index of Screenwriters